Douglas Scott.

BEINN LAOIGH.
telephoto from Tyndrum Road.

March, 1947.

THE SCOTTISH
MOUNTAINEERING CLUB GUIDE

THE
SOUTHERN HIGHLANDS

EDITED BY

J. D. B. WILSON, B.Sc.

INCLUDING AN

APPENDIX ON THE ROCK CLIMBS IN THE
ARROCHAR DISTRICT

BY

B. H. HUMBLE and J. B. NIMLIN

WITH 44 ILLUSTRATIONS AND MAP

PUBLISHED BY
THE SCOTTISH MOUNTAINEERING CLUB
SYNOD HALL, CASTLE TERRACE, EDINBURGH
1949

PRINTED IN GREAT BRITAIN BY
M^cCORQUODALE AND CO. LTD.

CONTENTS

		PAGE
FOREWORD	- - - - - - - - - - -	vii
INTRODUCTION	- - - - - - - - - -	ix
SUMMARY OF THE GEOLOGY OF THE SOUTHERN HIGHLANDS. Dr. J. Phemister	- - - - - - - - - -	1
I.	THE KILPATRICKS AND CAMPSIE FELLS - - - -	7
II.	THE OCHILS - - - - - - - - -	10
III.	THE LOMONDS OF FIFE (including Benarty, Cleish and Saline Hills) - - - - - - - - - -	16
IV.	COWAL AND ARDGOIL - - - - - - - -	20
V.	THE ARROCHAR GROUP - - - - - - -	31
VI.	BEN LOMOND AND SURROUNDINGS - - - - -	43
VII.	BEINN BHUIDHE, LORNE AND KNAPDALE - - -	52
VIII.	THE TROSSACHS HILLS - - - - - -	58
IX.	THE TYNDRUM GROUP - - - - - - -	66
X.	THE CRIANLARICH GROUP - - - - - -	72
XI.	THE LOCH EARN GROUP - - - - - -	83
XII.	BEN CHONZIE AND THE GLEN ALMOND GROUP - - -	90
XIII.	THE DOCHART GROUP - - - - - -	96
XIV.	THE FOREST OF MAMLORN GROUP - - - - -	100
XV.	THE KILLIN HILLS - - - - - - -	109
XVI.	THE LAWERS GROUP - - - - - - -	117
XVII.	GLEN ORCHY AND THE INISHAIL GROUP - - - -	125
XVIII.	THE LOCH LYON HILLS - - - - - -	134
XIX.	THE UPPER GLEN LYON AND WEST RANNOCH GROUP -	137
XX.	THE CARN MAIRG RANGE - - - - - -	143
XXI.	SCHICHALLION - - - - - - - -	150
APPENDIX 1.	ROCK CLIMBS IN THE ARROCHAR GROUP - - -	154
APPENDIX 2.	ROCK CLIMBS IN THE REMAINING DISTRICTS OF THE SOUTHERN HIGHLANDS - - - - - - -	164

ILLUSTRATIONS

Beinn Laoigh, telephoto from Tyndrum Road   *Frontispiece*

Pages

Dumgoyne and Campsie Fells from the Blane
valley   4

Maiden's Bower, Lomonds   5

Clach Bheinn from Loch Eck   .   .   .   20

Puck's Glen   21

Beinn an Lochain from Ben Donich   .   .   .   28

Cobbler, South Peak   .   .   .   .   between 28-29

Cobbler, North Peak   .   .   .   .   between 28-29

The Buttermilk Burn and the Cobbler   .   .   29

The Arrochar hills from Inversnaid   .   .   .   36

Loch Lomond from the slopes of Ben Vorlich   .   37

Ben Lomond from Ben Narnain   .   .   .   44

Panorama from Ben Reoch, with key. 2 pp.   between 44-45

Ben Lomond from near Tarbet   45

Beinn Bhuidhe   52

Western seaboard north of Easdale   .   .   .   53

Loch Lubnaig   60

Ben Venue   .   .   .   .   .   .   between 60-61

Beinn Laoigh from Beinn a'Chuirn.   .   .   between 60-61

Beinn Laoigh, summit   61

ILLUSTRATIONS—*Continued.*

Pages

Beinn Laoigh from above Coninish . . . 68

Point 2526-ft. from Loch Voil side . . . 69

Ben More from near Crianlarich . . . 76

Cruach Ardrain from Strathfillan . . between 76-77

Stobinian and Ben More from Glen Dochart between 76-77

Beinn Tulachain and Stob a'Choin . . . 77

Stuc a'Chroin from Ben Vorlich . . . 84

Loch Voil and Ben Vorlich 85

The Crianlarich hills from Beinn Achaladair . 92

Strathfillan, winter . . . . . between 92-93

View south from the Crianlarich hills . . between 92-93

Beinn Achaladair from Crannach wood . . 93

Beinn Dorain from above Auch 108

The peaks of Tarmachan from Creag na Caillich . . . . . . between 108-109

View from the summit of Lawers . . between 108-109

The Lawers group from the north-west . . 109

Schichallion and Loch Rannoch . . . 140

Spearhead Arête, Narnain . . between 140-141

Ben Ime from Narnain . . . between 140-141

The Brack, north face 141

The Cobbler from the upper corrie . . . 156

Creag Tarsuinn . . . . between 156-157

Ben Narnain, Summit Cliffs . . between 156-157

A'Chrois cliffs 157

Ben A'n, south face (line diagram) . . . page 178

FOREWORD

WHEN the editorship of this Guide was entrusted to me towards the end of 1946, the manuscript had already been in preparation for something over a decade and a number of chapters came to me in a near final form.

Due to the lapse of time, and for other reasons, it was thought best to rewrite the whole work in order to achieve unity of style and presentation.

For much of the preliminary work I am indebted to the late Mr. J. C. Thomson, and particularly so in respect of Chapters 14, 18 and 19. Much of the information contained in Chapters 7 and 9 was contributed by Mr. A. C. McLaren and my thanks are due to him as well as to Mr. E. C. Thomson who kindly gave me the benefit of his knowledge of the Crianlarich hills by writing Chapter 10. For the information contained in Chapter 3 I am indebted to Dr. J. H. B. Bell, as well as for his helpful advice. Dr. Phemister's excellent paper on the geology of the district forms an especially valued contribution. Thanks are also due to Mr. Malcolm Johnston, for his advice regarding the meaning of many of the Gaelic names.

I should like to thank those members and others who kindly submitted photographs, a selection of the best of which serve to lighten the somewhat dry matter of which the Guide is composed.

Without the help of the General Guide Book Editor, and the work of Miss M. B. Sharp in preparing the typescript, the Guide would surely have been further delayed, and my thanks are due to them in no small measure.

J. D. B. WILSON.

Dunblane, 1949

INTRODUCTION

THE area covered by this Volume of the Scottish Mountaineering Club's Guide is relatively extensive. On the south it is bounded by the Forth and Clyde Canal : on the east by the coast to the north side of the Firth of Tay : and on the west by the indented coastline north to Oban, but excluding the islands of the west. The peninsula of Kintyre falls to be included. The northern boundary is less naturally defined. It follows the railway from Oban east as far as Dalmally, then north-east by the line of Glen Orchy to join the West Highland line at Bridge of Orchy and so north to Rannoch. Loch Rannoch is the most northerly limit of the area, as the boundary runs south-east again from Kinloch Rannoch, first by the road to Pitlochry, then by the railway to Dunkeld, and thence to the Firth of Tay.

In the area covered are seventy tops over 3000 ft., of which forty-six are classed as separate mountains. All find a place in the Guide, as well as a number of peaks of sub-Munro height which are included when they are of special interest, or if they form isolated hills or groups. The Southern Highlands embrace Sections 1, 2 and 3 of Munro's Tables (S.M.C. General Guide Book).

Recommended maps are noted at the beginning of each chapter, and it will be found that the most generally useful are the sheets of the one-inch Ordnance Survey. In the half-inch scale, Bartholomew's sheets will be found to be excellent : in many ways the coloured contours of this series give a better idea of topography. On all maps anomalies are prone to occur, and it is not uncommon to find different spellings of the same name on any given sheet. The names and spelling adopted by the one-inch Ordnance Survey map have been used in every case except when no name occurs on that map, in which case the name is taken from the six-inch Ordnance Survey sheets (or Bartholomew's half-inch) and the fact so stated in the text. In isolated cases names appear on no map but are known locally.

In general, the heights given also agree with the one-inch Ordnance Survey maps. When the one-inch and six-inch maps are not in agreement, the six-inch is taken as correct. Where no height is stated on either of the Ordnance Survey maps, an aneroid height is shown in the text, or a computation has been made from map contours. In these cases the heights are given as approximate.

At the end of each Chapter will be found a list of centres relative to the district. The centres are arranged alphabetically and not in order of comfort. Nearest Youth Hostels are also indicated.

Under the general heading—Paths—are included the major routes in the various districts. In nearly every case actual tracks are used for at least part of the way. The evidence of a track, however, does not constitute evidence of a right-of-way. Where a route is in fact a right-of-way this is stated. Forestry Commission land, of which there is a good deal in the Southern Highland area, should be treated with special respect in this connection, and every care taken to do nothing to jeopardise the safety of trees, young or old.

The endeavour has been to obtain up-to-date and first-hand information on the state of paths and bridges, but it should be remembered that a storm may wash out sections of a track and carry away bridges. Paths themselves vary from season to season in their definition and according to the amount they are used. Grass tracks especially are prone to disappear unless used extensively.

Hill routes given in the text involve no rock-climbing as such. On some, a little very simple scrambling may be encountered, but there is a simple route to the summit of every mountain in the area. At the end of the main text is a section on the rock-climbs of the area. The bulk of the climbing is in the Arrochar district, and a Guide to this is being published separately (*Rock-climbing Guide to the Arrochar District*—Nimlin and Humble). The bulk of the information therein is included in the present work for the sake of completeness. Over large parts of the remainder of the mountains in the Southern Highlands are scattered rocks without continuous climbs. The positions of these are indicated in the hope that further investigation will yield satisfactory short climbs. A number of the mountains are better adapted for winter climbs under snow conditions than for rock ascents. For obvious reasons, no attempt at classification with respect to difficulty has been made on these winter routes: on pure rock-climbing routes the classification follows accepted practice, and in all cases is given assuming dry conditions. Abbreviations used in classification are: E.—easy; M.—moderate; D.—difficult; V.D.—very difficult; A.S.—an easy severe; S.—severe; V.S.—very severe. Regularity of classification is difficult to achieve and there is some considerable range within each group.

The bibliography at the end of each Chapter is compiled from relative writings in the *Scottish Mountaineering Club Journal* (*S.M.C.J.*) and the *Journal of the Cairngorm Club* (*C.C.J.*). References pertaining wholly, or largely, to rock-climbing routes are marked with an asterisk.

SUMMARY OF THE GEOLOGY OF THE SOUTHERN HIGHLANDS

By James Phemister, D.Sc.

THE topographic division of Scotland into Highlands and Lowlands corresponds to a remarkable change in the nature and structure of the rocks which compose the two types of country. The change is abrupt and takes place across a line, or rather zone, of fracture which is known to geologists as the *Highland Boundary Fault*. This fault cuts in a straight course across the region described in the present Guide. Traversing the Loch Fad hollow in Bute the Highland Boundary Fault skirts the coast at Toward and Innellan, and passing the mouth of the Gareloch crosses Loch Lomond at Balmaha. Thence, by Aberfoyle, its course lies along Glen Artney, and just clearing the mouth of the Sma' Glen, reaches the Tay near Murthly Castle. To all familiar with Perthshire and Cowal scenery, the reason for so naming this great fracture will be clear. On the north stand the craggy and rough mountains, on the south lie rounded, grassy hills.

Geology.—South of the Highland Boundary Fault, the rocks are mainly sandstone, conglomerates and mudstones of Old Red Sandstone age. They comprise both the Lower and Upper divisions of this formation. The Lower strata are typically of a dull red or chocolate colour while the Upper have brighter tints in red and yellow. A long interval of time elapsed between the deposition of the Lower and Upper Series, and during this interval the Lower strata were tilted steeply against the Highland Boundary Fault, folded and greatly denuded. The strata of the Upper Series lie flatly across these steeply inclined beds and cross the fault on to the Highland rocks. The fault is therefore of very ancient date. Nevertheless, the frequent earthquake shocks experienced near Crieff and Comrie indicate that small adjustments are still taking place along this line of weakness.

The " Old Red " rocks rise to considerable heights, for example, Uamh Mhor, only to the south of Glen Artney.

Younger strata occur at Helensburgh and Dumbarton, where Carboniferous sediments follow upwards on Upper Old Red strata. In south-east Bute lavas of Lower Carboniferous age appear.

Along the course of the Highland Boundary Fault near Callander, Aberfoyle, Innellan and Loch Fad appear strips of rock of Cambro-Ordovician age which have been preserved between branching fractures of the fault zone. These rocks, known as the Highland Border Series, include grits, cherts and shales, which, south-west of Aberfoyle, have yielded fossils. The Series also includes basic and ultrabasic igneous rocks which have been altered to greenstone and serpentine. As far as their actual area of outcrop is concerned, they are insignificant, but they are nevertheless of the greatest geological importance.

Save in the neighbourhood of Crieff, where some sediments and lavas of the Lower Old Red Sandstone age occur, the region north of the Highland Boundary Fault is built up of very ancient sedimentary rocks. These originally were pure sandstone, gritty and pebbly impure sandstone, sandy, calcareous and carbonaceous shales, and limestones, but before the Old Red Sandstone era were subjected to intense folding during which they were greatly altered by heat and shearing stress. The alteration affected both the texture and the mineral composition of the rocks and in parts of the region was so thorough that the rocks now bear no resemblance to sediments at all. It has been found that the degree of alteration, or metamorphism, as it is technically termed, increases from south-west to north-east and also in a transverse direction, from the fault north-westwards. Thus, in our region, the most highly altered rocks occur between Glen Orchy and Pitlochry. The less altered rocks near the fault retain the aspects of grits and shales but a pronounced cleavage of schistosity has been developed by the compressive crustal stresses. The shales have become slates and phyllites. The latter term is applied to those slaty rocks which show a silvery or greenish lustre on their splitting planes. The lustre is due to development of multitudes of tiny scales of muscovite and chlorite. The grits are now schistose grits, and show rudely parallel folia of mica and chlorite, elongated grains of quartz and drawn-out pebbles. With increase in degree of metamorphism the scales of white mica become larger, green chlorite is replaced by black mica, and the parallel disposition of the minerals becomes more perfect. Pink garnets appear in abundance in some bands. Such altered shaly rocks are termed mica-schists. Where the original shale was carbonaceous, the mica-schist is graphitic. The more siliceous rocks also lose their original sedimentary appearance and are converted to rocks in which folia composed mainly of quartz, or quartz and feldspar, alternate with more micaceous folia. They include rocks termed gneissose grits, siliceous schists, and granulitic gneisses. Pure sandstones have been recrystallized to quartzite, a rock composed of closely united quartz grains. Limestones have been converted to marble which is pure or contains a variety of minerals according as the original sediment was pure or impure.

This very varied assemblage of rocks is known as the Dalradian Series and for convenience of description it has been divided into groups which have been found to stretch, or strike, in a general north-east—south-west direction through the region. The groups have been given names derived from localities where the particular group is well-developed. Thus, from the Highland Boundary Fault north-westwards, there appear in succession the Leny Grits, Aberfoyle Slates (—Dunoon Phyllites), Ben Ledi Grits (—Ben Bheula Grits and Schists), Pitlochry or Glen Struan Grits and Schists, Loch Tay Limestone, Ben Lui Garnetiferous Mica-schists, Ben Lawers Schists (—Ardrishaig Phyllites), Ben Eagach Black Schists, Central Highland Quartzite, and Blair Atholl Series. To the north-west of the latter two groups the banded granulites of the Moine Series appear in Glen Orchy and between Glen Lyon and Loch Rannoch.

The groups enumerated above are not composed of one type of rock alone. The name indicates the most conspicuous type, but phyllites are found interbanded in the grit groups, quartzites in the schist groups, and *vice versa*. A peculiar kind of rock, not so far mentioned, occurs at intervals between the Loch Tay Limestone and the Ben Ledi Grits. This is a green schist which owes its colour to abundance of the green mineral chlorite and the yellow mineral epidote.

The foliation or schistosity of the rocks has in general a steep dip towards the north-west, but in places the direction or amount of the dip changes. For example, between Loch Earn and Glen Dochart the rocks lie flat. In eastern Cowal they dip south-east, in western Cowal north-west. Moreover, when examined in detail they are frequently found to be crumpled and contorted. Veins of quartz, also often contorted and drawn out by the crustal stresses, are numerous, particularly in the Ben Lawers Schists.

While the above description applies to all the region between the Tay and Kintyre, a change occurs in the ground around Loch Awe. There the rocks are in a low grade of metamorphism and consist of slates, phyllites and quartzites among which are interbanded green rocks representing interbedded lavas and intrusive sheets. These have been folded and metamorphosed at the same time as the other rocks of the region.

Influence of the rock-types on hill features.—The softer rocks, which belong to the Aberfoyle or Dunoon group, crumble easily and give rise to the smooth, undulating grass-covered hills which mark its outcrop from Toward to the Pass of Leny. The resistant schistose grits of the Ben Ledi group are denuded mainly by disruption along joints. The mountains built by rocks of this group, Ben Bheula, Venue, Ledi, Vorlich, Chonzie, are craggy and scarred by cliffs of bare, sharp rock.

Strongly metamorphosed mica-schists are also resistant but in a manner different from the hard, jointed grits. They split easily along but with difficulty across their schistosity. When their dip is steep, serrated crests rise above rough, knobby slopes at the foot of which lie screes of jagged schist.

Mica-schists, interbanded with siliceous schists, build the rugged country which stretches from Central Cowal to Aber-

A. D. S. Macpherson.

DUMGOYNE AND CAMPSIE FELLS FROM BLANE VALLEY.

September, 1928.

MAIDEN'S BOWER, LOMONDS.

J. H. B. Bell.

feldy and from Ben Lomond to Ben Lui. In Cowal and at the heads of Loch Goil and Loch Long a mica-schist containing conspicuous brown crystals of albite (a feldspar) is a prominent rock.

The soft calcareous schists which lie horizontally at Ben Lawers break down into good soil and yield smooth slopes there, but where they stand vertically the same schists, and the contiguous soft graphitic schists, prove resistant and give rise to such steep, craggy ground as is found along the Ben Eagach and Farragon ridge.

Homogeneous quartzites break down into screes which form smooth steeply inclined slopes. When no prominent direction of erosion is present the quartzite mountain assumes a conical form such as is exemplified by Shichallion.

Intrusive rocks.—In contrast to most of the Grampian Highlands this region contains no very large masses of intrusive rock. In the triangle between Lochs Tulla and Laidon, and Kinloch Rannoch, the southern part of the large " Moor of Rannoch Granite " appears. Other large masses of granite and diorite lie between Glen Fyne and Glen Falloch, and to the east of Glen Lednock. The heat of these intrusions has hardened and toughened the surrounding schists, and the latter, as at Carn Chois, may for this reason prove more resistant to denudiation than the adjacent intrusion. Smaller intrusive masses which vary in composition from black pyroxenite or hornblendite to granite, are dotted around the head of Loch Lomond. Large sheets of porphyry are numerous between Glen Shira and Lochgilphead and appear also to the south of Loch Tay. These intrusions are all of Lower Old Red Sandstone or somewhat earlier age.

More recent intrusive rocks include the great dykes which stretch east-north-east from Strachur and Dalmally, and the dyke-swarm which extends south-east through Cowal from the Mull volcanic centre. These dykes are dolerites or basalt, black or dark grey in colour. They are generally well jointed, are eroded easily and determine the trend of many of the streams which frequently have worked deep chasms along their courses.

B

Development of the topography.—The wide views obtained from the summits reveal the fact that the mountain tops keep a fairly constant level. The Highlands, in fact, represent a high plateau which has been vigorously dissected by river action. Though the rocks are highly folded there is no mountain chain. Though they are traversed by many powerful faults, the lines of these faults are not dominant topographic directions. For example, the course of Loch Lomond cuts across the great Highland Boundary Fault; the Loch Tay hollow is merely deflected in its central part along a great zone of fracture which runs from the head of Loch Tummel to Loch Vennacher.

The general aspect of the Highlands has been greatly modified by the action of ice. During the Ice-age the erosive action of glaciers smoothed the mountain tops, and swept the hillsides bare of scree. But in their turn the ice streams deposited hummocky moraine along the valley sides, threw crescentic barriers of terminal moraine across the mouths, and bore great pieces of rock far from the parent strata to leave them stranded as " perched blocks " or erratic boulders. Melt-waters from the glaciers formed large temporary lakes in which flat spreads of sand and silt were deposited. Around Loch Tulla lakes of this origin have left old strand-lines of the same type as the " Parallel Roads " of Glen Roy.

Since the Ice-age the agents of denudation have been ceaselessly at work and " in course of time, the rain and frosts will restore to the outline of our hills and mountains all the ruggedness which they possessed before they were swathed in the wintry folds of the ancient glaciers." (Sir A. Geikie, *Scenery of Scotland*, p. 220, 1901.)

Minerals.—Old workings for metallic ore are comparatively numerous in this region. The best known are the lead mines which occur west of Tyndrum. Lead ore, galena, has been sought also in Glen Orchy and Glen Creran. With the lead ore, zinc and copper minerals were obtained. Copper has been worked on both sides of Loch Fyne, and the ore was accompanied by the nickeliferous mineral, pyrrhotite or magnetic pyrites. Workings for copper exist also at Tomnadashan on the south side of Loch Tay.

I

THE KILPATRICKS AND CAMPSIE FELLS

Maps : O.S. One-inch Scale Popular Edition, Sheets 66
and 67. O.S. Half-inch Scale, Sheets 26 and 27.
Bartholomew's Half-inch Scale Revised, Scotland, Sheets
6 and 7. Bartholomew's Half-inch Scale, Great Britain,
Sheets 44 and 45.

THESE two groups, separated by wooded Strath Blane, are
the nearest hills north of Glasgow, and as such form a favourite
district for excursions on short days. Nowhere is the 2000-
foot contour reached, the highest top in the Kilpatricks
being just over 1300 ft. In the Campsies, Earl's Seat reaches
1896 ft., but to the east the hills are lower and finally merge
into the Carse of Stirling east of the Gargunnocks. They are
composed of lava sheets, very much worn down by ice in
ages gone, and some of the more prominent hills, such as
Dumgoyne, are the vent plugs of ancient volcanoes. The
volcanic ash has long since vanished, leaving the hard lava
cores to weather slowly. In many parts of the Campsies
evidence of ice erosion and transportation is to be seen, and,
geologically speaking, the hills are full of interest.

The Kilpatricks.—A number of private secondary roads
run off into the high ground from east and south. These
serve the numerous lochs and reservoirs in the hills, and
provide the walker with easy (although forbidden) access,
particularly from the Glasgow-Drymen road (A809). Burn-
crook's reservoir is the largest sheet of water in the area and
is approached by a fair road running up from West Carbeth,
about 2 miles from Blanefield. The road gives an easy
approach to Auchineden Hill, 1171 ft., to the north of the
reservoir. On a spur of the hill is situated the Whangie
from where there is a particularly pleasing prospect north to
the open country around the end of Loch Lomond, and on good
days a lovely view of the hills away up the loch, and beyond.

Fynloch Hill, 1313 ft., and Duncolm, 1314 ft., the highest points of the Kilpatricks, are more easily approached from the direction of Loch Humphrey, by the delightful road from Old Kilpatrick to the moors. Both hills give good views and the north-east side of Duncolm drops away steeply giving the summit a nice sense of height. The cliff is composed of basaltic columns. To the north and west the country is less interesting and completely trackless.

The Campsies are more extensive, but like the Kilpatricks have few tracks amongst the hills and across the high plateaux. The road from Lennoxtown to Fintry (B822) cuts high across the moor but between there and the Blane valley the plateau gives rough and heavy going. To the east is the Carron valley reservoir, at a height of 750 ft., along the north side of which a road runs from Fintry eastwards to Denny. To the east of the Crow Road (B822) the Fells become the Kilsyth Hills, the highest point being Meikle Bin, 1870 ft. It is approached most easily from a point on the road $1\frac{1}{4}$ miles north of the old Toll House near the highest point by way of Waterhead Farm. There are two tops, close together, the lesser being 80 ft. lower than the summit, which has a small cairn. From the higher hills to the north, Meikle Bin appears over the general plateau level of the Fells as an easily recognisable flattish cone. The view from Meikle Bin, as well as Earl's Seat some distance west in the Campsies, is good, and on a clear day extends from the Crianlarich hills to Merrick in the south. To the north is Little Bin, 1446 ft., which is reached from its higher neighbour after a dip of 700 ft. There is no cairn on the flattish top.

Apart from the scarped north side of the Gargunnocks behind Kippen, the hills east of Fintry present little of interest, and the finest part of the Campsies lies between Strath Blane and Campsie Muir.

Earl's Seat, 1896 ft., is the highest top in the range and lies near the western edge. Its top can be reached either from Campsie Glen, following Fin Glen, but keeping above the stream and contouring the western brow, or from Strathblane, following either the course of the Ballagan Burn or the ridge to the west of it, by Slackdhu. From the west, or

Dumgoyne direction, the Seat is reached over Clachertyfarlie Knowes, which are worth a visit, if only on account of the name. The whole way from Dumgoyne to Earl's Seat gives magnificent views northwards.

Dumgoyne, 1402 ft., is prominent in many views from the hills to the north, and is best ascended from the road south of Killearn. The summit should be approached from the north.

Facing the Blane valley the slopes of the hills are precipitous. The rock is loose and turfy, and easy ways through hard to find. Particularly is this the case above Strathblane, and the area is best avoided except by the rock-climber.

PATHS

The more southerly, and easterly, parts of the Kilpatricks have a number of private roads, closed to the tramper. The Campsies have very few paths across the rough fells, although, in the south, a number of cul-de-sac tracks lead towards the high ground. Four miles east of Lennoxtown and north of Twechar station a road runs to Dykehead and continues as a track to the Birken Reservoir, below Meikle Bin. From here it is possible to descend to the Carron Valley Reservoir, thence east to Carron Bridge. The Reservoir may also be reached from Kilsyth by a path up the east side of the Garrel Burn.

CENTRES

The district is near enough to Glasgow to permit of easy day excursions but there are hotels or inns at the following : Campsie, Carronbridge, Kilsyth and Strathblane.

Youth Hostel at Fintry.

BIBLIOGRAPHY
*" Practice Scrambles," by G. Thomson, *S.M.C.J.*, Vol. 2, p. 8.
*" The Whangie "—Notes by G. Thomson, *S.M.C.J.*, Vol. 2, p. 139.
" Hills near Glasgow "—Notes by H. B. Watt, *S.M.C.J.*, Vol. 2, p. 206.
" Saturday Hill Walks near Glasgow," by W. W. Naismith, *S.M.C.J.*, Vol. 15, p. 35.
*" The Campsie Fells," by J. N. Orr, *S.M.C.J.*, Vol. 21, p. 18.
*Chiefly of rock-climbing interest.

II

THE OCHILS

Maps : O.S. One-inch Popular Edition, Sheets 63 and 67.
O.S. Half-inch, Sheet 23. Bartholomew's Half-inch
Series, Revised, Scotland, Sheet 12. Bartholomew's
Half-inch Series, Great Britain, Sheets 45 and 48.

(1) Bencleuch, 2363 ft. - - - 2½ miles N.N.W. of Tillicoultry.
(2) Ben Ever, 2010 ft. approx. - ¾miles W.S.W. of (1).
(3) The Law, 2094 ft. - - - ¾ miles S.E. of (1).
(4) Andrew Gannel Hill, 2196 ft. - 1 mile E. of (1).
(5) Kings Seat Hill, 2111 ft. - - 2¼ miles N.W. of Dollar.
(6) Tarmangie Hill, 2117 ft. - - 1 mile N.N.E. of (5).
(7) Whitewisp Hill, 2110 ft. - - ¾ mile E. of (6).
(8) Innerdownie, 2004 ft. - - 1¼ miles N.E. of (7).
(9) Blairdenon Hill, 2073 ft. - - 5 miles E. of Dunblane and 2½ miles W.N.W. of (1).

THE early Celts were content to distinguish between the flat
ground of the Forth's meanderings and the hills to the im-
mediate north by naming the latter Uchil, meaning high,
from whence is derived their present name. This attractive
area of rounded, grassy summits measures some 28 miles
long by 8 at its broadest part, and lies between the level
reaches of Strathearn in the north and the broad plains of
the Forth to the south.

To the Forth, the Ochils present an imposing front, and
the crags on Dumyat, the most westerly outlier, form a
fitting side-piece for the Gateway to the Highlands at Stirling.
On their northerly side the hills fall away gently in long slopes
to Strathearn, and the range is divided into two unequal
portions by Glen Devon and Glen Eagles. The hills in the
western portion are higher than those to the east and the
summits are better defined.

It is an area well adapted to hill wandering, for, apart
from the steep southern slopes to the western end of the
range, there are few crags and no cliffs. There is, however,

ample opportunity for route finding over ground deficient in landmarks and amongst valleys which wind and weave amongst the tops in a disconcerting manner.

To the east of Glen Devon the district is traversed by a number of roads, that running from Muckart to Dunning being the most important as well as the highest. At its summit the road rises to over 1000 ft. and provides fine views north on the descent to Dunning.

Tops over 2000 ft. all lie in the portion west of Glen Devon.

Bencleuch, 2363 ft., called Glen Whappen Rig on some maps, is the culminating point of the Ochils, and in some ways is the most attractive hill of the range. It lies sufficiently close to the southern edge of the group to give a fine sense of height when on the top, and at the same time it is surrounded by rolling hill country which adds the necessary touch of remoteness to its summit. The hill is approachable on all sides, but the most pleasing routes lie from the south, up one or other of the glens descending towards Dollar, Tillicoultry or Alva, that from the last named being the easiest. A well-marked path runs up behind the town, and, contouring the south slopes of the Nebit (Middle Hill), 1437 ft., low down, reaches a col between Ben Ever and the Nebit overlooking Glenwhinnel at a height of about 1200 ft., by way of Silver Glen. Silver Glen was quite prosperous at one time, and, apart from silver, copper and lead have also been mined in the Ochils : abandoned workings are still to be seen amongst the hills. A way is now made up Glenwhinnel for about a mile, and the headwaters of the burn followed up easy slopes on the west of Bencleuch. An indicator pedestal of stone, and an Ordnance Survey cairn and shelter lie on the highest point immediately to the south-west of the fence running out to Ben Buck.

The summit is conical and commands a very extensive view. On a clear day the Cairngorms are just visible on the extreme horizon in the north, while nearer at hand, and more to the west, all the higher tops of the Southern Highlands stand around in proud array. The descent can be varied by way of one of the other glens to the south, or by **The Law,**

2094 ft., with a direct descent down steep grass slopes to the
Mill Glen behind Tillicoultry.   There is quite a good right-of-
way path up the slopes east of the Gannel Burn, which, if
followed, leads to Maddy Moss and an open pass between
Skythorn, 1970 ft. approx., and **Andrew Gannel Hill,**
2196 ft.   The slopes of the latter from this side are very easy.
The top is found on the south-east side of the fence which
crosses the hill from Bencleuch.   There is a second top a
little further to the south-east.

Kings Seat Hill, 2111 ft., is easily gained from Tillicoultry by the path mentioned above, or direct from Dollar
by the slopes west of Castle Campbell in Dollar Glen.   Alternatively the summit is easily included in the climb between
Bencleuch and Dollar.   There are two cairns, one 200 yards
north-west of the 2111 ft. point.

By continuing to follow the path from Tillicoultry up
the Gannel Burn and over the bealach west of Skythorn Hill,
one dips down close to the Broich water and reaches the
lonely cottage of Backhill west of Frandy Reservoir.   The
name is appropriate.   From the cottage one can continue
north by Glen Bee, and over the low col west of Craigentaggert
Hill, to Kinpauch and Blackford, the total distance from
Tillicoultry to Blackford Station being 12 miles.   From
Backhill, too, there is a path, some distance up the hillside,
leading to Frandy.

From Dollar to Glen Devon, a good path leads by the
Burn of Care to the gap east of Whitewisp Hill, and by the
west side of the Glenquey reservoir to the main road along
the Devon.   The distance from Dollar to the Glendevon
Hotel is 6 miles.

Glen Sherup also contains a reservoir which is served by a
road passing Glensherup Farm.   This road leaves the main
valley and crosses the River Devon about ¾ miles west of
Glendevon Church.   Glen Sherup is steep sided and is ringed
at the head by Scad Hill, **Tarmangie** and **Whitewisp.**
South of the reservoir lies **Innerdownie.**   The round of these
hills from Glen Devon gives a very pleasant walk which should
include Ben Shee, a nicely isolated little hill of 1691 ft., west
of the reservoir.   Its side facing Scad Hill is steep, and from

the col beneath an ill-defined path may be found leading up
the wet ground of the ridge ahead. From Scad Hill (1921 ft.)
the head of Glen Sherup is contoured and the county march
between Clackmannan and Perth followed to the top of
Tarmangie Hill. The summit is close to the edge of steep
scree and grass slopes and just to the north of the dyke
crossing the hill. From there it is an easy walk over short
grass to Whitewisp Hill by the nearly level ridge separating
Glen Sherup from the Burn of Sorrow. A dyke is followed
nearly all the way along the ridge. Innerdownie is reached
in about half an hour by the ridge of Bentie Knowe, and a
descent can then be made direct to Glen Devon, or by either
of the valleys east and west of the hill. There is a branch
fence to the dyke between Whitewisp and Innerdownie a
little east of the former hill. This leads down into Glen Quey.

West of Bencleuch the only hill over 2000 ft. is **Blairdenon** (2073 ft.), rising at the head of Glen Tye above
Sheriffmuir. It is approached most easily from the highest
point on the secondary road from Dunblane to Greenloaning,
by Sheriffmuir. The north side of Glen Tye is followed over
Glentye Hill and Mickle Corum to the summit of Blairdenon.
There are two tops of which the eastern one, at the junction
of three fences, is the higher. From here Bencleuch can be
reached over rough and peaty ground or a descent can be
made by way of Colsnaur Hill to Alva. A little to the east
of Blairdenon Hill lies the source of the River Devon amongst
peat bogs and it is interesting to reflect that the river's course
is so lengthy in spite of the fact that its beginnings and end
are separated by less than 5 miles in a straight line.

The most westerly point of the Ochils, Dumyat (1376 ft.),
rises steeply above the main road at Blairlogie. The quickest
approach is from Menstrie, by a rough track to the top.
The summit may also be reached from Bridge of Allan by
following the Sheriffmuir road and the very rough branch
leading off to Blairlogie. It is best to leave this road near the
reservoir and make for the top by way of the open gully some
distance west of the summit. For its height Dumyat commands a very pleasing outlook and on this account alone its
summit is well worth a visit.

To the east of Glen Devon the Ochils are lower and of less interest, and finally merge into the plain near Bridge of Earn. Apart from the roads over these hills, the most pleasant cross-country route is from a little west of Glendevon Hotel to Auchterarder. The distance is about 7 miles, the last part, from Coulshill, being along a farm road.

The Ochils give good ski-ing in the right conditions. The best running is to be had from Bencleuch, and on the slopes around Glen Tye. The western slopes of Ben Buck are especially favourable, while the descent from Bencleuch over Skythorn and Scad Hill, and the long ridge to Glen Devon is not difficult. The slopes of Ben Shee should be traversed on the north.

PATHS

Menstrie to Sheriffmuir.—An old road starts at Blairlogie, and, contouring the slopes of Dumyat, runs east, then north above Menstrie Burn. Finally it is on the north of Dumyat, and, passing a reservoir, joins the Sheriffmuir road at a height of 775 ft.

Tillicoultry to Blackford.—This is the most repaying of the Ochil paths and leads (see foregoing chapter) by Mill Glen, the eastern slopes above the Gannel Burn and a pass at 1850 ft. approximately, to Broich Water and Backhill. From here continue north by Glen Bee, and over the watershed to Kinpauch and Blackford.

Dollar to Glen Devon.—The right-of-way track leads, first above the east bank of the Burn of Sorrow, then, turning more north-east, climbs to a narrow pass and descends to Glen Quey. Beyond the reservoir a good road leads to Glen Devon.

Glen Devon to Auchterarder.—A track, faint at Glen Devon, leaves the main road about a mile west of Tormauchin Hotel and mounts the hillside in a north-easterly direction. It is followed to Coulshill farm, from whence a cart track leads to Auchterarder.

Centres

On the south and west of the Ochils are numerous towns
at any of which it is possible to stay : the most convenient
are Bridge of Allan, Dunblane, Dollar and Tillicoultry. It is
sometimes possible to arrange accommodation at Sheriffmuir
Inn, above Dunblane. In or near the village of Glen Devon
are three hotels, and on the north there are hotels at
Auchterarder.

Youth Hostel—Whitehead (Dunblane).

Bibliography

" The Ochils," Guide Book Article, *S.M.C.J.*, Vol. 6, p. 235.
*" Dumyat," by J. H. B. Bell, *S.M.C.J.*, Vol. 20, p. 238.
" May Day on the Ochils," by H. B. Watt, *C.C.J.*, Vol. 1, p. 73.

*Chiefly of rock-climbing interest.

III

THE LOMONDS OF FIFE
(including BENARTY, CLEISH and SALINE HILLS)

Maps : O.S. One-inch Scale Popular Edition, Sheets **68**
(and **64**). O.S. Half-inch Scale, Sheet **24**. Bartholomew's
Half-inch Scale Revised Edition, Sheets **13** (and **8**).
Bartholomew's Half-inch Scale, Great Britain, Sheets **45**
and **49**.

THE three hills of the range are conspicuous and easily
identified from afar off, and are situated to the east of Loch
Leven in the Kingdom of Fife.

The East Lomond (1,471 ft.) stands a little apart and is
the lowest top : the West Lomond above Strathmiglo is the
culminating height of the " Kingdom," being **1713** ft. To
the south-west, the inclined plateau known as the Bishop's
Hill has its highest point in Whitecraigs, **1492** ft.

The Bishop's Hill is quickly ascended from Kinnesswood,
near Loch Leven, there being a track most of the way. The
West Lomond is a little more difficult of access, but a quick
route can be made from Strathmiglo by following a secondary
road west for a short distance, then cutting across fields and
making a steep route up the wide gully to the plateau, east
of the summit. On the ascent one passes close under the
cliffs of Craigengaw. From the plateau a short steepish
climb up the final cone of the hill takes one to the summit
where there is a cairn, and a hollow of stones. The East
Lomond is very quickly climbed from the main road (A912)
between Falkland and New Inn. The way lies up the steep
old road by the Purin Den to a little wood high up on the
eastern shoulder, then through two fields by track up to a
dry-stone dyke. The top is then close at hand, and there is
an excellent indicator on the summit.

One of the main attractions of the Lomonds is the view.
From any of the tops it is good, that from the summit of the

West Lomond being the most extensive. From there on a clear day it is possible to see away to the Cairngorms in the far north, while rather nearer at hand are many old friends and familiar shapes. Far beneath is Loch Leven and the level ground around Milnathort, while, beyond, the rolling Ochils lead the eye westwards to the distant Campsies and the farther Arrochar hills. To the south is Arthur's Seat and the estuary of the Forth. The finest views are often to be had in late Spring when snow on the high hills away to the north and west help one to pick out the familiar outlines.

The most pleasant excursion is to traverse the range from west to east. From the road beyond Strathmiglo a hill road runs due south to the base of the hills and it is possible to find an upward track through the fir woods of Drumdreel. Beyond the woods are grassy slopes. These are contoured and the debris of a landslide crossed. About a mile beyond is the weird sandstone mass called the Maiden's Bower, with its curiously poised Bannetstane. Another mile of slightly upward contouring takes one by the high level track to Glenvale, the deep valley separating the West Lomond and Bishop Hill. This is also known as the Covenanter's Glen and on the Lomond side are some terraced cliffs of white sandstone in the middle of which is John Knox's Pulpit.

Beyond Glenvale are heather and grass slopes to the easterly top of the Bishop Hill. The going from here is rough and the best way follows the north edge of the plateau by a grassy dyke. Half an hour from Glenvale takes one to the middle Bishop top—a twin top with a small gap between. From there the highest and most westerly twin top is readily seen and can be reached in 20 minutes.

Back at Glenvale the West Lomond is a straightforward climb of a little over half an hour and from its summit a way is made eastwards by the north rim of the plateau. Some way along the rim it is possible to strike an old track which ultimately becomes a grassy road between dry-stone dykes near the col between the Lomonds. Over the col runs a seldom-used road from Falkland to Leslie. Beyond this, the grassy road continues by an old quarry, and then eastwards along the south slopes of the East Lomond. The road is followed for nearly a mile, when it is best to make a bee-line for the summit. The descent can be made by the eastern shoulder towards Purin Den, or directly north to Falkland by the steep track through the lower woods. The whole traverse takes 5 to 6 hours and covers 7 distinct tops, 5 of which are on the Bishop Hill.

Benarty—Cleish Hills—Saline Hills.—All three groups —grass or heather-covered dolerite escarpments—make pleasant hill traverses, either separately or in combination. There are a few broken crags here and there but nothing worthy of attention from a rock-climbing point of view. Where continuous crags exist, along part of the north front of Benarty and along the northern front of the Cleish Hills east of Loch Glow, they are unsatisfactory except for minor experimental purposes, the rock being much fractured and easy or in short, vertical, impossibly difficult walls.

Benarty, 1131 ft., can be traversed from the Scotlandwell-Lochore road over the minor eminence of Navity Hill (721 ft.) and then along the main ridge with a steep descent through a beech wood to a side road just east of the main Kinross-Cowdenbeath road near Blairadam station (2 hours from Scotlandwell to Blairadam). There are good views northwards over Loch Leven in marked contrast to the industrial area to the south.

The foregoing traverse can be continued directly westwards over the Cleish Hills, by simply crossing the main road and proceeding westward up a farm road (30 minutes) and then making for the hill crest. It is best to proceed fairly close to the craggy northern edge until in sight of Dumglow, the main top, 1241 ft. A subsidiary top of 1100 ft. is passed on the way. Less than 1½ hours will suffice from the main road to Dumglow. Thereafter the going is rough and very marshy to the last top, Wether Hill, 1100 ft., in about 50 minutes. The descent is very rapid and easy to the Dunfermline-Rumbling Bridge road (2½ miles from the latter). Dumglow can be climbed and descended in about 40 minutes from the nearest point on the Cleish road running below it on the north side.

Both Saline Hill, 1178 ft., and Knock Hill, 1189 ft., can be very quickly ascended from the refuse dumps of the old Steelend coalpit about 2 miles east of Saline village on the road to Kelty. Several of these hills are promising terrain for ski-ing in winter, as they are readily accessible yet carry a good deal of snow. Besides Cleish Hills and Saline Hill may be mentioned the little Cults Hill, 865 ft., close above the aforesaid Rumbling Bridge-Dunfermline road.

Visitors to the region should certainly visit the deep gorge of the Devon at Rumbling Bridge, and also the Cauldron Linn, a mile lower down. The latter is best approached from the south side by a side road, the railway line and a short field path. Both are impressive examples of erosion in the old red sandstone.

The traverse of the Lomonds, Bishop Hill, Benarty and Cleish Hills from Falkland to Rumbling Bridge has been accomplished on the following time schedule—Falkland 10 a.m.; E. Lomond 10.37; W. Lomond 11.51; W. Bishop 1.0 p.m.; over Benarty to Blairadam 3.21; Dumglow 4.50; Wether Hill 5.50 and Rumbling Bridge 7 p.m. (J. H. B. Bell and W. Omand, October, 1931.)

CENTRES

Hotels at Kinross and Rumbling Bridge. These are distant from the easterly hills, but a bus service runs via Strathmiglo.

BIBLIOGRAPHY
" The Fife Lomonds," by W. Brown, *S.M.C.J.*, Vol. 3, p. 38.
" Guide Book Article," *S.M.C.J.*, Vol 6, p. 235.
" The Lomonds," by J. H. B. Bell, *S.M.C.J.*, Vol. 18, p. 280.
*" The Lomonds Rock Climbs," by J. H. B. Bell, *S.M.C.J.*, Vol. 18, p. 344.
*Chiefly of rock-climbing interest.

IV

COWAL AND ARDGOIL

Munro's Tables—Section 1.
Maps : O.S. One-inch Scale Popular Edition, Sheets 71,
65 and 61. O.S. Half-inch Scale, Sheets 26 and 22.
Bartholomew's Half-inch Scale, Sheets 11 and 7.
Bartholomew's Half-inch Scale, Great Britain, Sheet 44.

(1) **Cowal,** said to be named after Comghal or Comgall, a
chief of the Dalriada Scots in the sixth century, is a large
promontory about 36 miles long and 17 miles broad at its
widest. It is bounded on the south by the Kyles of Bute,
stretching in a curved line between Loch Fyne on the west
and the Firth of Clyde in the east. Its east coast is formed
by the waters of the Clyde and Loch Long, out of which,
further north, Loch Goil cuts into the land and separates
Cowal from Ardgoil and Ardgartan. North of these the
boundary runs by the county march from Arrochar to Glen
Fyne. For the purpose of this section, however, the northern
boundary is taken as Loch and River Goil and Hell's Glen.
The hills immediately to the north are described in the next
section, while the Arrochar hills are a chapter unto themselves. The western shores are washed by Loch Fyne, which
curves around gradually from Ardlamont Point on the
southern tip of Cowal to end some 2 miles north-west of
Strome beyond the mouth of Glen Kinglas.

It is a district rich in beauty, and offers in miniature
much that is best in Highland scenery. South of Hell's Glen
and the River Goil, Cowal possesses no hills over 3000 ft. and
is pre-eminently a district for the walker. Most ready access
to the southern part of the district is by sea. A fair steamer
service makes Dunoon within easy reach of Glasgow, and this
popular resort, or Kirn, makes an admirable starting point
for the many walks in the southern part of the district.

R. M. Adam.

CLACH BHEINN FROM LOCH ECK.

June, 1934.

PUCK'S GLEN.

B. H. Humble.

Ardentinny Hotel on the west shore of Loch Long is reached
by road, and is a useful base for exploring the hills on both
sides of Glen Finart. Whistlefield on the shores of Loch Eck
is also a good centre for this area. Lochgoilhead is convenient
for the hills in the north. For the hills to the west of Loch
Eck, that jewel of Central Cowal, some form of conveyance
is almost a necessity. A good road runs from Strachur, by
Loch Eck to the Holy Loch, and Strachur itself may be
reached easily by road from Arrochar by Glen Croe and Glen
Kinglas, or from Inveraray by the head of Loch Fyne.

Cowal hills over 2000 ft., and south of Hell's Glen and
the River Goil, comprise the following, and are divided into
seven groups thus :—

(1) Cruach nan Capull 2005 ft., 5½ miles W.N.W. of
Dunoon and 3½ miles S.E. of the head of Loch
Striven. This is the highest point of the low hills
south of Glen Lean.

(2) Beinn Ruadh, 2178 ft., 2¼ miles W.N.W. of Ardentinny,
is the highest point on the promontory between
Loch Eck and Glen Finart.

(3) Beinn Mhor, 2433 ft., 2¾ miles S.W. of Whistlefield
Inn.

(4) Beinn Bheag, 2029 ft., 1¾ miles N.E. of (3) and almost
opposite Whistlefield.

(5) Clach Bheinn, 2109 ft., 1¾ miles S.E. of (3).

(6) Creag Tharsuinn, 2103 ft., 1¼ miles W.N.W. of (3).
These form a group to the west of Loch Eck.

(7) Cruach a' Chaise, 2069 ft., 2¼ miles north of Ardentinny.

(8) Creachan Mòr, 2156 ft., ⅓ mile N.W. of (7).

(9) Cruach Eighrach, 2100 ft., ½ mile N.W. of (8).

(10) Cruach a' Bhuic, 2084 ft., 1 mile N.W. of (9).

(11) Beinn Bhreac, 2043 ft., ½ mile N.W. of (10).

(12) Sgurr a' Choinnich, 2148 ft., 1 mile N. of (11).
Form an almost continuous ridge, with only slight
dips, running parallel to, and to the north-east of,
Glen Finart.

c

(13) Beinn Bheula, 2557 ft., 3½ miles W.S.W. of Lochgoil-
      head and 3¼ miles N.N.E. of Whistlefield Inn.
(14) Beinn Dubhain, 2114 ft., ⅞ mile S.W. of (13).
(15) Carnach Mòr, 2079 ft., 1 mile W.N.W. of (13).
          These are the group N.E. of the north end of
      Lock Eck and are separated from the following by
      the Bealach an Lochain and Curra Lochain.
(16) Beinn Lochain, 2306 ft., 2½ miles W. of Lochgoilhead.
(17) Beinn Tharsuinn, 2037 ft., ¾ mile N.E. of (16).
(18) Nameless Point, 2155 ft., ½ mile N.E. of (17).
(19) Mullach Coire a' Chuir, 2098 ft., 2¼ miles N.W. of
      Lochgoilhead.
          This group forms the high ground to the N.W. of
      the head of Loch Goil and is separated from the
      following by a drop of 1000 ft. to the headwaters of
      the Allt Canachadan.
(20) Cruach nam Mult, 2001 ft., 1⅛ miles N. of (19).

Cruach nan Capull, 2005 ft., may be approached from
Loch Striven by the path on the west side of the Inverchaolain Glen as far as the Bealach na Sreine (there is also a
fair path on the east side of the Glen), or from Glen Kin by a
path leading to the same point. The track about the Bealach
is indistinct. From this point the way lies over Leacann nan
Gall, 1838 ft., in a northerly direction and on to the summit
of Cruach nan Capull after a dip of 150 ft. The most pleasant
approach, however, is from Dunoon over Bishop's Seat. The
road to the reservoir is followed and then the left bank of
the Balgie burn to the flattish moor lying below the twin
tops of the Bishop's Seat. From the top a descent of 600 ft.,
at first west, leads easily to the Bealach na Sreine and the
ridge then followed as before. Descent from Cruach nan
Capull is easy by way of the ridge forming the east side of
Corrachaive Glen and into Glen Lean, or a way can be made
along the south ridge leading to Loch Striven. The views
from these hills are fine and give a good panoramic picture of
Cowal. From Cruach Neuran, 1988 ft., about 2 miles north-
west of Cruach nan Capull, it is possible to see Glasgow on a
clear day. This top makes a good finish to a day's hill walk

from Dunoon. There is a path from the head of Loch Striven by the eastern shore of the loch to Inverchaolin, to which point it is possible to drive from Dunoon.

The hills of the promontory between the Holy Loch and Glen Finart culminate in **Beinn Ruadh, 2178 ft.**, which may be gained from Inverchapel near the south end of Loch Eck by following the Inverchapel burn by its right bank and contouring the slopes of Creag Liath. The view of the Beinn Mhòr group is good, but the best view of the Arrochar Hills is to be had from Kilmun Hill rising towards the southern tip of the promontory.

Beinn Mhòr, 2433 ft., is the highest and the most interesting hill of the group lying west of Loch Eck. It is seen to advantage from the road descending to Loch Striven from Glen Lean, and from this point occupies an isolated and imposing position. It is best ascended from the farm at the head of Glen Massan by the long slope over Sron Mhòr, **1669 ft.** The top is flattish and the cairn lies at the south-west edge where the ridge drops away to Sron Mhòr. It is also possible to cycle to the foot of Glen Bernice from whence the top may be gained in about 1½ hours by following the stream to the watershed between Loch Eck and Glen Shellish and, after turning sharp left, by easy slopes to the summit. A more interesting route is to follow the south branch of the Bernice stream to the shoulder running out to Meall an t-Sith and contouring from there into the south-west corrie. This side of Beinn Mhòr is characterised by broken cliffs and pinnacles, but the right-hand side leads easily to the flattish ground near the summit. Scrambles of varying degrees of difficulty are possible in the corrie.

The descent of Beinn Mhòr can be made by way of **Clach Bheinn, 2109 ft.**, on which there are some rocky pinnacles. The descent from Beinn Mhòr involves a dip of almost 800 ft. and a subsequent rise to Clach Bheinn of over 450 ft., by way of the bounding ridge of Coire an t-Sith. From Clach Bheinn the descent is easy to the south-east and the Allt Corrach.

Beinn Bheag, 2029 ft., lying to the north of Beinn Mhòr, may be approached by way of the col at the upper end of

Glen Bernice. The ridge west of Beinn Mhòr, from which it is separated by the Garrachra Glen, culminates in **Creag Tharsuinn,** 2103 ft., which shows a steep face to the east, considerably broken by outcropping rock.   The easiest approach is from Glenmassan Farm by a track disappearing beyond Garrachra.   From there a diagonal approach leads to the Bealach nan Sac, and to the summit of Creag Tharsuinn by the ridge.

The watershed between Glen Finart and Loch Goil consists of a long knolly ridge of summits, of which the highest, **Creachan Mòr,** is 2156 ft.   The most southerly top is Am Binnein, easily approached from Ardentinny by the road to Glenfinart House.   After crossing Finart Water the Knap path is taken and followed for ½ mile.   From there strike left through the trees and follow the hillside upwards to the top in about 1½ hours from Ardentinny.   The path to Knap lies some distance up the hillside and has many delightful situations : it continues to Carrick, crossing Knap burn, and rising well up above the headland of Rudha nan Eòin, and is not marked on either the one-inch Ordnance Survey or half-inch Bartholomew maps.

Beyond Am Binnein, which is really a spur of **Cruach a' Chaise,** 2069 ft., the ground rises easily to the flattish top of the latter peak.   From here the whole ridge may be followed in a north-westerly direction to Sgurr a' Choinnich, 2148 ft., over four intervening summits and a number of indeterminate knolls.   It is nearly 4 miles long and drops nowhere below 1800 ft.   From Sgurr a' Choinnich a descent can be made west by way of Coire Ealt in which there is a Forestry Commission path open all the year.   Alternatively, the main ridge may be followed rather north-east to Cnoc na Tricriche and a descent made to Loch Goil by the east shoulder of that hill and the left bank of the Carrick Burn to Carrick.

If the ridge walk above mentioned has not afforded sufficient exercise, **Beinn Bheula,** 2557 ft., may be included without much additional effort.   The col between Cnoc na Tricriche and Beinn Bheula is rather over 1800 ft. and affords quick access to the steeper slopes beyond.   Height is quickly gained on the broken slopes and, crossing a subsidiary top at

2507 ft., the summit is reached in less than an hour from the Cnoc. The main top of Beinn Bheula lies close to the edge of the steep east face and is marked by a fair-sized cairn. The east face is rocky and should be avoided in mist. Beinn Bheula's outlying tops, **Beinn Dubhain,** 2114 ft., and **Carnach Mòr,** 2079 ft., are of little interest by themselves, but the round of the hills from the Loch Eck road at Bridgend makes a pleasant hill walk of 5 hours. From Lochgoilhead, the quickest way to Beinn Bheula is by the Lettermay Burn as far as the branch coming from Curra Lochain. A way is made up this branch and the shoulder of Beinn Bheula on the left followed to the top. Probably the easiest route of all to the top is direct from Loch Eck side by Coire Aodainn.

The range of hills shutting in Loch Goil on the north-west may also be traversed in one expedition. The most southerly top, **Beinn Lochain,** 2306 ft., is conveniently approached from Lochgoilhead by the Lettermay Burn to Gleann Bàn, separating Beinn Lochain and Beinn Tharsuinn to the north. The ridge straight ahead is then followed to the top, which lies some way back. From here the way to the north is followed over **Beinn Tharsuinn,** 2037 ft., and an unnamed top of 2155 ft. to **Mullach Coire a' Chuir,** 2098 ft. The dips between the tops are nowhere great, the lowest col being over 1600 ft., and the hills command a pleasing vista of Ardgoil and the Arrochar group. Descent from Mullach Coire a' Chuir can be made by the ridge facing the Brack or by a more circuitous route in the opposite direction to the col south of Cruach nam Mult and Gleann Canachadan. The direct descent is to be preferred unless it is intended to include Cruach nam Mult, 2001 ft., and descend into Hell's Glen.

The area around Loch Eck forms the southern part of the Argyll National Forest Park, the Beinn Mhòr range being included. The northern boundary of this part of the Park is roughly on a line between Carrick Castle on Loch Goil and Strachur to the west. Certain areas, adequately marked, and all below 900 ft. altitude, are reserved for afforestation.

The extensive and beautiful forest garden at Benmore is open to the public, and is well worth a visit. Close by, in the delightful gorge known as Puck's Glen, is a rest house designed by Sir Robert Lorimer. This is panelled with different woods drawn from every type in the estate. The view to Beinn Mhòr, through the trees, is exquisite.

(2) **Ardgoil** is the strip of country lying between Glens Croe and Kinglas on the north, and Hell's Glen and the River Goil on the south. The most southern part, or Argyll's Bowling Green, forms the wedge between Loch Goil and Loch Long. The hills in this section are higher and more rugged than those of the southern part of Cowal, and form a connecting link, as it were, with the Arrochar peaks to the north. The name, Argyll's Bowling Green, does not appear to be in use prior to 1750, nor is it shown in the old edition of the one-inch Ordnance Survey, although the six-inch applies the name to a small plot of ground between Mark and The Saddle. It seems likely that the name, applied originally to a restricted area, has come to cover a much greater tract of ground.

Lochgoilhead, in the west of the district, and Arrochar are the best centres, although it is possible to climb direct from Mark on the west shore of Loch Long after approaching by fishing boat from Portincaple or by road from Ardgartan. The road does not continue beyond Mark.

From south to north the hills over 2000 ft. are :—

(1) Beinn Reithe, 2141 ft., 2 miles N. of Mark.
(2) Cnoc Coinnich, 2497 ft., 1½ miles N. of (1).
(3) The Brack, 2580 ft., on a line between Lochgoilhead and Arrochar and distant 3 miles from either place.
(4) Ben Donich, 2774 ft., 2¼ miles N.E. from Lochgoilhead.
(5) **Beinn an Lochain,** 3021 ft., 1¼ miles S.W. of Butter-bridge in Glen Croe.
(6) Beinn an t-Seilich, 2359 ft., 1 mile W. of (5).
(7) Stob an Eas, 2400 ft., 1 mile W.S.W. of (6).

The first three hills form part of the backbone of Argyll's Bowling Green, the most southern top of the range being Clach Bheinn, 1433 ft., due west of Mark.

The traverse from Clach Bheinn to **Beinn Reithe,** 2141 ft., involves crossing Tom Molach and the Saddle, 1704 ft., but the going is easy. The col between Tom Molach and the Saddle, at under 1000 ft., forms an easy route from Mark to Beach on Loch Goil. South of Tom Molach is the only

Lochan of any size in Ardgoil. The Saddle presents a steep
and rocky face to the south and is most easily approached
from the south-west. Its summit is rocky. North of the
Saddle the ridge continues towards Beinn Reithe by way of
the Bealach na Diollaid at 1352 ft. and presents no difficulty.
From Beinn Reithe to **Cnoc Coinnich,** 2497 ft., it is necessary
to swing around the corrie by lumpy ground rather west, with
the col at 1732 ft., and gain the Cnoc by its south-west ridge.
From the summit it is possible to descend to Coilessan by the
Glen of that name, or by the area called Garbh on the one-
inch map. This spot is well named and is strewn with boulders
large and small, the largest being upwards of 50 ft. high. It
is also possible to continue the ridge walk to The Brack by
descending 800 ft. to the col at 1600 ft. and ascending by the
south-west ridge, over a small subsidiary top, to the summit.
Descent from there is easiest by the west slopes to the col
north of the headwaters of the Allt Coire Odhair and so to
Glen Croe. It is necessary to follow the Forestry Commission
path to avoid the plantation.

The Brack, 2580 ft., throws out a great shoulder to the
east towards Ardgartan, very rough and craggy, which gives
a pleasant route from Arrochar and is equally useful for the
descent. Facing Glen Croe the mountain shows a fine steep
side of broken cliffs upwards of 500 ft. high on which are a
variety of rock climbs. A descent on this side is to be avoided
by the walker. From Lochgoilhead a path leads up Donich
Water and the Brack is easily climbed from this side, preferably from the col between it and Cnoc Coinnich.

Ben Donich, 2774 ft., is said to be named after a local
saint, and commands the finest view of Ardgoil. If
approached from the direction of the Brack, the east ridge,
although craggy in parts, is nowhere difficult and the views
across Glen Croe are always fine. The summit is flattish,
the cairn lying near the edge of the south slopes. Across
Gleann Mòr, through which a road runs from Lochgoilhead
to the Rest and Be Thankful in Glen Croe, Beinn an Lochain
looms grandly, the peaks of Cruachan being visible over its
left shoulder. From Lochgoilhead the traverse of Ben Donich
makes a pleasant excursion, best done from south to north.

The somewhat uninteresting southern slopes lead directly to the summit with no intervening tops and the expanding views at one's back invite frequent halts. From the cairn it is necessary to go a little way north-east before striking the long, well-defined, north ridge facing the Rest and Be Thankful. The road through Gleann Mòr is reached at its highest point. Taken in the reverse direction, of course, the traverse is even easier, for transport is possible to the highest point in Gleann Mòr, and there remains considerably less than 2000 ft. to be ascended on foot.

Beinn an Lochain, 3021 ft., is the only peak over 3000 ft. in Cowal, south of Glen Kinglas and Glen Croe. The Ordnance Survey one-inch Map (Popular Edition) gives its height as 2992 ft., but the actual summit is about 150 yards N.E. of this point, and on the six-inch map is shown as 3021 ft. Loch Restil, at a height of 800 ft., lies below the steep and craggy east face of the mountain, and on the south side, lower down, steep slopes flank Gleann Mòr.

The most usual approach is up the north-east ridge facing Butterbridge in Glen Kinglas, this point being reached from the 4 miles distant Cairndow Hotel on Loch Fyne, or from Arrochar by the Rest and Be Thankful road. When descending the north-east ridge in mist it is well to remember that a large subsidiary spur leaves the main ridge in a northerly direction at about the 2250 ft. contour. This is perfectly easy to descend, but leads west of Butterbridge and to a possibly unfordable Kinglas Water.

If making the ascent from Lochgoilhead follow the Gleann Mòr road as far as the bridge crossing the Allt Glinne Mhòir and take to the hillside above the left bank of the stream issuing from the corrie between Beinn an Lochain and Beinn an t-Seilich. For about 1000 ft. the way is steep until the upper corrie is reached at which point the way lies east up easy slopes overlooking the steep ground facing Gleann Mòr.

Beinn an t-Seilich, 2359 ft., and **Stob an Eas,** 2400 ft. contour, are seldom visited but are accessible from either end of Hell's Glen to the south or by the ridges running out to Glen Kinglas in the north. There is no bridge over Kinglas water between the west end of the Glen and Butterbridge,

BEINN AN LOCHAIN FROM BEN DONICH LOOKING ACROSS GLEANN MOR.

August, 1934. *B. H. Humble.*

W. Inglis Clark.

COBBLER, NORTH PEAK.

D. Scott.

THE BUTTERMILK BURN AND THE COBBLER.

so that Beinn an t-Seilich would be more easily ascended from the south. The two hills form roughly parallel ridges, the highest point of Stob an Eas lying above small cliffs at the south end. The summit of Beinn an t-Seilich lies towards the north end although there is a top of nearly equal height at the south.

Nearly the whole of Ardgoil, east of Gleann Mòr and the River Goil, forms part of the northern area of the Argyll National Forest Park.

PATHS—(1) COWAL

Colintraive to Dunoon by the coast.—Road or track is followed the whole way. Approximate distance—32 miles. This may be shortened by driving the first 6 miles from Colintraive, and the last 14 miles into Dunoon.

Inverchaolain to Dunoon by Glen Kin.—A very re-paying walk this, by the path which leaves the road a little north of Inverchaolain, and, following the north side of the deeply cut glen of that name, crosses the Bealach na Sreine at 1100 ft. Thereafter it drops into Glen Kin and winds through the woods to Ballochyle Bridge. A little further on the main road is reached.

Loch Eck by the west shore.—A rough road runs from Benmore Farm to Bernice, thereafter a track continues by Stuck to Glenbranter and the main road joined at Bridgend. The distance is about 9 miles.

Loch Eck to Lochgoilhead through the hills.—A Forestry Commission path climbs up Coire Ealt from Craig-brack, $\frac{1}{2}$ mile from the north end of the loch. This is followed to the col beneath Beinn Bheula and the descent made to Lochgoilhead on the far side by way of the Lettermay Burn. The way over the col and northwards is trackless.

(2) ARDGOIL

Lochgoilhead to Ardgartan by the hills (*N.B.*—There is *no* track via the coast).—Alternative routes exist. The path up Donich Water is followed in both cases to where the glen bends north-east. The glen can now be followed to the col between Ben Donich and The Brack and a descent made to Glen Croe by the Forestry Commission path through the plantation, or, alternatively (and preferably), a way is made over the col north of Cnoc Coinnich and into the Coilessan Glen. The going here is trackless and somewhat boggy until a path is encountered lower down by the burn. The lochside road is then followed to Ardgartan.

CENTRES

Ardentinny, Ardgartan, Arrochar, Dunoon, Kirn, Lochgoilhead, Strachur and Whistlefield all have hotels ; it is sometimes possible to arrange a bed at Mark also, but this cannot be relied upon.

Youth Hostels are found at Ardgartan, Glen Loin (Arrochar), Loch Eck (Whistlefield), Strone (Dunselma, near Dunoon), Tighnabruaich (Kyles of Bute).

BIBLIOGRAPHY

" Cowal," Guide Book Article, *S.M.C.J.*, Vol. 6, p. 172.
*" Beinn an Lochain," by H. Raeburn, *S.M.C.J.*, Vol. 7, p. 242.
" The Brack," by W. Inglis Clark, *S.M.C.J.*, Vol. 9, p. 19.
*" The Brack—Elephant Gully," by H. Raeburn, *S.M.C.J.*, Vol. 12, p. 209.
*Note on the above by J. M. Wordie, *S.M.C.J.*, Vol. 12, p. 294.
*" Clach Bheinn Pinnacles," by Allan Arthur, *S.M.C.J.*, Vol. 12, p. 235.
" Argyll's Bowling Green," by F. S. Goggs, *S.M.C.J.*, Vol. 12, p. 323,
" Cowal and its Hills," by S. M. Penney, *S.M.C.J.*, Vol. 11, p. 313,
" Coast and Hill Paths round the Firth of Clyde," by B. H. Humble, *S.M.C.J.*, Vol. 23, p. 68.
" Rest and Be Thankful " Stone, *S.M.C.J.*, Vol. 12, p. 344.

V

THE ARROCHAR GROUP

Munro's Tables—Section 1.
Maps : O.S. One-inch Scale Popular Edition, Sheets 61
and 62. O.S. Half-inch Scale, Sheet 22. Bartholomew's
Half-inch Scale (Revised), Sheet 11. Bartholomew's
Half-inch Scale, Great Britain, Sheet 48.

(1) Ben Arthur, 2891 ft. - (The Cobbler)	-	2 miles W. of the head of Loch Long.
(2) **Ben Narnain,** 3036 ft. -	-	1 mile N.E. of (1).
(3) A' Chrois, 2785 ft. (The Cross) -		2 miles N.N.E. of Arrochar.
(4) **Ben Ime,** 3318 ft. - - (Butter Mountain)	-	3¾ miles N.W. from Arrochar.
(5) **Ben Vane,** 3004 ft. - - (Middle Mountain)	-	3¾ miles N.N.W. from Arrochar.
(6) **Ben Vorlich,** 3092 ft. -	-	2½ miles S.W. from Ardlui.

IT is only within fairly recent years that this fine group of
hills has been accorded the attention it deserves. In small
compass, and within easy reach of Glasgow, the area has now
become as popular a week-end climbing centre as any in
Scotland, and the reasons for this are not far to seek.
Although not of very great altitude the hills rise almost directly
from sea level, and thus present their full height value ; the
group is compact and accessible from most quarters ; the
views from the tops are unexcelled, embracing loch, sea and
hill ; and lastly the rock-climbing possibilities are of a high
order.

The hills lie to the north of Loch Long and are bounded
on the east by Loch Lomond. They are separated from the
other hills of Cowal by the deep valley of Glen Croe and
Kinglas Water, and from the lower hills to the north-west
by Strath Dubh-uisge.

The first four of the summits above mentioned lie within
the confines of Argyll, while Ben Vorlich and Ben Vane are

enclosed by the county march of Dunbartonshire. Beinn an Lochain, west of Glen Croe's summit, is often included amongst the Arrochar Hills, but is described under Cowal in the present work.

It must be admitted that the area is one of heavy rainfall, and, unfortunately, as the hills lie so close to the sea they seldom accumulate snow to the extent of our higher Bens. In winter the hills are often icy, and the climbing at that time can become very hard indeed.

Arrochar is the best centre, but, on the periphery of the group, Ardlui and Inverarnan to the east, and Cairndow at the head of Loch Fyne, are useful alternatives. The motorist has a wider field of choice as the district is well served by roads, while, from Glasgow, the West Highland line runs direct to Arrochar, bringing the area well within the range of day excursions.

Ben Arthur (The Cobbler), 2891 ft. Although one of the lowest, The Cobbler is certainly the most important and interesting mountain of the group. Its three strange, rocky points, and its excellent position as a viewpoint, combine to place it in the front rank of our Scottish hills. The crooked peaks can be seen from many points afar off, and thousands of tourists, passing by train on the West Highland line, have marvelled at the strange outline. Few, seeing the mountain for the first, or hundredth, time can fail to be impressed. Who first applied the name, Cobbler, is obscure, and it is indeed hard to find any likeness to a cobbler in the shape, but it is interesting to note that some of the peaks of the Eastern Alps, whose shapes are often spectacular and whose summits tend to end in perpendicular drops have the name Schuster (or Cobbler) applied to them. John Stoddart (*Local Scenery and Manners in Scotland,* 1799-1800) writes : " This terrific rock forms the bare summit of a huge mountain, and its nodding top so far overhangs the base as to assume the appearance of a cobbler sitting at work, from whence the country people call it *an greasaiche cròm,* the crooked shoemaker."

The name Cobbler is properly applied only to the centre peak, which is also the highest, but the name is commonly used to cover the whole mountain. The south peak (on left, seen from Arrochar) is familiarly known as Jean, or sometimes the Cobbler's Last : the other peak to the north of the main top is the Cobbler's Wife or north peak.

For long, the Cobbler had a reputation of inaccessibility, and indeed it must be admitted that the climb up the final rock tower is not without difficulty, but the mountain can be climbed with perfect ease from any direction as far as its rocky heart. From **Arrochar,** there is a choice of two routes : the first, not so much used nowadays, is by way of the prominent stream descending direct to Loch Long from the corrie. The road is followed round the end of the loch past Succoth as far as the Allt a' Bhalachain (Buttermilk Burn) and a muddy path is taken on the west side of the stream. The lower reaches of the hillside are afforested. The path follows the stream course steeply upwards for about 1200 ft. to where the angle eases and The Cobbler once more comes into sight. This point is reached more conveniently by following the path starting at the south bank of the Allt Sugach near the Youth Hostel and mounting the steep slopes beyond. The path then traverses into the corrie at a height of between 1200 and 1500 ft. The left bank of the Buttermilk Burn is now followed over boggy ground until some rocky outcrops on the slopes of Narnain are passed and a collection of large boulders reached. These are the Narnain Boulders which provide a useful landmark in misty weather, as well as a number of entertaining scrambles. They lie quite near the stream, and a rude shelter, built with loose stones, can be used as an uncomfortable resting place. It is, in fact, a well-known " howff."

From here again there is a choice of routes. One leads up the main stream towards the col between Narnain and The Cobbler's north peak, which can then be traversed to the dip beneath the main top. The north ridge and peak are rough but not difficult and a well-worn track leads over the rocky parts. The alternative is to cross the burn near the Boulders and follow a stream coming from the main corrie. The going is hard over bogs until the rocky ground at the head of the corrie is reached, where a rough path may be found leading steeply to the depression in the ridge between the north and centre peaks. From here a scramble leads to the summit. The dip between the centre and south peaks may also be attained from the corrie, although the going is steep.

A grassy hump lies to the back (west) of the true summit, which consists of a narrow wall of rock, vertical on three sides and steeply sloping to the south. The ordinary and easiest route of ascent begins where a number of fallen rocks abut on the north-east corner. A few feet up, the wall is split by a narrow fissure, through which the climber passes. This leads to a commodious ledge on the west side which is then followed towards the south-west corner of the tower, where a short wriggle in a second fissure brings the summit to hand. The outlook is delightful.

From the col south of the main peak a way may be made up the rocks of the south ridge, but this is more ambitious and should not be undertaken by those with no experience of rock-climbing. The angle is not excessive, and the holds are good, but it should be remembered that the rock becomes very slippery in wet weather. The route is at first up a steep slab by way of a crack in the middle, and thence up the ridge direct to the top.

From **Glen Croe** the ascent is steep and uninteresting, but nowhere difficult, and may be made anywhere from the road beyond the limit of the plantations. The col between the south and centre peaks is the point on the ridge most easily gained from this side.

From **Upper Inveruglas** on Loch Lomondside the way to The Cobbler is longer but very beautiful. The new roads, made in connection with the Loch Sloy Hydro-Electric Scheme, help, and lead well up past Coiregrogain. The Coiregrogain Burn is followed and a route made on the south side up grassy slopes to the col between Ben Ime and The Cobbler. The north ridge of the latter is then followed to the top, the distance from Upper Inveruglas to the summit being a little over 4 miles. Coiregrogain can also be reached from Arrochar by the road and path up Glen Loin, the distance being 3 miles.

To the top of The Cobbler's **South Peak** there exists no absolutely simple route, although the south-west side of the peak can be ascended in perfect safety if due care is taken. The easiest route starts on the south-west where steep grass slopes abut on the screes below. Considerable variation is possible, and the route is not hard to find. For those completely inexperienced in rock-climbing, a descent should be made by the same way.

The steep drop to the col between "Jean" and The Cobbler is not really difficult, but here again it is well to remember that in wet weather, especially, the rocks become very slippery. From the col the normal route makes use of a prominent ledge running obliquely right from a little above the gap. From near the far end of this a shallow chimney, changing presently to a grassy ledge, will be observed sloping up to the left. This leads to the western edge of a broad shelf which is crossed, and a way made directly up two short but steep rock pitches to the top, which is reached some yards west of the extreme summit.

The **North Peak** is traversed easily along the ridge by a well-worn track. The peak is probably the most impressive of The Cobbler summits, whether seen from the south or from the west, where the overhanging top appears to advantage.

A traverse of the three peaks from south to north is a popular expedition of moderate difficulty. It is customary to include an ascent of the Right-angled Gully on the North Peak (for details see the section on Rock Climbs) but this is not essential. The main difficulties are then concentrated between the South and Centre Peaks.

Ben Narnain, 3036 ft.—Rising direct from Glen Loin, Narnain is a most attractive mountain, although it is somewhat overshadowed by its more interesting neighbour, The Cobbler. The best general view of Narnain's east face is to be had from Cruach Tairbeirt (1364 ft.) separating Glen Loin from the shore of Loch Lomond. From here the mountain stands up proudly, and its summit, which is hidden from Arrochar by the huge buttress descending towards

Succoth, is well seen. The summit is flat and easily recognisable from other tops by its high plateau, cut off on three sides by steep cliffs. From Narnain the view is even finer than from The Cobbler, for the latter peak is itself included. Particularly at sunset, the outlook to the west, and down the reaches of Loch Long, is exceedingly fine.

On the slopes facing The Cobbler are numerous outcrops of rock and much shattered debris of fallen cliffs. Near the top, and surrounding the Sugach Coire the rocks are more continuous, forming a range of precipices of considerable height. The lower slopes of the hills are afforested, being part of the Argyll National Forest Park.

The usual approach to the top is from Succoth by the long slopes immediately to the south of the prominent rock face visible from the road. Higher up one bears right to the easy ridge leading up to a subsidiary top separated from Narnain by a slight dip. From this top, Cruach nam Miseag, Narnain lies straight ahead with a line of cliffs guarding the upper plateau. The rocks are best avoided on the right (north), where a wide gully will be found leading in due course to the stony summit. Alternatively, by contouring the slopes under the cliffs to the left, it is soon possible to strike through broken rocks and so gain the top from the south side. There are two small cairns on the summit plateau.

An attractive alternative route to Narnain is given by the path leading up the south bank of the Allt Sugach. From the track a way is made into the impressive Sugach Coire above, and the ridge ahead gained by screes to the north-east of Narnain. To approach the hill from the other side, it is best to follow the Buttermilk Burn (see under routes to The Cobbler) by the path to the Narnain Boulders, and make for the top by the course of a little burn descending in a wide gully. Alternatively, continue on up the left bank of the Allt a' Bhalachain to the bealach between the north peak of The Cobbler and Narnain. From here turn right, up the easy shoulder leading to the flat top of the latter peak.

From Upper Inveruglas the route is the same as to The Cobbler as far as the Narnain-Ime Bealach (Bealach a' Mhaim), when the shoulder of Narnain mentioned above is

A. D. S. Macpherson.

THE ARROCHAR HILLS FROM INVERSNAID.

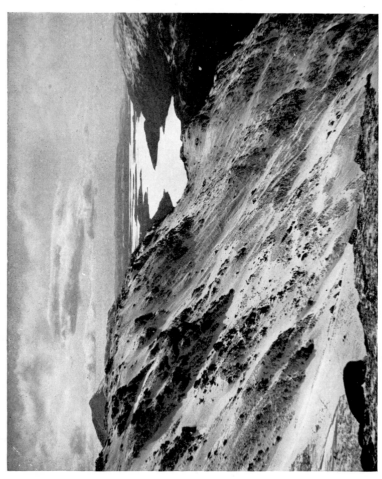

A. D. S. Macpherson.

followed upwards. The slopes bounding Coiregrogain are steep but not difficult.

A description of Narnain would be incomplete without reference to its caves and boulders. The latter have been mentioned in the section on the usual Cobbler routes : they lie close to the Allt a' Bhalachain, south of Narnain, near the 1500 ft. contour, and provide a variety of short, well-marked scrambles. The A' Chrois caves are harder to find. They lie on the slopes of A' Chrois 300 to 400 ft. above Glen Loin and may be reached by following the road on the west side of Glen Loin past the hostel. A little over a mile from the head of the loch a track leads diagonally up the hillside to a maze of boulders : near these the caves are to be found. They consist of deep and, in places, very narrow fissures, and are connected by tunnels and intriguing subterranean passages.

A' Chrois (or Feorlin), 2785 ft.—From Glen Loin, A' Chrois is not seen to advantage, but from a little above Upper Inveruglas, or from the road to Loch Sloy, the peak presents a bold and formidable appearance. The grass slopes facing Coiregrogain are among the steepest in the country. To the north of the peak the hillside is considerably broken by outcropping rock, whilst on the south, too, a short way below the summit, there are a number of low cliffs and short gullies. The hill is connected to Narnain by a most attractive ridge circling Coire Sugach, and the two hills are often combined in a pleasant high level excursion.

From Glen Loin follow the path up the south bank of the Allt Sugach to a bridge over the stream, which is crossed, and climb the hill by the little ridge bounding the Sugach Coire on the north. A small stream descends from near the ridge a short way east of Creag Tharsuinn, and this forms a useful route of descent, especially in misty weather. The only other route from Glen Loin makes use of the very definite lane through the trees. It is found on the south bank of the burn just to the north of the A' Chrois Caves.

There is a fine outlook over the more remote Arrochar hills from the top of A' Chrois, and Ben Vane stands up beautifully across the deep trench of Coiregrogain, while due west is the symmetrical cone of Beinn Ime. Nearer at hand

D

the abrupt step below the summit of Narnain is well seen in profile. The top also affords an uninterrupted view over Loch Lomond.

From Narnain, the ridge to A' Chrois is easy to follow in good weather, but it sports a number of subsidiary tops and rocky protuberances which can be quite misleading in mist. The slopes on both sides of the ridge are steep, and on the Sugach side precipitous. From Coiregrogain the ascent is hard work all the way up steep grass. It is best to contour the hillside and approach the summit from the east. On the way some remarkable cracks in the earth may be encountered. Some of these appear to be about 50 ft. deep, and it is well to remember their presence if descending in the dark.

Beinn Ime, 3318 ft.—This is the highest mountain of the Arrochar Group and presents a cone of comparative steepness when seen from the north or south. It is hidden from Arrochar by the mass of Narnain, but from The Cobbler the peak is obvious in the north. Facing Coiregrogain the slopes of Beinn Ime are broken by cliffs, while seen from Ben Vorlich, on the opposite side of Loch Sloy, the peak stands up very much aloof, head above its neighbours.

The quickest route from Arrochar is by the Allt a' Bhalachain to its headwaters, and the col between The Cobbler and Narnain. Flattish ground is crossed to the Bealach a' Mhaim and the broad gently sloping south ridge of Beinn Ime rising straight ahead is followed to the summit. There are two tops, the northern being the higher, and adorned by a large well-built cairn.

Although the highest of the group, the mountain does not possess the finest view. The surrounding hills present their less interesting sides, and the middle distance is somewhat cut off by intervening heights. It is, however, a good point from which to work out the topography of the district.

From the Coiregrogain side Beinn Ime is best approached by the northern tributary of the Allt Coiregrogain. There is a sheepfold at the branching of the burns. From the headwaters of the stream it is easy going to the Glas Bealach north of Beinn Ime, from whence, turning left, the summit is gained quickly by the north ridge. By following the south branch of the Allt Coiregrogain a more direct, but steeper, ascent may be made by the wide scree gully to the south of the cliffs. If desired there is an easy descent to Glen Croe by Croe Water which descends the valley immediately north of The Cobbler.

Ben Vane, 3004 ft., throws down a ridge to the south-east, separated from the similar ridge of Ben Vorlich by Inveruglas Water. Both hills have resounded to the noise of rock drills, and the new roads up Coiregrogain, and to Loch Sloy, have destroyed the unspoilt solitude of the valleys. The hill is easily ascended by the ridge descending towards Coiregrogain. Outcrops of rock vary the ascent, and from the top, where there is a small cairn on the south edge of the summit plateau, a good ridge leads, first west, then north, to Beinn Dhubh, 2509 ft., over which the descent can be made north to Loch Sloy. The water level has been raised 140 ft., and the Loch now extends nearly 1 mile north of its original limits. A path contours the western slopes above the loch and this track forms a convenient way of return from Beinn Dhubh to the road and Coiregrogain.

Ben Vorlich, 3092 ft. (north top 3055 ft.), occupies a larger area than any of the other Arrochar mountains, and is the only one wholly within Dunbartonshire. It shows to advantage from A' Chrois, and from points on the north shore of Loch Katrine. From the Loch Lomondside road the summit is visible from a point a little south of Ardlui.

Ben Vorlich's west side dips steeply to Loch Sloy in grassy slopes and precipitous steps ; its east side is more gentle and is intersected by a number of corries, two of which run well back into the hill, and are very beautiful. The most northerly of these, Coire Creagach, is the largest, and for most of its length is lightly wooded. Coire na Baintighearna is also worthy of a visit.

From Ardlui the easiest route to the top follows the Stob na Coinnich Bhacain ridge rising behind the hotel. The slopes are fairly steep but provide easy going to the Stob, which is crossed and the ridge followed south-west, then south, to the small cairn on Vorlich's north top. From here a dip of less than 200 ft. leads directly to the main summit, the cairn of which is perched on the edge of a cliff overlooking the Loch Sloy side. The view is superb, the nearer mountains being finely grouped, with Beinn Ime lording it over its satellites. Away down the loch, too, the pastoral ground round Balloch offers rich contrast to the high hills in the north.

The ridge descending towards Upper Inveruglas is a little tiresome in the ascent on account of false tops, but can be recommended for the descent. The most pleasant way up the hill from this side is to follow the road to Loch Sloy, and strike straight up, making for a very shallow corrie just below the ridge. From there to the top is easy going between rocky knolls.

The waters of Loch Sloy are taken by a tunnel through Ben Vorlich to a surge chamber on the slopes of that hill above Loch Lomond. For access to the eastern end of the tunnel a road has been constructed diagonally across the hillside above Upper Inveruglas. Scenically this road is very fine and from it Ben Vorlich is easily ascended.

PATHS

Arrochar to Inveruglas.—Branch off the main road near Shire Bridge just north of Arrochar and follow the delightful road and path through Glen Loin, thence by a well-marked track contouring the hillside. This leads to Coiregrogain and the road to Inveruglas. Total distance 4 miles.

Inveruglas to Ardlui by Loch Sloy.—The road to Loch Sloy is private and closed to motor traffic. At the south end of the loch where the road ends, a path continues on the left (west) of the great dam. This path contours the slopes of Beinn Dhubh a good distance above the water-level, and eventually leads to the new road at the north end of the loch. From here strike north-east round the head of the loch and make over to the Strath Dubh-uisge by a rather faint and boggy track.

Inveruglas to Butterbridge by Loch Sloy.—As above to the north end of the loch, and then by the new road direct to Butterbridge in Glen Croe.

Glen Falloch to Glen Fyne by the hills.—The new cul-de-sac roads running up the Lairig Arnan and the Dubh Eas start opposite Glen Falloch farm, a mile north of Inverarnan, and give easy access to two routes to Glen Fyne from Glen Falloch. For the first, follow the new road to its end (taking the left branch at the fork), and make for the low col of the Lairig Arnan. Descend to Glen Fyne via the Allt na Lairige by an ill-defined track. The second route leads to the head of Loch Fyne. Follow the new road up the Dubh Eas to its end, and cross the low col north of Meall nan Caora. Descent is by the Allt Coir' an Longairt into Glen Fyne.

Glen Falloch to Dalmally by the Dubh Eas.—The Dubh Eas gives access to Beinn Laoigh and Ben Oss to the north, as well as the beginning of a fine route to Dalmally. It is the route of an old drove road and right of way from Glen Falloch to Socach. From the end of the new road in the Dubh Eas the Allt nan Caorrunn is followed to where the stream bends north to the slopes between Beinn Laoigh and Beinn a' Chleibh. A tributary stream, the Allt a' Mhinn, is then followed past a bothy and fank, to the low pass on the west of Beinn a' Chleibh. Here, the old drove road passes through a wall. This section is wet, and the descent on the far side of the bealach, by way of the Allt a' Chaorain, is little drier. When the railway is reached near the foot of Coire Ghaill at Socach a good track is found leading to the main road 1½ miles east of Dalmally. The distance from Glen Falloch to Dalmally by this route is a little over 12 miles.

CENTRES

The following are the most convenient; there is hotel accommodation at each: Ardlui, Arrochar and Inverarnan.

Youth Hostels are found at Ardgartan and Glen Loin (Arrochar).

BIBLIOGRAPHY

" Notes on Cobbler," by W. W. Naismith, *S.M.C.J.*, Vol. 3, p. 161
" Ben Arthur," by A. E. Maylard, *S.M.C.J.*, Vol. 3, p. 272.
*" The Cobbler Climbs," by H. C. Boyd, *S.M.C.J.*, Vol. 5, p. 153.
*" The Arrochar Group," Guide Book Article, *S.M.C.J.*, Vol. 6, p. 172,
*" Narnain and Vorlich," by W. Inglis Clark, *S.M.C.J.*, Vol. 7, p. 66.
*" Coire Sugach," by J. Gall Inglis, *S.M.C.J.*, Vol. 7, p. 70.
*" Coire Sugach and Narnain," by R. G. Napier, *S.M.C.J.*, Vol. 7. p. 179.
*" The Rocks of Coire Sugach," by S. G. Shadbolt, *S.M.C.J.*, Vol. 9, p. 143.
*" Cobbler Calling," by B. H. Humble, *S.M.C.J.*, Vol. 21, p. 392.
*" Rock Climbs on the Cobbler," by J. B. Nimlin, B. H. Humble, G. C. Williams, *S.M.C.J.*, Vol. 22, p. 221.
" Ben Narnain," by J. Stewart, *C.C.J.*, Vol. 5, p. 211.

*Chiefly of rock-climbing interest.

VI

BEN LOMOND AND SURROUNDINGS

Munro's Tables—Section 1.
Maps : O.S. One-inch Scale Popular Edition, Sheets 62
and 66. O.S. Half-inch Scale, Sheet 22. O.S. Tourist
Map of Trossachs and Loch Lomond. Bartholomew's
Half-inch Scale, Scotland, Sheets 7 and 12. Bartholomew's
Half-inch Scale, Great Britain, Sheets 44 and 48.

Ben Lomond, 3192 ft., is the most southerly Scottish mountain over 3000 ft., its summit standing $2\frac{3}{4}$ miles north by east of Rowardennan on the east shore of Loch Lomond. With the possible exception of Ben Nevis, it is the most popular and frequently ascended mountain in Scotland. No doubt its dominating position over the famous loch at its base, coupled with the fact that the mountain is visible from many parts of the Lowlands of Scotland, combine to ensure its popularity. The references in literature show that its fascination is not of recent date alone, but that the mountain exercised its charms upon many who passed along the shores of Loch Lomond in the years gone by.

One of the earliest records of an ascent of the Ben appeared in a poem, dated 1785, inscribed on a pane of glass in the old inn at Tarbet. Unfortunately the pane is no longer there. John Stoddart's *Remarks on Local Scenery and Manners in Scotland during the years* 1799-1800 describes the north side of Ben Lomond as " exciting a degree of surprise, arising almost to terror : this mighty mass which hitherto had appeared to be an irregular cone placed on a spreading base, suddenly presents itself as an imperfect crater, with one side forcibly torn off, leaving a stupendous precipice of 2000 ft. to the bottom."

Stoddart made the ascent and recorded his impressions of the summit " far above the clouds of the vale . . . it

43

seemed as if I had been suddenly transported into a new state of existence, cut off from every meaner association and invisibly united with the surrounding purity and brightness." Modern climbers will find nothing to argue with in this description, even if rock-climbers can cavil legitimately at Stoddart's estimate of the height of cliff to the north of the summit.

The derivation of the name is uncertain. One writer gives it from an old British word, Llumnan, signifying a beacon (*Tartanland*, p. 170), and this certainly fits the mountain. It is interesting to note that the Fife Lomonds are of the same shape and there again " beacon hill " seems applicable. Also strange is the fact that Loch Leven lies at the foot of the West Lomond of Fife, and Loch Lomond was at one time called Loch Leven, and the River Leven flows from the south end of the loch. It seems likely, therefore, that the hill name has been applied to the loch also. Another suggestion is that the name is traceable from " leamh-monadh "— the elmwood mountain, while a third possibility would be from the Gaelic " loman " meaning a banner or shield.

Geologically, Ben Lomond consists of a hard mass of mica-schist dipping steeply to the south-east. The summit mass rises sharply on all sides and from most points of view appears conical. It is, however, more in the form of a curved ridge, or " demicrater," the slopes on the loch side descending more or less abruptly, and on the other falling away in broken cliffs. The corrie below these cliffs is unusually steep and appears, as one ascends it, to have no floor at all. The actual summit of the Ben is at the top of the huge bastion enclosing the corrie on the west. From the top, the ridge extends south-east for a short distance, then, bending north-east, dips steeply to Glen Dubh.

Below the summit mass the mountain throws out a long, broad spur of easy gradient to Sròn Aonaich, 1893 ft., in the south. To the west, the slopes are broken by the Ben's satellite top, Ptarmigan, 2398 ft., beyond which the hillside falls steeply to the beautifully wooded shore of Loch Lomond. The broad ridge connecting Ptarmigan to its loftier neighbour

E. C. Thomson.

BEN LOMOND FROM BEN NARNAIN.

4

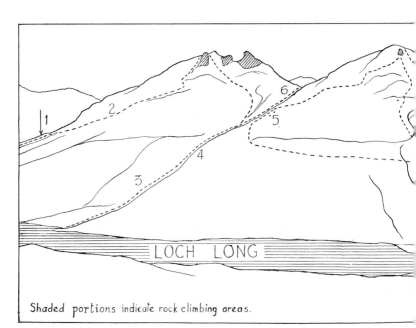

Shaded portions indicate rock climbing areas.

EN REOCH.

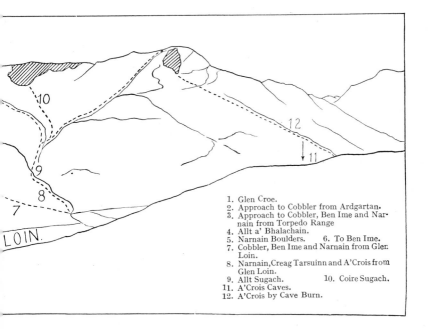

1. Glen Croe.
2. Approach to Cobbler from Ardgartan.
3. Approach to Cobbler, Ben Ime and Narnain from Torpedo Range
4. Allt a' Bhalachain.
5. Narnain Boulders.   6. To Ben Ime.
7. Cobbler, Ben Ime and Narnain from Glen Loin.
8. Narnain, Creag Tarsuinn and A'Crois from Glen Loin.
9. Allt Sugach.   10. Coire Sugach.
11. A'Crois Caves.
12. A'Crois by Cave Burn.

BEN LOMOND FROM NEAR TARBET.

Hugh Gardner.

May, 1883.

offers a col at about 2250 ft. and encloses a gentle, south-facing corrie. On the north the slopes of the mountain are steep.

Like so many other Scottish hills, it is in winter that the Ben is at its best. When the ground is hard and the upper slopes covered in deep snow, the northern corrie often presents an alpine appearance, and even the easy ascent from Rowardennan is not without difficulty. There is an interesting account of an early winter ascent recorded in Vol. 1 of Colonel Hawker's *Diary* of 1812. The winter must have been severe that year in Scotland, as elsewhere, for on page 59 we read : " To get to the most elevated point of the shoulder we found impossible, as the last 50 yards was a solid sheet of ice, and indeed for the last ½ mile we travelled in perfect misery and imminent danger. We were literally obliged to take knives and to cut footsteps in the frozen snow, and, of course, obliged to crawl all the way on our hands, knees and toes, all of which were benumbed with cold. . . . " Provided adequate equipment is carried the modern climber is unlikely to encounter such difficulties on the normal route from Rowardennan, although in the gullies of the northern cliffs, routes of considerable technical difficulty may be made in the right conditions.

The mountain can be ascended on all sides, if the cliffs on the north side are avoided. The usual, and easiest, approach is from **Rowardennan Inn,** reached by road from Balmaha. There is a path of easy gradients nearly the whole way and the ascent offers no difficulty other than that of a steady plod. From the hotel the track ascends gently to the north-east, bending round to the end of the south shoulder, and follows the ridge thereafter to the foot of the final peak, which is ascended by a zigzag. From the top of the zigzag the path is nearly level to the summit. In wet weather the track in many places becomes almost a watercourse, and very muddy, but in normal conditions average time to the summit would be about 2½ hours.

From **Inversnaid** (hotel) the quickest route to the summit is made by following the Rowchoish track as far as the Cailness Burn whose right bank is then ascended and a way

made to the north ridge of the mountain, the lowest point
being a little over 1500 ft. at the col connecting Ben Lomond
with Cruinn a' Bheinn. The ridge leads by pleasant slopes
directly to the summit, and for part of the way a path may be
found.

From **Aberfoyle** (hotels) there is a choice of routes, all
of them fairly long. Probably the quickest is to follow the
Loch Ard road to the west end of the loch, whence a branch
road leads south, and past the aqueduct of the Glasgow
Corporation Water Works. Just before the pipe-line is
reached, a path branches off to the left which follows the
course of Duchray Water. This path is taken, and, after
crossing the stream, the other bank is followed to a knoll
at the foot of the Bruach Caoruinn Glen. A descent beyond
the knoll brings one to another stream and from here a few
hundred feet of ascent leads to an easy gradient along the
hillside on the north bank of the Bruach Caoruinn Burn as
far as a broad moor, reached in about 1 hour after leaving
the Duchray Valley. The moor is crossed to its southern
margin and a way made to the shoulder of the Ben in a
further ¾ hour, when the Rowardennan path will be reached
and followed to the summit. This route is one of easy
gradients, but is dull from the Bruach Caoruinn Glen to the
shoulder.

An alternative route, much used by those staying at
Ledard Youth Hostel, is to take the Loch Chon road at the
head of Loch Ard, and cross Chon Water about 1 mile beyond
the branch, where there is a ford. From there a rough cart-
track is followed to the dip in the hill and a descent made to
Stronmacnair on the other side. From here the direct but
dull approach is to cross the stream a little below Loch
Dubh and ascend to the lowest point of the ridge beyond—
about 1250 ft.—on the north of Beinn a' Bhàn. A slight
descent may then be necessary to the watershed between
two streams. Ascend the bluff beyond and work south
round the head of the streams to the foot of the peak where
the Rowardennan path will be found. This direct-line approach is seldom used ; a more repaying way is to follow the
path beyond Loch Dubh, and cross the stream to Comer,

when a steep but interesting route to the summit may be made by following the true right bank of the stream from the corrie. Cross the stream about the lower end of the corrie, and ascend steeply to reach the gap in the ridge just to the south of the summit. This route gives good views of the summit cliffs, and forms a very pleasant glissading descent in the right conditions.

An alternative route from Comer would be to follow, roughly, the course of the Caoruinn Achaidh Burn. The south side is followed for a few hundred yards and the stream then crossed above some linns. Thereafter the hillside can be ascended following the trend of the stream. In about 1 hour from Comer, a sloping moor is reached with the north shoulder of the Ben right in front. A steepish climb leads to the shoulder and the Inversnaid route is joined.

From **Stronachlachar** (reached by steamer from the Trossachs or by road from Inversnaid) the road is taken as far as Frenich Farm at the head of Loch Chon. Thence a ridge of about 1000 ft. has to be crossed and an almost equal descent made to Comer, where the routes described above are joined. By crossing the glen a little above Comer, some descent is saved.

The view from the summit is most extensive, and on a good day amply repays the effort of an ascent by any route. The indicator was erected in 1929 and replaced in 1933. Beneath, to north and south, is Loch Lomond, bisected by the projecting height of Ptarmigan. To the east, Loch Ard nestles amid its wooded hills and, beyond, the Lake of Menteith is visible. The Carse of Stirling and the Forth estuary stretch to the horizon in the east and are flanked on the north by the Ochils and Lomonds of Fife. Further south are the Campsie Hills and Kilpatricks, and, afar off, distant Tinto. The peaks of Arran appear over Bute to the south-south-west, with the Mull of Kintyre and the sea beyond, and a little further north, the Paps of Jura. Across Loch Lomond are all the Arrochar Hills, Crois, Narnain, Vorlich, Vane, Ime and The Cobbler. Mull is visible in the north-west with Ben Cruachan closer, and Ben Lui over the head of Loch Lomond. Just to the right of this, Ben Nevis rises bluff beyond the Blackmount and Glencoe Hills. To the north are the Crianlarich Hills, Ben Chabhair, Cruach Ardrain, Ben More and the rest, and to the right again are the peaks of the Lawers massif. Further round, Stuc a' Chroin and Ben Vorlich appear between Ben Vane and Ben Ledi, with Ben Venue almost immediately in front.

So much for the view from the Ben. Views of the Ben are had from many directions. Seen from away to the east, say, from Stirling Castle or the Ochils, the mountain shows a beautiful outline, especially at sunset. The long gradual ridge to the south is in marked contrast to the steep slopes of the north and east sides. Impressive near views are had from Gleann Dubh, beneath this east side, and from Ptarmigan in the west, while, early on a calm summer's morn, before the traffic starts along the Loch Lomond road, Ben Lomond seems to live its name, " beacon-hill," and stands, timeless and serene, above the placid waters of the loch.

Surrounding District of Loch Lomond.—Apart from the beauty of the loch itself and the many delightful spots on its shores, the enclosing hills are well adapted for wandering at medium heights. There are numerous tracks, and the whole district is well established as a playground for trampers from Glasgow and further afield. The most suitable centres for exploring the district are Rowardennan, Inversnaid, Inverarnan, Ardlui, Arrochar, Tarbet and Luss. The shores are served by roads, that on the west being the main route from Dumbarton to Crianlarich, while on the east a secondary road runs from Balmaha as far as Rowardennan. Beyond that a well-marked and delightful path, through woods for the most part, leads to the Stronachlachar-Inversnaid road some ¾ mile east of Inversnaid. From the hotel at Inversnaid the way to Ardlui is rougher, but a track is found most of the way. About 1 mile north of the hotel a group of caves is passed beneath Sroin Uaidh, and these are said to have been of use to the Clan MacGregor for hiding cattle in times of trouble. The loch is by now very narrow, and after some 3 miles its head is reached. To cross the River Falloch, however, it is necessary to continue on to Benglass Farm where there is a bridge.

Apart from the massif of Ben Lomond, the country to the east of Loch Lomond is devoid of hill interest. To the west of the loch, however, the hills are higher and are cut into by several fine glens.

The finest hill walk in this area, and one giving very comprehensive views, is the round of Beinn Eich (2302 ft.) and Doune Hill (2409 ft.), starting from Luss and finishing by way of Glen Douglas. A fair road leads from Luss to Edentaggart at the entrance to Glen Mallochan and from the farm a way is made up the gently sloping east ridge of Beinn Eich to the summit. Doune Hill lies nearly 2 miles off to the north-west and is reached along the ridge of Beinn Lochain after a drop of some 500 ft. From the summit of Doune Hill a descent can be made north into Cona Ghleann and the road reached in Glen Douglas.

The hills south of Glen Luss form a continuous chain with its highest top in Beinn Chaorach (2338 ft.). The latter is readily approached from the path in Glen Luss, and a descent may be made directly to Glen Fruin from any point on the bending ridge. In Glen Fruin a good road leads to Helensburgh or Loch Lomondside, or, alternatively, a path north-west over the low hills leads from Auchingaich to Garelochhead.

An attractive high-level approach to Arrochar can be made from Inverbeg on the west shore of Loch Lomond opposite Rowardennan, by way of Beinn Bhreac (2233 ft.) and Ben Reoch (2168 ft.). The two hills command magnificent views.

Cruach Tairbeirt (1364 ft.), lying between Glen Loin and Loch Lomond, offers a viewpoint out of all proportion to its height, and is easily ascended on all sides.

North of the Tarbet-Arrochar road the hills fall more correctly into the Arrochar Group and are considered separately in that section.

PATHS

Helensburgh (or Rhu) to Glen Fruin.—Two paths lead over the elevated ground north of Helensburgh : both join the secondary road near the Fruin bridge at Ballymenoch in Glen Fruin. The westerly path is the better and leads across the hillside in a north-easterly direction from Rhu.

Glen Fruin to Garelochhead.—A good road runs the length of Glen Fruin and beyond Auchingaich. From Strone a rough cart track leads over a low col and descends in a little over 1 mile to the Gareloch at Lennox Bank. In addition, a path strikes north-west from Strone and reaches Garelochhead from a northerly direction.

Luss to Garelochhead.—Following the glen above the left bank of Luss Water, the glen road degenerates beyond Edentaggart into a farm track which, however, continues by Glen Luss to a point beyond Beinn Eich. From here the way on is trackless to Glen Fruin, reached most easily by the low bealach west of Beinn Chaorach, but from Strone the path is again obvious, over the low ridge ahead, to the Gareloch.

Loch Lomond to Loch Long, via Glen Douglas.—A rough road runs the length of Glen Douglas and along the north bank of Douglas Water. Distance from Inverbeg to Gorten—6 miles.

Rowardennan to Inversnaid.—A beautiful path, through trees for the greater part of the way, leads by Cailness to the Stronachlachar-Inversnaid road, at the old Garrison.

Inversnaid to Ardlui by Loch Lomondside.—A somewhat faint path is found most of the way. From Inversnaid the way is very little above the lochside to the rocky bluff ahead, after which the track is faint. Continue close to the water's edge for a little over 2 miles until a large headland is reached. By climbing a little way up the back of the bluff a track will be found leading on to the head of the loch. To cross the River Falloch, it is necessary to continue north to Benglass Farm, where there is a bridge.

CENTRES

Aberfoyle, Ardlui, Arrochar, Garelochhead, Inverarnan, Inverbeg, Inversnaid and Rowardennan. At each of these places is an hotel. Youth Hostels are found at Auchendennan (2¼ miles Balloch), Inverbeg (opposite Rowardennan), Glen Loin (Arrochar) and Ledard (west end Loch Ard, 4½ miles Aberfoyle).

BIBLIOGRAPHY

*" Ben Lomond by the Cliffs," by W. I. Clark, *S.M.C.J.*, Vol. 4, p. 331.
" Ben Lomond," by A. E. Maylard, *S.M.C.J.*, Vol. 3, p. 140.
*" Notes on Ben Lomond Cliffs," by James Maclay, *S.M.C.J.*, Vol. 3,
     p. 343.
*" Guide Book Article," *S.M.C.J.*, Vol. 6, p. 112.
" Ben Lomond, May, 1902," by W. C. Newbigging, *S.M.C.J.*, Vol. 8,
     p. 87.
              *Chiefly of rock-climbing interest.

VII

BEINN BHUIDHE, LORNE AND KNAPDALE

Munro's Tables—Section 1.

Maps : O.S. One-inch Scale Popular Edition, Sheets 61 (Bheinn Bhuidhe), 60, 65. O.S. Half-inch Scale, Scotland, Sheets 22 (Beinn Bhuidhe), 21, 25. Bartholomew's Half-inch Scale Revised, Scotland, Sheets 11 (Beinn Bhuidhe) and 7. Bartholomew's Half-inch Scale, Great Britain, Sheets 48 (Beinn Bhuidhe), 44 and 47.

Beinn Bhuidhe, 3106 ft. (The Yellow Mountain) — 4 miles north from head of Loch Fyne.

THE large area of Argyll west and north-west of Loch Fyne is practically devoid of interest for the mountaineer. It comes to its highest point in the extreme east, in the tract of mountainous country between Glen Shira and Glen Fyne, and culminates in Beinn Bhuidhe. For the rest, it is an area of heathery uplands and knolly hills, deeply indented on the west coast. Loch Awe cuts right through the centre of the area, coming within 3 miles of the sea at its south-west end, and stretching away to the north-east to the peaks of Cruachan, a distance of 25 miles. Between the loch and the Firth of Lorne are a number of smaller sheets of water lying in the folds between the low hills. Of these, the largest is Loch Avich. Between Loch Awe and Glen Fyne the country becomes more mountainous and is cut into by two large glens abutting on Loch Fyne. These are Glens Aray and Shira, of which the first is a through glen carrying the road between Dalmally and Inveraray, while the second, after pursuing a nearly level course north from Loch Shira, curves round the north of Beinn Bhuidhe and is joined to Glen Fyne by a col at a little over 1100 ft.

(1) **Beinn Bhuidhe,** 3106 ft.—This somewhat remote peak is not so often climbed as it deserves, but can be taken without undue fatigue from various directions. Lying as it

April, 1926.

BEINN BHUIDHE.

P. Donald.

September, 1938.

I. D. B. Wilson.

does between the lovely and fragrant upper reaches of Glen
Fyne and Glen Shira, it is remarkable for its botanical
treasures.

The summit is the highest point on a narrow 4-mile ridge
running roughly from south-west to north-east, and having
steep slopes to north and south. The south face is the steeper,
and has some rocks here and there along its length, although
none of the outcrops are of any great extent. Of the ridge
itself, the narrowest and best defined section lies immediately
north-east of Beinn Bhuidhe summit.

The mountain is accessible from all directions but is
reached most conveniently from Inveraray, by either Glen
Shira or Glen Fyne. For those with a car, the latter is the
quicker route as the transport can be used as far as the head
of Loch Fyne, the nearest point, on any main road, to the
mountain. With permission, motors may be taken up Glen
Fyne as far as the Lodge. Beyond the Lodge there is a very
rough cart road to Inverchorachan, at which place the track
is left and the steep slopes above are climbed. Follow the
grassy north bank of the principal stream over the first steep
rise to a fine little " cirque " with a waterfall, then keep well
to the right. At about 2000 ft. one comes into view of the
final rampart of the mountain and the ridge is gained at a
col ½ mile north-east of the summit. From here a pleasant
climb up the narrow ridge brings one to the bulky cairn on
the highest point.

If approaching the mountain from Inveraray, by Glen
Shira, the narrow road up the glen is followed to Rob Roy's
House at the foot of Brannie Burn, and from here the long
and gradual south-west ridge is followed to the summit. A
nearly level shoulder is passed just above the 2000-ft. contour
and a further top (Stac a' Chùirn) has to be crossed before
the rise to the top of Beinn Bhuidhe is reached. The dip
between the two tops is only slight.

From Ardlui, or Inverarnan, the way is longer, and
involves the crossing of a ridge and a descent into Glen Fyne.
Two ways are open. The first follows the Dubh Eas path
for 3 miles and then crosses into the head of Glen Fyne by

E

the side of the Allt Coir' an Longairt. A footbridge over the
River Fyne leads to the ridge of Ceann Garbh (2635 ft.), which
is climbed to its summit. Beyond this top the ridge bends
more to the south and descends to a col at 2400 ft. before
climbing to a second subsidiary summit $\frac{3}{4}$ mile to the south-
west. This second top—a rather pleasing little summit—is
crossed and a descent of 300 ft. made on the other side. The
north-east ridge of Beinn Bhuidhe is then at hand.

Alternatively, from Ardlui one can go up the Allt Arnan
and cross the Lairig of that name, north of Beinn Damhain.
There follows a longish descent to Glen Fyne which is reached
on the wrong side of the river from Inverchorachan. Once
across the river (which may be difficult in times of flood) the
route to Beinn Bhuidhe's summit is as described under the
approach from Inveraray.

The approaches from Dalmally are again long. The
easiest is to follow the main road east to Socach then go up
the Eas a' Ghaill and the Allt Coire Lair. The watershed
beyond is crossed by wet ground about the 1400-ft. contour
and a descent made down Coire an Taillir. Cross the Fyne
and climb the slopes of Ceann Garbh contouring into a little
corrie high up and reaching the main ridge south-west of the
Ceann.

The other route from Dalmally follows the Allt Mhaluidh
past the almost invisible ruins of Uachdar Mhaluidh, and over
the western shoulder of Beinn Bhoidheach. The going is
heavy and trackless all the way. Pass below Lochan Beinn
Bhreac on its right, and descend to the Shira. From here a
way is made direct to the summit of Beinn Bhuidhe by easy
and uninteresting slopes.

Due to its isolated position the mountain commands a
magnificent view. The Ochils are visible away to the east
beyond the Arrochar and Trossachs hills, while in the west
and south-west a glorious panorama of distant islands is
unfolded beyond the low hills of Lorne and Knapdale. To
the north-west the peaks of Cruachan look particularly fine :
beyond, and to the right of them, the Glencoe and Lochaber
mountains are easily recognisable.

(2) **Lorne.**—The beauty of the district is largely confined
to the coastal area, along which runs the road from Oban to
the Crinan Canal and Lochgilphead. From the south shore
of Loch Feochan a secondary road branches off west at
Kilninver and goes by way of Seil Island to Easdale. The
main road continues south-east at Kilninver, and reaches
Kilmelfort after skirting above the rugged little Pass of
Melfort. From the bay there is a charming view to the west.

Between the coast and Loch Awe is a large tract of heathery
upland with numerous small lochs lying between the ridges.
The area is crossed by a right-of-way road, suitable for motor
traffic, from Kilmelfort to the west shore of Loch Awe by way
of Loch Avich. In addition are two paths by which the
district may be crossed (these are described at the end of
this section), as well as the road running from Taynuilt by
Glen Lonan to Oban, and the well-known and repaying drive
from Taynuilt to Kilchrenan by Glen Nant.

Loch Awe is one of Scotland's largest lochs and is the
longest in the Southern Highlands area. Its extent, however,
is not as great as that of Loch Lomond, as Loch Awe is little
wider than ¾ mile over the greater part of its length. Like
many of the greater lochs of the Highlands, it is studded here
and there with wooded islands, some of them of considerable
antiquarian interest. Inishail—" green Inishail "—was at
one time the site of a Cistercian nunnery, as well as being for
long the burial place for the clans who inhabited the shores
of the loch. Authoritative articles on this island and the
others of Loch Awe are to be found in *S.M.C.J.*, Vol. 12.

To the east of the loch the country is again heather-clad
and knolly, but offers little of interest to the mountaineer.
Above the west side of Glen Aray the slopes of Mullach nam
Maol, 1668 ft., are very steep and lead to the high plateau
beyond. The summit of the Mullach affords a fine view over
the north end of Loch Awe and of the peaks of Cruachan.

PATHS

Loch Awe to Kilninver by Loch Avich and Loch
Scamadale.—Follow the Loch Avich road from the west shore
of Loch Awe, and leave it by the path which cuts up the

hillside in a northerly direction from a point well above the north shore of Loch Avich and leaving the main road near the top of a steep rise. The path leads over the shoulder of Meall Odhar and beyond to Loch na Sreinge. A little way beyond this a path leaves on the right up the Allt Dearg. The main route continues straight on, crossing the stream and entering the little valley of the Allt Braglenmore. The path is now well defined and leads by the north shore of Loch Scamadale and the valley of the Euchar to the main road 2 miles south of Kilninver. Distance from Loch Avich is 10 miles.

Kilchrenan to Kilmore by Loch Nant and Stor Loch.— A farm track leaves the Glen Nant road on the west side, just out of the village of Kilchrenan, and leads to Achnamady. It is followed for nearly a mile when a way is made directly towards the higher ground ahead. Some high, rough moor is passed before Loch Nant is reached. The path continues by the Abhainn Càm Linne and passes along the north side of Stor Loch before reaching the Allt an Loin Mhoir $1\frac{1}{2}$ miles beyond the west end of the loch. The Loin stream is crossed, and without losing height the path continues for a short way across the slopes on the west side of the little valley. It then crosses the low ridge above and descends into the upper part of Glen Feochan, which is then followed to Kilmore. The total distance along the path from Kilchrenan to Kilmore is 12 miles.

---

(3) **Knapdale.**—From the Crinan Canal a narrow neck of country runs south to West Loch Tarbert, and is cut into from the Sound of Jura by two sea-lochs—Loch Sween and Loch Caolisport. On the east, the area is bounded by Loch Fyne, and is divided into North and South Knapdale by the road from Achahoish to Inverneil.

From Loch Sween across to Loch Fyne the ground rises and falls in a fairly uniform series of parallel folds, running north-east and south-west. In the main it is an area of rough moorland with numerous small tops, having a generally characteristic shape—a sharp, wave-like crest—impressive when viewed end-on.   The sides of these crests are often rocky.

Access is best gained from Ardrishaig or from the old mill road running south from Dhail Farm near Cairnbaan.   Alternatively, the hills can be gained from the west by the tracks from Achnamara, or by the Lussa Water.   Certain points on the Kilmory-Knap road south of Dunrostan are also convenient starting points.

The hills are well adapted for walking and afford fine westward views.   Cnoc Reamhar above Caol Scotnish is a grand viewpoint for Loch Sween, whilst from the other tops it is possible to see Islay, Jura, Mull and Ardnamurchan, as well as the familiar shapes around Arrochar.   The highest summit is Cruach Lusach, 1530 ft.

The hills of South Knapdale are higher but are of less interest than those immediately to the north.   They culminate in Sliabh Gaoil, 1840 ft., and run in a single range to the south-west.   The easiest approach to the highest part of the range, which is near the north-east, is from the Lochgilphead-Tarbert road from near Meall Mor cottage.   The hills afford pleasing vistas to the ranges of Cowal and to the rocky peaks of Arran to the south-seat.

CENTRES

Beinn Bhuidhe area :   Hotels at Dalmally and Inveraray ; Youth Hostel at Dalmally.

Lorne :   Hotels at Connel, Ford (south end Loch Awe), Kilchrenan (and Taychreggan), Kilmelfort, Oban, Port Sonachan and Taynuilt.

Knapdale :   Hotels at Ardrishaig, Cairnbann and Lochgilphead.

BIBLIOGRAPHY

" Ben Bhuidhe," by S. M. Penney, *S.M.C.J.*, Vol. 7, p. 124.
" The Islands of Loch Awe," by W. Douglas, *S.M.C.J.*, Vol. 12, pp. 65, 137, 189; Vol. 13, p. 73.
" Ramblings about Lorn," by A. C. McLaren, *S.M.C.J.*, Vol. 17, p. 314.

VIII

THE TROSSACHS HILLS

Maps : O.S. One-inch Scale Popular Edition, Sheet 62.
O.S. Half-inch Scale, Sheet 22. O.S. Tourist Map of
Trossachs and Loch Lomond. Bartholomew's Half-inch
Scale Revised, Scotland, Sheet 12.   Bartholomew's
Half-inch Scale, Great Britain, Sheet 48.

(1) Ben Venue, 2393 ft. (Hill of $1\frac{1}{4}$ miles W.S.W. Trossachs Pier.
the Caves or, possibly, the
Mountain of Milk)

(2) Ben Bhreac, 2295 ft. (Speckled 1 mile W. by S. of (1).
Hill)

(3) Ben A'n 1520 ft. - - - $\frac{3}{4}$ mile N.W. of Trossachs Pier.

(4) Ben Ledi, 2873 ft. (locally, 4 miles W.N.W. of Callander.
Hill of Light ; may also be
Beinn le Dia, the Hill of God)

(5) Stuc Odhar, 2081 ft. (The 1 mile S.W. of (4).
Dun-coloured Peak)

(6) Ardnandave Hill, 2332 ft. (The $1\frac{1}{2}$ miles N. of (4).
Height of the Stags)

(7) Ben Vane, 2685 ft. (The Middle $2\frac{1}{2}$ miles S.W. of Strathyre.
Mountain)

(8) Beinn an t-Sithein 1871 ft. 1 mile W.N.W. of Strathyre.
(The Hill of the Fairy Knoll)

(9) Point 2526 ft. - - - 2 miles S. of Monachylemore.

(10) Stob Breac, 2250 ft. (The $1\frac{1}{4}$ miles S.E. of Inverlochlarig.
Speckled Point)

(11) Stob a' Choin, 2839 ft. (The 2 miles S.W. of Inverlochlarig.
Dog's Point)

THIS is the classic ground of the Scottish Highlands, and
although none of the hills attain an altitude of 3000 ft. the
scenery amongst them is widely and justifiably famous. To
the tourist, a visit to Scotland is hardly complete without a
visit to the Trossachs. The raising of the water level of Loch
Katrine, and the over-civilisation of the loch's eastern end,
has robbed the scene of a good deal of its charm, but the
Trossachs still combine that sylvan beauty and rugged

grandeur pictured in *The Lady of the Lake*. Luckily, too, for the climber, the Trossachs hills have remained unchanged : the summer visitors are for the most part content to view the loch from the road end. From the surrounding hills it is usually hard to pick out the evidence of civilisation amongst the clustering trees around the loch end.

Lochs Katrine and Arklet, and their catchment area, belong to Glasgow Corporation, and the road on the north of Loch Katrine is closed to motor traffic, although it is sometimes possible to obtain permission if it is necessary to drive further than the Trossachs. The road is not continuous to the west end of the loch but is being extended at present, and in the meantime a good walking path and rough road runs from the surfaced road end to Glengyle, and back on the south side of the loch to Stronachlachar. Beyond there the path continues to Royal Cottage : thereafter the way is rough and trackless round the north of Ben Venue to within 1 mile of Achray.

From the south and west the area is easily reached by Aberfoyle and the fine road over the hills to Achray. This road (A821) gives beautiful views as one approaches from the south, although Ben Venue shows to better advantage from the road along Loch Venachar. This latter road forms the route from Callander and the east.

To the north the area is bounded by the Balquhidder Valley which runs west almost to the head of Glen Gyle and separates the Trossachs hills from the Crianlarich group further north. The River Balvag, flowing from Loch Voil by Balquhidder then south by Strathyre to Loch Lubnaig, forms the eastern boundary of the area, while the district may be said to extend far enough south to include the hills enclosing Loch Katrine on the south.

Ben Venue, 2393 ft., is the dominating height about Loch Katrine, and is well seen from the road along Loch Venachar. Its twin tops make the hill easily recognisable from most angles. It shows a bold front to the Trossachs, rocky and deeply shadowed most of the year, and after rain seamed by waterfalls. The caves, from which the hill gets its name, are to be found low down near the loch, and are marked Coire na Uruisge (Goblin's Cave) on the Ordnance Survey map.

From Achray Hotel the route to the summit lies at first through woods by a pleasant path on the south of Achray Water, then by a rough track towards the hill. Make for, and up, a wide grassy gully between rock outcrops, and bear right to the first top (2386 ft.). The second and higher top is reached along the ridge in 10 minutes. The view is open and extensive, and embraces a pleasing combination of loch and mountain, while the contrast between the low hills to the south and the giants of the north and west is particularly striking.

The descent can be made easily by the route of ascent or, if making for Aberfoyle, over Creag Tharsuinn and by way of the Ledard Burn to Loch Ard.

Beinn Bhreac, 2295 ft., may be included without difficulty if the northern slopes of Creag Tharsuinn are contoured, and a descent to Aberfoyle made as before. Beinn Bhreac has three distinct tops, that nearest Ben Venue being the highest. The slopes to Loch Katrine are easy, but often wet.

Ben A'n, 1520 ft., is a most effective feature of the Trossachs, its rocky cone standing up proudly above the silver birches around the end of the loch. It is, however, only a spur of the featureless hill, Meall Gainmheich, behind, and is connected to it by a slight drop. Bartholomew's half-inch map gives the height of Ben A'n as 1750 ft., while the Ordnance Survey one-inch shows two small 1500 ft. contours but no height. There is a good deal of clean bare rock on Ben A'n facing south and the whole hill dries quickly after rain. The view from the top is out of all proportion to the height. The Arrochar hills stand up well, beyond the end of Loch Katrine, while Ben Venue, across the Trossachs, shows its full height and impressive steepness. On the rocky south face of Ben A'n are many heathery ledges, delightful for a contemplative halt, and all around the base of the rocks the birch woods stretch downwards to the loch. The best route to the summit is from the east. Leave the main road at the fence separating the woods from the grounds of the Trossachs Hotel, and follow the track through the woods at first parallel to the

J. D. B. Wilson.

LOCH LUBNAIG.

May, 1938.

5

September, 1940.

BEN VENUE

R. M. Adam.

April, 1922.

BEINN LAOIGH FROM BEINN A' CHUIRN.

Hugh Gardner.

Easter, 1905.   *Rev. A. E. Robertson.*

BEINN LAOIGH, SUMMIT.

fence, and then by a deep-cut burn. There is a short boggy stretch, just before the end of the woods, followed by open ground. The final cone of the hill lies ahead across a plateau of bracken and heather. This stretch ends at another burn, which is crossed, and the path divides. The route now slopes up to the right through a shallow corrie and circles the top of it to approach the summit from the north-east. The summit is rocky, with two small tops.

A good path also leads from Loch Katrineside, following the left bank of the stream entering the loch about 200 yards west of the Trossachs pier at a sharp bend in the road. This path goes through the birch woods to a boggy clearing which is crossed. Thereafter the way is trackless and lies up across rough and steep ground above the first tier of rocks to join the route described above, east of the summit. Care is required in places above the lowest tier of rocks.

It is also possible to reach Ben A'n from the west by striking up through the woods and following the stream which falls from near the little col to the north of the summit, but there is no track and the going is heavy in places.

Ben Ledi, 2873 ft., is conspicuous from the Carse of Stirling, rising in a commanding position, in the angle formed by Lochs Venachar and Lubnaig. Being partially isolated on the southern edge of the Highlands, between the lowlands to the south and the mountains of the north, it commands a very fine view which embraces nearly all the higher hills from Ben Nevis to Tinto and from the Cairngorms to Arran. Of the nearer hills, Ben Vorlich alone is hidden, lying behind Stuc a' Chroin.

The usual route of ascent is dull and long, by way of the south-east ridge rising behind Coilantogle Farm on the Trossachs road. There is a faint track on the lower part of the hill at the first steepish rise; thereafter the ridge is followed to the top in about 2 hours from the road. There are numerous short, steeper rises, and the actual summit is not seen until it is almost gained. The top is flattish and has a large, low cairn.

A quicker and more interesting way to the top is from the east, crossing the River Leny by the bridge about 1 mile short of the south end of Loch Lubnaig, and making direct up the hillside. Height is quickly gained to about the 1500-ft. contour, where a fence is crossed and a way made rather south to the ridge. This route avoids the rocks on the east face of the hill some distance below the summit. The ridge is gained about the 2000-ft. contour.

The finest approach, however, is by the Stank Glen to the north of the hill. A road runs from the above-mentioned bridge over the Leny, past Coireachrombie Farm to Stank, and from there a good path winds up the hillside on the south of the stream, and into the Stank Glen. The lower part of the hillside is afforested, and there is a fine waterfall in the stream near the 750-ft. contour. After passing a deer fence the path is more nearly level and follows the stream closely. Half a mile above the falls the path is left and a way made over grass to the large boulders lying beneath the steep hillside on the south. Above the boulders the slopes are covered by masses of fallen rocks and, higher up, crazy pinnacles. This chaos is best avoided by following the true right bank of the stream descending from the little corrie to the north of the summit. From the lip of this corrie a way is made west, up the steep and pleasant spur enclosing the corrie on the north. When descending from the summit in mist it is easy to pass this spur and continue too far north, whence a descent can be made over rough and steep ground into the Stank Glen. The spur abuts on the summit ridge about 300 yards north of the main top, and not far below its level.

On the col, 1 mile north of the summit, is the little Lochan na Corp, said to be so named after a funeral party, on its way to St. Brides burial ground, had disappeared beneath its ice one winter's day. The south-east ridge of Ben Ledi descending to Coilantogle quite often gives good ski-ing, as do the slopes running down to Duart north of Brig o' Turk.

The ridge running parallel to Ben Ledi on the west culminates in **Stuc Odhar,** 2081 ft., a rather featureless hill, easily ascended from Brig o' Turk. The road up the valley to Duart is very beautiful, especially in its lower reaches where it winds through woods, and by falls in the river.

Ardnandave Hill, 2332 ft., in the angle of Loch Lubnaig, is an impressive sight from the main road along the lochside. Its eastern shoulder shows a precipitous face of rock towards the loch, and its northern side has several small corries high up in the hillside. From the top there is a good view up Strathyre to Balquhidder, while Ben Ledi in the south takes on an unusual aspect. The summit is most easily reached from Stank at the south end of Loch Lubnaig by going up the steep shoulder directly behind the farm, and following the ridge over intervening knolls to the highest point. The going on the ridge is heavy, and the lower part of the shoulder above Stank is afforested.

Ben Vane, 2685 ft., is a retiring hill and seldom climbed. Its conical top is well seen from the main road along Loch Lubnaig, a little north of Ardchullarie. The quickest way to the top, but giving an ascent of little interest, is from Laggan Farm on the west shore of Loch Lubnaig. The road to this point from Strathyre is passable for motors. The stream is followed west for some distance, almost to the low watershed ahead, and a way made up the long slopes on the left to gain the summit by the south-east side.

The hill throws out a long ridge to the south, ending at Duart at the mouth of Glen Finglas. The top of this ridge is nearly level, or only gradually sloping, for over 1 mile south of the summit : where it drops more steeply to Duart are some scattered rock outcrops which afford fair " bouldering." Ben Vane can be traversed conveniently *en route* from Brig o' Turk to Balquhidder, but the slopes to the north of the hill give heavy going to the track end in Glen Buckie.

The little peak between Glen Buckie and Strathyre, called **Beinn an t-Sithein, 1871** ft., affords a fine view of the Crianlarich hills and may be ascended from Strathyre by a good path in about 1¼ hours. The path crosses the hillside diagonally to a point south of the summit and then continues to Immereon in Glen Buckie. It is left above some butts and high heathery ground traversed over a number of knolls and minor tops to the main summit. The descent can be made north, then east, to Bailefuill and the road to Strathyre regained.

The south side of the Balquhidder and Lochlarig valley is bounded by more or less steep slopes, especially west of Loch Doine. These are intersected by corries running south and the hills so formed have their highest summits overlooking the main valley. The road past Lochs Voil and Doine is passable for cars to Inverlochlarig, and shortly before reaching that point a branch leads to a bridge over the river to Blaircreich. **Stob Breac,** 2250 ft., may be easily climbed from this direction. The summit is at the north end of a long undulating ridge with several subsidiary tops stretching towards Loch Katrine. Descent can be made to the Invernenty Burn east of the hill and a return to Blaircreich by a faint track. This track continues eastwards from the burn to Monachyle Tuarach opposite Monachylemore. From here the slopes of Ceann na Baintighearna (2277 ft.) are easy and pleasant and lead back by a gradual ridge from the Ceann to the nameless **Point,** 2526 ft. This is the highest point on the ridge, which drops again gradually to the south by heavy and complicated ground.

Stob a' Choin, 2839 ft., is isolated, and may be climbed from Portnellan on Loch Katrine by the long and wet approach up the Allt a' Choin, but is more conveniently reached from Inverlochlarig. A path continues along the north side of the river which is forded a little over 1 mile west of Inverlochlarig. There is no bridge. North of the summit the slopes are steep, and in places rocky, but by following the right bank of the stream flowing from the bealach west of the top (Bealach Coire an Laoigh) the going is easy. The summit is rocky and affords a fine outlook over to the high hills of the Crianlarich group. In particular, Beinn Chabhair stands up most impressively.

PATHS

Round of Loch Katrine.—From Trossachs by road and path along the north shore of the loch to Glengyle. The path continues on the south side to Stronachlachar and Royal Cottage, after which the way is trackless to within a mile of Achray.

Brig o' Turk to Balquhidder through the hills.—
From Brig o' Turk a roughish road leads to Achnahard in
Glen Finglas. From here a faint track continues north-west
but is soon lost, and a pathless way has then to be made up
Gleann nam Meann by the stream. At the head of the glen,
steer a course due north and over the open pass (1350 ft.
approximately). About a mile further on, and after rounding
the hillside on the right, a track will again be found. This
leads to Glen Buckie and thence to Balquhidder. The trackless part of this route is fully 5½ miles, and the going near
the watershed rather heavy.

Strathyre to Balquhidder over the hills.—Cross the
Balvag and mount the hillside ahead by the path crossing
diagonally from right to left. The path traverses the shoulder
of Beinn an t-Sithein and descends on Immereon in Glen
Buckie. From here the road leads north to Balquhidder.

CENTRES

For the south and western hills of the group the following
are the most convenient (there is hotel accommodation at
each) : Achray, Callander and Trossachs. Youth Hostel at
Brig o' Turk.

For the northern hills of the group the best centres are
Kingshouse Hotel and Strathyre. Youth Hostel at
Monachylemore.

BIBLIOGRAPHY

*" Ben A'n," by H. C. Boyd, *S.M.C.J.*, Vol. 4, p. 155.
" Stob a' Choin," by A. Frazer, *S.M.C.J.*, Vol. 4, p. 247.
" Ben Venue," by A. W. Russell, *S.M.C.J.*, Vol. 4, p. 298.
*" Cliffs of Ben A'n," by W. W. Naismith, *S.M.C.J.*, Vol. 5, p. 52.
" Guide Book Article," *S.M.C.J.*, Vol. 6, p. 238.
*" Ben A'n," by J. B. Nimlin, *S.M.C.J.*, Vol. 23, p. 134.
*" Ben A'n," by Geo. Williams, *C.C.J.*, Vol. 3, p. 363.
" On Ben Ledi," by F. R. Coles, *C.C.J.*, Vol. 4, p. 8.
" A Week-end in and around the Trossachs," *C.C.J.*, Vol. 4, p. 149.
*Chiefly of rock-climbing interest.

IX

THE TYNDRUM GROUP

Munro's Tables—Section 1.
Maps : O.S. One-inch Scale Popular Edition, Sheets 61
and 62. O.S. Half-inch Scale, Sheet 22. Bartholomew's
Half-inch Scale, Scotland, Revised, Sheet 11. Bartholomew's Half-inch Scale, Great Britain, Sheet 48.

(1) **Beinn Dubhchraig,** 3204 ft. 5 miles W. of Crianlarich.
(Mountain of the Black Rock)

(2) **Beinn Oss,** 3374 ft. (Mountain 1½ miles E.S.E. of (3).
of the Elk)

(3) **Beinn Laoigh,** 3708 ft. (Moun- 6 miles E. of Dalmally.
tain of the Calf)

(4) **Beinn a' Chleibh,** 3008 ft. 1 mile S.W. of (3).
(Mountain of the Chest or,
possibly, the Creel)

THIS noble range, standing as it does on, or very close to,
the main watershed of Scotland, catches the eye and commands attention from whichever angle it is viewed. The
prospects from the summits are among the most extensive in
the Highlands, and the ridges provide delightful walking.
Although many of the corries are steep and rocky, there is
little scope for the rock-climber, and it is in the winter months
that these hills give of their best to the serious mountaineer.

The group is a favourite haunt of deer as it lies close to
the forest at the heads of Glen Fyne and Glen Shira, and
above the great moor north of the Dubh Eas of Glen Falloch.
White hares are also plentiful, as are ptarmigan on the slopes
over 2000 ft.

Beinn Dubhchraig, 3204 ft., is one of the mountains so
finely seen as one enters Glen Falloch from Loch Lomond ;
it also shows up well from the head of Strathfillan. Historic-
ally it is of interest, for the battlefield of Dailrigh lies at its
foot. The action was fought in 1306, between Robert the

66

Bruce and the MacDougals of Lorn, the former being forced to retire. Lochan nan Arm, the tiny circular lochan lying almost hidden among the moraines at the foot of the Coninish Glen, is reputed to hold some of the armour and weapons discarded in the ensuing flight.

The mountain can be climbed most conveniently from either Crianlarich or Tyndrum, although the approach from Ardlui in the south is also repaying. For the latter route, follow the Glen Falloch road to a point almost opposite the Falls of Falloch and make a way up the left bank of the Allt Fionn Ghlinne. The easiest approach is directly up the hillside by the broad ridge ahead, or alternatively proceed by Loch Oss and strike up to the bealach between Beinn Oss and Beinn Dubhchraig. From this col, about 2580 ft., it is an easy climb to the summit where there is a good-sized cairn. The route just described gives fine views down Glen Falloch, but the going is a little heavy south of Loch Oss.

From Crianlarich the above route may also be followed by going along the Glen Falloch road for about 3 miles to Croiteonan and contouring round the hillside into the Fionn Ghlinne. The preferable route from Crianlarich, or from Tyndrum, is, however, to leave the main road at Dailrigh, and make almost directly for the summit by the burn which joins the Allt Gleann Achrioch some 500 yards above the railway bridge. There is a bridge at the foot of the Achrioch Burn as well as one $\frac{1}{2}$ a mile up the Abhainn Coninish. The way is very pleasant by a lightly wooded gorge with the stream coming over several waterfalls. Above the gorge the going is easy up the hillside to join the ridge a little north of the summit.

Alternatively, from Dailrigh, the Allt Gleann Achrioch can be followed for about 1$\frac{1}{2}$ miles and the summit gained from that point in a nearly direct line. The gorge route is the more picturesque, but both give fine views to the north and east.

Beinn Dubhchraig is easily climbed by its round north ridge which runs down to a point almost opposite Coninish Farm. The farm is reached by the rough road along the north side of the Abhainn Coninish from Dailrigh ; or by the path starting from the L.M.S. Station at Tyndrum and

contouring the hillside into the Coninish Glen.   Opposite the
farm is a bridge over the stream, and the north ridge, rising
ahead, is followed past the tiny lochan to the summit.

Beinn Oss, 3374 ft., is perhaps a better viewpoint than
anything else, although the steep, broad ridge leading to the
Oss-Dubhchraig col gives a very pleasant climb under snow
conditions. From the mountain's top, where there is a small
cairn, one gets a magnificent view of Ben Laoigh.   The
mountain is usually climbed in conjunction with Beinn
Dubhchraig, by any of the routes above described, or from
Ardlui by the track up the Dubh Eas.   The southern slopes
of the hill are somewhat uninteresting : the easiest approach
is to follow the Dubh Eas track to a point beneath the Lui-Oss
col and ascend by way of that bealach.

Beinn Laoigh, 3708 ft., is one of the best-known mountains of the Highlands, and from hill-tops afar off its shapely
summit can be seen standing well above its surrounding
neighbours.   In its winter coat of snow, whether seen from
Beinn Oss or from further points such as Dalmally or the foot
of the Coninish Burn, Beinn Laoigh has all the attributes of
an alpine peak.   Its sweeping lines rising to the two little
tops make it unmistakable, whilst the curtain of steep snow
descending from the almost level summit ridge suspended
between the tops offers a never-failing challenge to the
climber.   It is this north-eastern corrie that is the mountain's
chief attraction, but it is a side that should not be lightly
undertaken by inexperienced climbers.   In the late spring, or
after heavy snowfalls and thaw, the wide gullies of the corrie
are subject to avalanche.   The snow debris low down in the
corrie in early summer bears witness to the size of the cornices
which form on the summit ridge during the winter.

Beinn Laoigh, or Ben Lui, to use its familiar name, slopes
off in easy gradients to the south and east, where it is joined
to Beinn Oss by a bealach about 2340 ft.   The northern
shoulder dips steeply in three distinctive steps known as
Ciochan Beinn Laoigh and is well seen in profile from Loch
Awe.   To the west, the stony slopes of the mountain run down
to a col at 2561 ft. and so join up with the satellite peak,
Beinn a' Chleibh.

J. E. MacLaren.

BEINN LAOIGH FROM ABOVE CONINISH.

January, 1928.

May, 1937.   J. D. B. Wilson.

POINT 2526 FT. FROM LOCH VOIL SIDE.

From Dalmally, the easiest route to the top is to follow
the Tyndrum road to opposite the mouth of Eas Daimh, a
distance of 4 miles. A beautiful fall, Eas Morag, marks this
burn about 400 yards above its junction with the River
Lochy, and just above the mouth of the burn, on the right
bank, are the ruins of Airidh nan Ciochan. It is necessary
to ford the Lochy unless it is preferred to continue on the
road for a further 1½ miles, where there is a bridge at Glenlochy
crossing, and contour the slopes of Beinn Dubh so as to gain the
Eas Daimh. Once in the Eas Daimh valley, make directly
for the summit up long and steepish slopes of grass. There
is a bridge over the burn at Eas Morag. Alternatively,
instead of pushing direct for the summit from Eas Morag, a
pleasant route lies over the second step of Lui's northern
shoulder. From there slant upwards and across the big
northern rockface ; higher up a rough track will be found
running over ledges. This leads round the shoulder of Stob
Garbh, and gives a sudden and glorious view of the summit
of the ben.

From Dalmally, too, it is possible to ascend Beinn Laoigh
over Beinn a' Chleibh, by taking the Tyndrum road to Corry-
ghoil, and the branch road to Socach, and ascending Beinn a'
Chleibh by its broad ridge facing the farm. From the top,
there is a drop of less than 500 ft. to the col, and steep, stony
slopes lead from there to the summit of Beinn Laoigh. This
route is probably more pleasant in descent. When snow-
covered, the slopes on Beinn Laoigh leading to the Beinn
a' Chleibh col require care.

From Ardlui it is necessary to go up the Dubh Eas gorge
and across the broad moor either directly for the south-east
ridge of Beinn Laoigh, or the Beinn a' Chleibh or Beinn Oss
bealachs, and so to the summit. The latter is the preferable
route from this side.

The approach up the Coninish road from Tyndrum or
Crianlarich is repaying. It is possible to cycle as far as
Coninish, there being bridges over the streams between Beinn
Chuirn and Meall Odhar. From Tyndrum use the pedestrian
path starting behind the " Oban " Station and follow it to the
Coninish road, a distance of 1½ miles. A rough track goes

F

on beyond Coninish, and unless it is intended to climb the mountain by one of the routes in Coire Gaothach ahead or by its bounding ridges it is best to continue by the Allt an Rund and ascend to the top by the northern shoulder and the Ciochan Beinn Laoigh. (For routes in Coire Gaothach, see section on rock climbs.) If descending by way of Beinn Oss, there is a useful bridge over the Coninish opposite the farm, as well as a bridge at the mouth of the burn coming out of the corrie between Beinn Oss and Beinn Dubhchraig ¾ mile above Coninish.

The summit ridge of Beinn Laoigh is narrow and supports a top at each end, the actual summit lying at the southern extremity. It is marked by a large cairn, that on the northern and lower top being a good deal smaller. In winter the ridge is usually heavily corniced above Coire Gaothach. The view is superb, extending from Ben Nevis to the Campsies, and from Mull to the Ochils. Cruachan appears to great advantage over Strath Orchy, and the Crianlarich group is sufficiently close to make the details plain.

Beinn a' Chleibh, 3008 ft., is rather a " lumpish " hill, dwarfed by its higher and more interesting neighbour. It is, however, a fine viewpoint and is often climbed in the descent from Beinn Laoigh. From Socach, about 3½ miles from Dalmally, the obvious route lies up the broad west ridge of the mountain descending directly towards the farm. It is nowhere difficult and leads without intervening tops to the undulating summit ridge of Beinn a' Chleibh. This ridge is broad and is graced with three cairns. The smallest, at the south-east end, marks the highest point of the hill. If ascending from the Eas Daimh valley it is necessary to make for the Beinn a' Chleibh-Beinn Laoigh bealach, and climb to the summit from there. The slopes above the corrie, and facing Beinn Laoigh are precipitous in parts and are seamed by long shallow gullies.

PATHS

Tyndrum to Dalmally by Coninish.—A good track starts behind the "Oban" Station, and crossing the shoulder of the hill low down, joins the rough road ¾ mile east of Coninish.

The path continues beyond the farm to the Allt an Rund, but disappears before the col ahead is reached. Cross the col under the Ciochan Beinn Laoigh and descend by the north side of the Eas Daimh after crossing the stream by the bridge at Eas Morag. There is no bridge over the Lochy at the foot of the Eas Daimh, and in times of flood it may be necessary to turn north round the slopes of Beinn Dubh and make for the bridge at Glenlochy Crossing. The main road has then to be followed to Dalmally.

Glen Falloch to Dalmally by the Dubh Eas.—This route has been described under the Arrochar group and follows the line of an old drove road. The distance from Glen Falloch to Dalmally by this route is 12½ miles.

CENTRES

The following are convenient (each place has a good hotel):—Crianlarich, Dalmally and Tyndrum.

Youth Hostels at Crianlarich and Dalmally.

BIBLIOGRAPHY

*" Old and New Routes on Ben Lui," by James Maclay, *S.M.C.J.*, Vol. 4, p. 106.

*" Note on South Rib," by H. C. Boyd, *S.M.C.J.*, Vol. 4, p. 177.

" Some Hill Walks from Tyndrum," by J. H. Bell, *S.M.C.J.*, Vol. 9, p. 1.

*" Eating Between Meals," by J. A. Garrick, *S.M.C.J.*, Vol. 17, p. 190.

" The Spell of Ben Lui," by Rev. C. R. P. Vandeleur, *S.M.C.J.*, Vol. 21, p. 93.

" Reflections on Lui and Neighbouring Hills," by C. E. Andreae, *S.M.C.J.*, Vol. 23, p. 177.

" Beinn Laoigh," by J. Rose, *C.C.J.*, Vol. 1, p. 15.

" Snow Climbs in Perthshire, by W. Barclay and E. R. Beard, *C.C.J.*, Vol. 4, p. 177.

*Chiefly of rock-climbing interest.

X

THE CRIANLARICH GROUP

Munro's Tables—Section 1.

Maps : O.S. One-inch Popular Edition, Sheet 62. O.S. One-inch Special Tourist Map, '' The Trossachs and Loch Lomond.'' Bartholomew's Half-inch Scale, Revised, Scotland, Sheet 12. Bartholomew's Half-inch Scale, Great Britain, Sheet 48.

(1) **Beinn Chabhair,** 3053 ft. (The Mountain of the Antler) — 3½ miles E.N.E. from Ardlui.

(2) **An Caisteal,** 3265 ft. (The Castle) — 3¾ miles S. from Crianlarich.

(3) **Beinn a' Chroin,** East Top, 3104 ft. (The Mountain of the Cloven Hoof) — 4¼ miles S. by E. from Crianlarich.

(4) Beinn a' Chroin, West Top, 3078 ft. — ⅝ mile W. by S. of (3).

(5) **Beinn Tulaichean,** 3099 ft. (The Knolly Hill) — 4 miles S.E. by S. from Crianlarich.

(6) **Cruach Ardrain,** 3428 ft. (The High Heap) — 3 miles S.E. by S. from Crianlarich.

(7) Stob Garbh, 3148 ft. (Rough Peak) — 2½ miles S.E. from Crianlarich.

(8) **Ben More,** 3843 ft. (Great Hill) — 3 miles E. by S. from Crianlarich.

(9) **Am Binnein,** Stobinian, 3827 ft. (The Pinnacle) — 1 mile S. from (8).

(10) Stob Coire an Lochain, 3497 ft. (Peak of the Corrie of the Small Loch) — ½ mile S.E. by S. from (9).

(11) Meall na Dige, 3140 ft. (The Round Hill of the Ditch) — 1 mile E. from (9).

(12) Stob Creagach, 2966 ft. (The Rocky Point) — ¾ mile N.E. from (11).

(13) Meall an t-Seallaidh, 2793 ft. (The Round Hill of the Sight) — 1⅝ miles N.N.E. from Balquhidder.

(14) Creag MacRànaich, 2600 ft. contour — 1 mile N.N.E. of (13).

72

THIS fine chain of hills, which contains some of the best-known and most frequented peaks in the Southern Highlands, extends in an east and west direction for about 17 miles from Inverarnan, in Glen Falloch, to Glen Ogle. It is bounded on the west and north by Glen Falloch and Glen Dochart, on the east by Glen Ogle, and on the south by Loch Voil and Loch Doine, and the River Inverlochlarig at their head. Its broadest point in a north and south direction from near Luib to Loch Doine is between 5 and 6 miles.

The group is for the most part formed of massive grits and crumpled mica-schists belonging to the Highland Metamorphic series. There are many small intrusive dykes of basalt, and the whole group has weathered evenly to give mainly grass-covered hills with bracken on their lower slopes. While there are small outcrops of rock on practically all parts of the chain, there are no extensive rock faces; consequently, though short rock scrambles might be made at a few points, the whole group is really devoid of rock-climbing interest. Lying at a considerable distance from the sea, however, these hills usually carry good quantities of snow until the springtime.

For purposes of description the whole group may be conveniently split into five sections. The first four of these, counting from the west, all contain one or more mountains rising to over 3000 ft., the fourth culminating in the twin peaks of Ben More, 3843 ft. and Stobinian, 3827 ft. The easternmost section is lower, reaching from 2500 ft. to 2700 ft., and is seldom visited even by hill-walkers though pleasant cross-country hill-walks may be made through the glens traversing it from Glen Dochart to Loch Voilside and Balquhidder. The grassy southern slopes of these hills slanting down to Loch Voil and Loch Doine are known by the general name of the Braes of Balquhidder (pronounced Balwhidder).

The best general views of the western part of the chain are from Strath Fillan to the north-west, and from the southern slopes of Beinn Chaluim. From Strath Fillan, Cruach Ardrain stands up well and the higher masses of Ben More and Stobinian form a magnificent background. The stretches of the Fillan Water, both above and below the point where it is crossed by the Tyndrum to Crianlarich road, are beloved by artists so that the group of mountains from this angle is a favourite subject at exhibitions of Scottish landscapes. The view from the southern slopes of Beinn Chaluim is probably less satisfactory from the purely æsthetic point of view, but it has the advantage of showing the full height of the peaks across the glen and may therefore be expected to give as much satisfaction to the mountaineer.

The view of the group from the north-east is magnificent, but it is so predominantly Ben More and Stobinian that description is deferred until these mountains are described. Another fine view of the group is from the road or railway between Balquhidder and Kingshouse stations. From this side the individual tops are not well seen with the exception of Creag MacRànaich, but the succession of shoulders, one behind the other, all sloping down to Loch Voil makes a grading of light and shade of great beauty which is especially well seen in an evening light.

The peaks of the group are readily accessible from every side owing to the fact that it is bounded by main roads on west, north and east, while a branch road suitable for motor cars runs along the southern boundary from Kingshouse Hotel for a distance of 8 miles through Balquhidder to Inverlochlarig Farm. The only section of the boundary not covered by a motoring road is a stretch of 9 miles from Inverlochlarig to Benglass Farm in Glen Falloch over the pass between Beinn Chabhair and Parlan Hill. This pass at a height of 1800 ft. separates the Crianlarich group from the hills to the south.

Beinn Chabhair, 3053 ft. (pronounced Ben Chabar, rather like Lochaber but with the second " a " noticeable).— It is the most westerly peak of the group and its southern slopes contain the furthest head-waters of the River Forth by its northern tributary, the Rivers Balvaig, Leny and Teith.

On a clear day it is conspicuous from a number of viewpoints in Glasgow, particularly from the summit of Ruchill Park, and it is also well seen from Loch Long.

Lying comparatively remote from the centres of population, it is the least visited of the " Munros " of the group.

The little inn at Inverarnan in Glen Falloch, 2 miles north
of Ardlui, is the best starting point for the ascent, the summit
lying 3 miles to the east. Its south, east and north sides are
of steep grass much broken by outcrops of rock. The west
side, sloping down for 1400 ft. to Lochan Beinn Chabhair is
less steep, but it is also broken in part by small outcrops.
A long ridge runs down in a west-north-westerly direction in
a series of rocky hummocks for 1000 ft. to Ben Glas, which
in turn broadens out into the sides of Glen Falloch.

The most enjoyable route is to ascend by Lochan Beinn
Chabhair and the west face and to come down the ridge to
Ben Glas. Cross the Falloch by the Benglas Farm bridge
200 yards north of Inverarnan Inn. A false path will be seen
sloping up the hill-side to the left. A real and very useful
path will be found starting only 30 ft. higher up the hill, at
a large tree above the farm gate on to the hill, and running
parallel to the false one. This path slopes north and left in
a series of zig-zags through the birches and bracken to the
ruins of a cottage at about 700 ft. to 800 ft. In conditions
of soft snow it may be advisable to make for the ridge, while
in a high wind the burn route will probably be the more
sheltered. Going by the burn, at this point turn south-east
and traverse upwards to the right, skirting below the lower
slopes of Meall Mòr nan Eag, till the upper section of the
Ben Glas Burn is reached about the 1250-ft. contour. A
pleasant heathery scramble follows for 250 ft., after which,
for ½ mile or so to the Lochan, it is inclined to be spongy.

From Lochan Beinn Chabhair to the summit is a quick
ascent of 1400 ft. pleasantly varied by the small outcrops.
The summit is well distinguished by a substantial cairn
2½ ft.—3 ft. in height.

The view from the summit is not substantially different
from that from the other Glen Falloch hills though its higher
neighbours to the north-west naturally limit the horizon in
that direction. It is especially well placed for the view down
Loch Long and a little known but delightful hill, Binnein an
Fhidhleir, on the north side of Glen Kinglas, is well seen
from this point.

An attractive feature of the descent over Ben Glas is the

beautifully situated Lochan a' Chaisteil at a height of just under 2000 ft. "The Castle Loch" is so called from the castle-like appearance of the cliffs which drop sheer into the water. This is a charming spot on a hot day. The line for the ruined cottage, and the top of the path, from here, is the railway viaduct over the Dubh Eas.

Beinn Chabhair can be approached from the Crianlarich direction by means of a bridge over the River Falloch at Derrydaroch (3¼ miles). Cut across the moor to the Allt a' Chuilinn from which the Ben Glas ridge can be struck at Stob Creag an Fhithich or a direct route can be made for the summit up the north-west slopes. In heavy spate the Allt a' Chuilinn can be crossed by a foot-bridge 100 yards above its entrance to the Falloch. Parties descending the Allt a' Chuilinn and making for Inverarnan can cross the Falloch by a foot-bridge at Falls of Falloch.

Beinn Chabhair is separated from An Caisteal by a drop of about 1000 ft. Being a good deal broken by outcrops it seems more. In severe winter conditions in mist, continue along the summit ridge south-east for about 100 yards from which point a good start will be made on the descent to the An Caisteal col.

Beinn Chabhair can also be climbed from the south-east by approaching it along the road leading from Kingshouse to Inverlochlarig Farm. This expedition is pleasant, easy and interesting, provided some means of conveyance is available as far as Inverlochlarig.

The road by Loch Voilside has already been referred to in the general description of the group. When the mouth of the Ishag Burn is reached, a slanting course is taken gaining height on the lowest southern slopes of Beinn a' Chroin instead of following the banks of the Inverlochlarig River closely. The southern Allt a' Chuilinn is reached at about the 1400-ft. contour. From this point the ridge from An Caisteal to Beinn a' Chroin looks remarkably fine and serrated, while the route up the south-east side of Beinn Chabhair to the south ridge can be examined at leisure. There is a variety of ways up through the many fine outcrops on this side, but the easiest and most direct one passes on the right

7

R. Young.

BEN MORE FROM NEAR CRIANLARICH.

CRUACH ARDRAIN FROM STRATHFILLAN.

D. J. Fraser.

Hugh Gardner.

STOBINIAN AND BEN MORE FROM GLEN DOCHART.

April, 1934.

of the very lowest outcrops and on the left of a much larger one half-way up to the south ridge.

An Caisteal, 3265 ft., and Beinn a' Chroin, East Top, 3104 ft., West Top, 3078 ft.—An Caisteal lies 1 mile north-north-east of Beinn Chabhair and 3¾ miles south of Crianlarich. The West Top of Beinn a' Chroin, lying ¾ mile south-east of An Caisteal, is separated from it by a 2650-ft. col. The East Top lies about ⅝ mile further east. The two hills are generally combined in one expedition from Crianlarich. An Caisteal sends down two ridges to Glen Falloch, one north-west over Stob Glas, 2323 ft., and the other north-north-west over Sron Gharbh, 2322 ft. The latter ridge is called Twistin Hill and is separated from Stob Glas by the Allt Andoran. An Caisteal is generally ascended by Twistin Hill. Access is gained by leaving the Glen Falloch road 1¾ miles south-west of Crianlarich and crossing the Falloch by a good bridge immediately below the point where it takes a right-angled turn into the main glen. The ascent from Derrydaroch, where there is another bridge over the Falloch, is more tedious apart altogether from the extra distance from Crianlarich.

The ascent of the West Top of Beinn a' Chroin (small cairn) from the An Caisteal col is steep. Three parallel terraces sloping upwards to the left look tempting, but in icy conditions these need considerable care and it is better to bear to the right when the rocks are reached. This takes one on to the south face where the snow is not generally so hard. Even if it is intended to shorten the expedition by omitting the East Top of Beinn a' Chroin (the higher top—small cairn) it is best to continue towards it at least as far as the lowest point between the two tops before striking down to the left on to the north ridge. There is a bridge over the burn coming out of the An Caisteal-Beinn a' Chroin corrie just where it joins the main upper glen (Coire Earb). Another bridge spans the upper Falloch just below the point where it is met by a small burn coming down from Hawk Craig. This is useful if it is desired to make a direct route across the moor to Crianlarich instead of continuing down the Falloch to the road.

The sharp drop on the west side of the West Top of Beinn a' Chroin is the best feature of the two mountains and makes the mountain easily identifiable from north and south. An unexpected view of it is obtained from a boat in the middle of Loch Tulla.

Beinn a' Chroin is also occasionally climbed from Balquhidder via Inverlochlarig, and it is a fine expedition to do the traverse between Crianlarich and Balquhidder in either direction. An Caisteal can be included but otherwise the ascent or descent of the north ridge of Beinn a' Chroin's East Top will be taken. In descending on the south side of Beinn a' Chroin from the East Top, it is best to make for the right bank of the east branch of the Allt a' Chroin. A small ridge running south on the east side of Lochan a' Chroin is more prominent than would be supposed from the very small bend in the contours of the Popular Edition Map. This little ridge bounds a shallow corrie to the east and it is easy to land in this corrie by mistake when looking for Lochan a' Chroin on the way up.

Cruach Ardrain, 3428 ft., is the favourite winter ascent from Crianlarich. A full length view of its north face is obtained from the village, from which the summit lies just three miles to the south-east. There is individuality in the outline of the summit ridge and, when plastered in snow, the north face, scarred by the Y-Gully, is an impressive sight.

The " tourist " route is up the south-west side of the Allt Coire Ardrain till under the north face of the mountain. Then bear to the right up easy slopes on to the saddle of the ridge terminating in Grey Height. From here it is an easy walk up the west side of the final peak to the top.

An alternative route is over Stob Garbh on the east side of Coire Ardrain and up the north east-side of the face to the summit. The slopes are steep and require care when iced.

Parties that do not feel that they have had sufficient exercise sometime walk out for 1 mile to the south-east to the summit of Beinn Tulaichean and back.

A fine expedition is to traverse Beinn Tulaichean and Cruach Ardrain from Strathyre or Kingshouse to Crianlarich. The walk up Loch Voil and Loch Doine to Inverlochlarig is very beautiful. The south-west end of Beinn Tulaichean is very easy going, keeping clear of the rough boulder-strewn slopes immediately to the east of the summit.

Coire Ardrain occasionally gives good ski-running when snow is plentiful. It is a trifle boulder-strewn, but the slopes are very favourable.

Ben More, 3843 ft., is one of the best known and most popular mountains in Scotland. It and its twin brother, Stobinian, are the highest mountains in the British Isles south of Strathtay, by several 100 ft. They are seen from far and wide, but the most impressive aspect is from the road on the north side of Glen Dochart between Killin and Auchlyne. They tower over the various reaches of the river all along this road, Ben More a huge sugar loaf sweeping down for 3000 ft. to the depths of the glen, Stobinian beautifully contrasted by its tapering cone so fascinatingly cut off flat at the top, the two connected by a perfect saddle dipping for nearly 1000 ft. below the summits.

The view from the summit of Ben More is impressive in its extent. Rhum, Jura, Ailsa Craig, the Merrick in Galloway, Glasgow, Stirling Castle, the Wallace Monument, Edinburgh and the Cairngorms can all be seen in suitable conditions.

Owing to its height it is one of the first mountains to catch new snow in the autumn and, standing well inland, the north-east face of Stobinian carries snow often well into the summer.

Benmore Farm, only 2 miles east of Crianlarich, is the usual starting point, but climbers from Luib will leave the road at a point 3 miles further east. In high summer, when the last snow has disappeared, no mountain is so safe to climb ; 3300 ft. of a steep, grassy climb lands one on the summit, where there are two cairns a little apart. The more southerly one is higher. A shallow scoop on the north-west face sometimes dignified by the name of the " Coire " forms practically the only break in its sugar loaf contours as seen from Benmore Farm. Keeping the Coire on one's right is the shortest and easiest route to the top. In winter this so-called Coire can carry a lot of deep, soft snow slightly corniced along its north edge, and owing to its steep angle it is inclined to avalanche. There have been one or two accidents as a result. The slopes above the Coire are steep and it is common here to find a covering of loose, soft snow on the top of hard ice. Particular care should therefore be taken to keep control on this part of the hill in such conditions as its appearance is deceptively easy. Many years ago one of a party without ice-axe slipped over some small rocks on the north side of this bounding edge and was killed. The place where the body was found is marked by an iron cross.

The drop to the Bealach-eadar-dha Beinn between Ben More and Stobinian is about 1000 ft. Neither it nor the corresponding ascent to Stobinian, where there is a fair-sized cairn, presents any more difficulty than the rest of the hill.

Stobinian is sometimes climbed from Glen Carnaig over Stob Coire an Lochain. To do so, leave the Loch Doine road before it begins to descend to Carnaig bridge and go up the east side of the glen until clear of Stob Invercarnaig. Then strike up on to the south ridge leading up to Stob Coire an Lochain. When Glen Carnaig is full of deep, soft snow it is advisable to go further along the road past the Carnaig bridge and so straight up Stob Invercarnaig on to the ridge at once. The going on the ridge is delightful, with a very gradual ascent and fine views all round. A short climb takes one from Stob Coire an Lochain to Stobinian, the descent from Stob Coire an Lochain being scarcely perceptible. Returning from Stobinian to Balquhidder the route should be varied by striking down to the east from Stob Coire an Lochain to the little lochan which gives it its name and then up Meall na Dige. From Meall na Dige, where there is a small cairn a few yards north of the actual summit, a fine view is obtained of the east side of Stobinian and the corrie just to the north of Stob Coire an Lochain. The descent is continued over Am Mam and Meall Monachyle to Monachyle-more, by the well-defined south-east ridge. If descending towards Luib, Stob Creagach may be added by passing along the knolly ridge connecting that hill with Meall na Dige. Below the actual summit the slopes are rocky and broken-up, but a way through is not hard to find. From the top, the descent towards Luib is by the open north-east ridge called

Leacann Riabhach. About 1 mile from the top, at a dip in the ridge, the slopes to the left give easy access to Coire Chaorach and so to the road a little over 1 mile west of Luib station.

The corries to the east of Stob Coire an Lochain give good ski-ing, as does the gradual ridge of the peak running out to Stob Invercarnaig. This ridge often retains a band of snow just below its crest late on into the year.

PATHS

Crianlarich to Monachylemore.—The fine pass at the head of the Ben More Glen is much used by hostel folk *en route* between Crianlarich and Monachylemore. From Ben More farm a faint track is found on the right bank of the stream which is followed directly to the deeply cut pass ahead. Descent on the south side of the watershed is by the Inverlochlarig Glen and gives some heavy going. From Inverlochlarig the road runs east to Monachylemore, and beyond.

To the east of Meall na Dige lies about 7 miles of tangled moor, peat hags and head waters, cut into on the south side by the three glens of Monachyle, Kirkton and Kendrum.

Luib to Monachylemore.—It is a delightful walk from Luib Station to Monachylemore where there is a Youth Hostel. On leaving the station strike up the hill, keeping the crags of Creag an t-Sasunnaich on the right. A mile of bog jumping takes one to the Cairn marked on the map, which is a conspicuous feature from the glen below, though not very noticeable from the moor. Once down into the glen, which at the top is impressively wild, a well-marked track is struck on the right-hand side of the burn. The walk down Monachyle Glen is charming.

Ledchary to Balquhidder.—An intermittent track leads up the Ledchary Burn from Ledchary. This can be used on the way to Lochan an Eireannaich under the picturesque crag of Meall an Fhiodhain. The Kirkton Glen on the south side of this pass has been thickly planted by the Forestry Commission, but a good path leads from the pass through the trees to Balquhidder.

Killin Junction to Edinchip, by Gleann Dubh and Glen Kendrum.—It is worth while to do this from Kingshouse to Killin Junction, taking the two tops of Creag MacRànaich on the way. Coming from Kingshouse, a grass track leaves the main road just before the first house at Balquhidder Station is reached, taking one pleasantly through woods to Edinchip House, which is avoided on the lower side. The track up the east side of the Kendrum Burn should be followed until well under the cliffs of Creag MacRànaich. A pleasant scramble can then be made up a grass gully breaking the row of cliffs at the south-east corner. The north top of Creag MacRànaich is slightly the higher of the two. The rim of the corrie round to Meall Sgallachd is reported to carry good cornices considering its comparatively low elevation. A track leads down the east side of the Gleann Dubh Burn to Braeval near Killin Junction Station.

CENTRES

Good hotels are found at each of the following places :—
Crianlarich, Inverarnan, Kingshouse (Balquhidder), Lochearnhead and Luib.

Youth Hostels at Crianlarich and Monachylemore.

BIBLIOGRAPHY

*" Cruach Ardrain," by N. W. Face, Notes, *S.M.C.J.*, Vol. 3, p. 306.
" Creag MacRàniach," by A. W. Russell, *S.M.C.J.*, Vol. 4, p. 247.
*" Leum an Eireannaich," by J. Gall Inglis, *S.M.C.J.*, Vol. 5, p. 246.
" The Crianlarich Group," Guide Book Article, *S.M.C.J.*, Vol. 6, p. 195.
" Avalanche on Ben More," by W. G. Macalister, *S.M.C.J.*, Vol. 12, p. 124.
" Creag MacRànaich," by W. Inglis Clark, *S.M.C.J.*, Vol. 14, p. 203.
" The Highlands in June," by J. G. Stott, *S.M.C.J.*, Vol. 14, p. 259.
" Day Trips by Rail," by J. Dow, *S.M.C.J.*, Vol. 19, p. 33.
" In Defence of Ben More," by E. C. Thomson, *S.M.C.J.*, Vol. 19, p. 238.
*" Beinn a' Chroin," Notes, *S.M.C.J.*, Vol. 20, p. 453.

*Chiefly of rock- or snow-climbing interest.

XI

THE LOCH EARN GROUP

Munro's Tables—Section 2.
Maps: O.S. One-inch Scale Popular Edition, Sheets 62
and 63. O.S. Half-inch Scale, Scotland, Sheets 22 and 23.
Bartholomew's Half-inch Scale, Scotland, Revised,
Sheet 12. Bartholomew's Half-inch Scale, Great Britain,
Sheet 48.

(1) **Ben Vorlich, 3224 ft.**   -   - 4 miles S.E. from Lochearnhead.

(2) **Stuc a' Chroin, 3189 ft.** (Hill 1¼ miles S.W. from (1).
of the Cloven Foot)

(3) Beinn Each, 2660 ft. (Hill of the 1⅜ miles S.W. from (2).
Horses)

(4) Uamh Bheag, 2181 ft. (Little 4½ miles N.E. from Callander.
Cave)

RISING south of Loch Earn, and bounded on the west by
Strathyre and Loch Lubnaig, these hills form a beautifully
compact group. To the south and east the ground slopes off
in great moors and low hills, the highest top in the area south
of Glen Artney being only slightly in excess of 2000 ft.

The higher hills of the group are well seen from the south,
say, from Stirling, when both Vorlich and Stuc a' Chroin
stand up grandly behind the rolling moors and low hills
south of Glen Artney. From the north, too, Stuc a' Chroin
shows a bold outline, particularly when seen from Glen Ogle :
the north buttress, descending steeply from the summit,
makes an impressive background to the heather-and-grass
slopes behind Edinample. Seen from the east, near Crieff, or
from the west by Loch Voil, Ben Vorlich is particularly
shapely, and assumes the form of a steep cone. From the
north side of Loch Earn, opposite Ardvorlich, the mountain
appears more massive.

Access to the two higher hills is most easy from the south shore of Loch Earn by way of Glen Ample or Glen Vorlich. From other directions, long glens leading into the heart of the group are usually followed. These, having roads for most of their length, lead easily from Comrie in the east, or Callander in the south.

In common with the greater part of the Southern Highlands, the rock of this group is mica-schist and the hills show the characteristic smooth grassy slopes broken here and there by small cliffs and many outcrops. In winter the two higher hills are generally snow-covered, but they seldom accumulate as much snow as the greater mountains to the north and west. It is usual for Ben Vorlich to be clear of its winter coat at least a month before the last of the snow disappears from Stobinian.

Ben Vorlich, 3224 ft.—Although the mountain from most angles appears either as a simple cone, or as a gently curving ridge, it is in fact rather more complex, having ridges which give it a peculiar propeller-like twist. In all, there are four of these ridges, the two main ones from the summit being the south-east to south ridge leading down to Dubh Choirein, and, in the opposite direction, the north-west to north ridge connecting the mountain to the low top called Ben Our (2400-ft. contour) above Edinample. A short distance west of the summit are two further ridges, one on each side of the mountain. The first of these faces a little east of north and dips steeply into Glen Vorlich; the second is a short ridge dropping to the south-west and connecting with the north-east spur of Stuc a' Chroin at the Bealach an Dubh Choirein.

To the north, Ben Vorlich is mostly steep grass with small cliffs towards the east ; on the other side, on the slopes above the upper part of Gleann an Dubh Choirein, are long tongues of scree and broken-up ridges of reddish rock.

The mountain may be climbed from Lochearnhead or St. Fillans, via Ardvorlich or Edinample, from Callander by the Keltie Burn, or from Comrie by way of Glen Artney.

By far the shortest and most simple route is that starting from Ardvorlich, reached from Lochearnhead or St. Fillans

STUC A' CHROIN FROM BEN VORLICH

G. R. Donald.

August, 1938.

J. D. B. Wilson

LOCH VOIL AND BEN VORLICH.

by the road along the south side of Loch Earn. Behind the farm a path leads up the very lovely glen to Bealach Dearg on the east of Ben Vorlich and thence by way of Dubh Choirein to Glen Artney or Callander. This path is followed for a little over 1 mile from Ardvorlich, when it is necessary to leave it and strike up the rounded north ridge of the mountain. The upper part of the ridge is steep and very broad, and in mist it is well to remember that it abuts on the summit ridge west of the top. The remains of a fence are encountered on the highest ridge, and this is then followed almost due east to the summit. There are two tops close together and connected by an almost imperceptible drop : the more easterly is the summit and has a moderate-sized cairn. The view north-west is very fine, while close at hand, Stuc a' Chroin shows its steep sides to great advantage.

From Edinample, a little over 1 mile from Lochearnhead, the way to the summit is rather longer. The path up Glen Ample is followed to the farm, and a little beyond, and the Allt a' Choire Fhuadaraich then leads eastwards towards the Bealach an Dubh Choirein. From the col the south-west ridge is followed to the top. Part of the way up Choire Fhuadaraich gives heavy going and it may be found preferable to leave the stream after breasting the steep rise above Glen Ample and make directly up the slopes of Creagan nan Gabhar, and thence to the summit by the easy slopes of the north-west ridge. Parts of this route give very pleasant ski-ing when snow is plentiful.

The way from Callander involves a long trudge up the Keltie Valley, and beyond. It is possible to take a car as far as Luirgeann some 2 miles from Callander, but this cannot be recommended. Beyond the farm, the road is quite possible for bicycles almost to Arivurichardich, after which it is neces-sary to walk. The right-of-way path leading to Glen Artney is now followed just north of the Allt a' Bhacain, and over a low col to the Allt an Dubh Choirein. On the left bank of this stream there is a rather faint track to Dubh Choirein, which point having been reached, it only remains to ascend the broad and gradual south-east ridge to Ben Vorlich's summit. The distance from Callander to the summit is fully 10 miles.

G

From Comrie it is possible to drive to Glenartney Lodge and make use of the other end of the right-of-way leading over to Arivurichardich and Callander. Leave the Glen Artney road on the left and a little way short of the Lodge, and follow the well-marked path up a gradual slope, and over the low bealach to the Allt an Dubh Choirein, when the route described above is joined.

Stuc a' Chroin, 3189 ft.—Probably the most effective feature of this mountain is the prominent rocky buttress descending from the summit to the Bealach an Dubh Choirein, beneath Ben Vorlich. As the two mountains are often climbed in a single expedition it comes about that this north-east buttress of Stuc is the usual way of ascent, although it is by no means the easiest route to the summit. From the top of Ben Vorlich the broken fence is followed down to the Dubh Choirein col by way of the steep south-west spur. The buttress of Stuc rises straight ahead, and although not difficult it requires care in places. There are a number of steep, rocky steps most readily avoided by keeping a little to the right of the crest. The summit is flattish and has two cairns ; the first one reached overlooks the cliffs to the east, while the second, and higher, lies a little way south and commands a very pleasing view of the steep side of Ben Vorlich across the Dubh Choirein.

If Stuc a' Chroin is to be climbed by itself, it is most approachable from Glen Ample. The path from Edinample is followed up the glen to the farm, after which a faint track traverses grassy slopes some distance above the burn. Half a mile beyond the farm strike up the slopes on the left, and make for the top of Creag Dhubh. From the farm, the Creag appears as a peak in its own right, but the slopes lead continuously to more level ground beyond, around the 2000-ft. contour. From there a broad ridge is followed to the top.

From Callander, the road by Keltie Water is taken to Arivurichardich, and from there the south-east ridge of Stuc a' Chroin can be gained at the col north-west of Meall Odhar. This ridge is long and gradual but leads directly to the summit. There is now a sizeable sheet of water at the mouth of Gleann a' Chroin (not marked on the Ordnance Survey maps). It is the Callander Water Works reservoir.

A very charming ridge runs between Stuc a' Chroin and **Beinn Each,** 2660 ft., by way of a number of rocky bumps and little cols. This can be used equally well in descent or ascent, the climb over Beinn Each and so on to Stuc being a pleasant way of reaching the latter summit. A fence runs the whole length of the ridge, winding somewhat tortuously above the upper end of Gleann a' Chroin. Beinn Each's north ridge, leading to the Bealach nan Cabar, is steep but presents no difficulty. It is usual to approach Beinn Each from Ardchullarie on Loch Lubnaig, by a very pretty path through the larches above the farm. This path leads over into Glen Ample, but it should be left before the highest point is reached, and a way made up the slopes of Beinn Each on the right. The hill's eastern side is steep and rocky, but the long line of cliffs shown on the Ordnance Survey map further east and on the south side of Gleann a' Chroin do not exist. These slopes, although broken in places by rock outcrops, are for the most part steep grass and scree.

South of Glen Artney is a large area of very rough moorland, culminating in **Uamh Bheag,** 2181 ft., with long, wide spurs running out eastwards. Uamh Bheag commands what is probably the best near view of Stuc a' Chroin and Ben Vorlich, and has, in addition, some interesting caves in its slightly lower shoulder, called Uamh Mhòr. From Burn of Cambus, 1½ miles from Doune along the Callander road, a rough road leads to Loch Mahaick and Severie. This is passable for cars almost to the end, from where a gradual rise over thick heather leads to Uamh Mhòr. The caves are to be found on the western shoulder at the prominent scarp of rock and close to a tiny rift valley, known locally as " Rob Roy's Cattle Fank." From here it is only a short climb north-east to the top of Uamh Bheag.

PATHS

Callander to Comrie by Glens Keltie and Artney.— The route has been described almost in its entirety in the

foregoing chapter.   From Callander take the road to the Golf
Course : a little way up the steep hill a path breaks off to the
right and leads to the Brackland Falls.   It is worth while
making the small detour to see the fine gorge below the falls.
After the initial height is gained, the road runs almost levelly
along the west side of the valley, some distance above the
Keltie, and 3½ miles from Callander the river is crossed and
the right-of-way path branches off the road just short of
Arivurichardich.   The track now makes a little north of
east, up the Allt a' Bhacain, and contours the hillside at the
watershed to drop again into the mouth of the Dubh Choirein
Glen.   From here there is a splendid view of Stuc a' Chroin
and Ben Vorlich, before the path, after crossing the stream,
mounts a small rise over the Monadh Odhar and passes into
Glen Artney.   The Artney road is joined just short of Glenartney Lodge, and is then followed to Comrie.   The total
distance from Callander is a little over 16 miles.

Callander to Ardvorlich by the hills.—Follow the above
route until the Allt an Dubh Choirein is crossed, and take the
rather faint path along the north bank of the stream.   This
leads to Dubh Choirein, when a way has to be made over the
pass east of Ben Vorlich (2200 ft. approximately).   A path is
found again in Glen Vorlich on the far side of the pass.

**Loch Lubnaig (Ardchullarie) to Edinample by Glen
Ample.**—From Ardchullarie Farm an alpine path climbs
through the thick larch woods, and then along the hillside
to the watershed.   This part is wet and virtually trackless.
Keep to the right side of the Burn of Ample after crossing
the pass and descend Glen Ample.   The track will be found
within 1 mile of the top and improves as it descends.   Below
Glenample Farm it crosses the burn by a bridge and leads
through trees to Loch Earnside.

Centres
Hotel accommodation is available at the following places :
Callander, Comrie, Lochearnhead, St. Fillans and Strathyre.

Youth Hostel at Comrie.

BIBLIOGRAPHY

*" Stuc a' Chroin's East Face," by W. Brown, *S.M.C.J.*, Vol. 3, p. 19.

" Ben Vorlich and Stuc a' Chroin," by G. Thomson, *S.M.C.J.*, Vol. 3, p. 107.

" A Saturday Afternoon on the Face of Stuc a' Chroin," by J. Gall Inglis, *S.M.C.J.*, Vol. 6, p. 102.

" Ben Vorlich (Perthshire) Group," Guide Book Article, *S.M.C.J.*, Vol. 6, p. 200.

*" The North-east Face of Stuc a' Chroin," by W. Garden, *S.M.C.J.*, Vol. 11, p. 278.

" Notes on Vorlich and Stuc, by J. H. A. McIntyre, *S.M.C.J.*, Vol. 14, p. 92.

" Some Hill Roads in Scotland," by W. A. Smith, *S.M.C.J.*, Vol. 14, p. 95.

" Ben Vorlich and Stuc a' Chroin," by J. C. Murray, *C.C.J.*, Vol. 2, p. 11.

" Christmas Monday on Vorlich and Stuc, by H. McRobert, *C.C.J.* Vol. 4, p. 37.

*Chiefly of rock-climbing interest.

XII

BEN CHONZIE AND GLEN ALMOND GROUP

Munro's Tables—Section 2.

Maps: O.S. One-inch Scale Popular Edition, Sheets 56 and 63. O.S. Half-inch Scale, Scotland, Sheet 23. Bartholomew's Half-inch Scale Revised, Scotland, Sheet 12. Bartholomew's Half-inch Scale, Great Britain, Sheet 48.

Ben Chonzie, 3048 ft. (Hill of the 5½ miles N. of Comrie. Cry of the Deer; possibly Hill of Weeping)

BETWEEN Strathtay and Strathearn there is a large tract of elevated moorland, into which cut several beautiful glens. The culminating point, and the only mountain in this group over 3000 ft., is Ben Chonzie. In addition, however, are many lesser tops in the area, of which the largest group lies to the north of Glen Almond, and near its head. The highest point in this series of flat tops is Creagan na Bheinn, 2909 ft. Between the heads of Glen Almond and Glen Lednock is a smaller, although rougher, group of summits culminating in Creag Uigeach, 2840 ft.

The main glens intersecting the large plateau are :—

(1) Glen Lednock, on the S.W. of the area, by which one can cross, by a right of way, from Comrie to Ardeonaig on Loch Tay.

(2) Glen Turret, which runs N.W. from Crieff to the foot of Ben Chonzie.

(3) The Sma' Glen, 5½ miles N.E. of Crieff, in which runs the road to Amulree.

(4) Glen Almond, running 11 miles in a W.N.W. direction from Newton Bridge in the Sma' Glen.

(5) Strath Bran, extending 10 miles S.W. from Dunkeld to Amulree. At the last-named place the glen turns N.W. and becomes Glen Quaich, in which, amid pastoral scenery, lies the lovely little Loch Freuchie.

Between Glen Quaich and Glen Almond is a track by way of a low col in Glen Lochan. This glen runs in a south-westerly direction from Loch Freuchie to Auchnafree and contains a number of lochans and steep walls to the north.

Ben Chonzie, or Ben-y-Hone, is well seen from the highest point on the Muir of Orchill road (A822) from whence it appears as a flat-topped mass rising above Strath Earn. The deep valley running into the hills immediately behind Crieff is Glen Turret ; the loch at its head, however, cannot be seen from the Orchill road.

The nearest point of approach is Comrie, but the mountain can also be reached from Crieff or Amulree, while Ardeonaig on Loch Tay is a more distant, but still useful, base. At each of these places there is an hotel.

From Comrie the quickest route to the summit is to follow the Glen Lednock road to Invergeldie, then by the path north-east up the right bank of the Innergeldie Burn for about $1\frac{1}{2}$ miles, when a direct line can be made up the even slopes on the right to the summit plateau. A fence is reached high up on the mountain and this can then be followed to the summit, beyond which the wires continue down the steep slopes to the east. At the top, a branch fence runs off in a north-westerly direction, the large, well-built summit cairn lying just to the south of the junction. There is a fine view of the Lawers group over the lower hills around the head of Glen Almond, and a good glimpse southwards down Glen Turret to Strathearn, but the view down into Glen Lednock is interrupted by a shoulder of the mountain.

An alternative and more interesting route from Comrie, if more laborious, is to follow the path through the gorge of Glen Lednock to the Deil's Cauldron. Follow the Lednock road from the town to a point just past the last houses and take the path turning off to the right. Above the gorge the main road is regained and followed for $\frac{1}{2}$ mile, when it is again left and the river crossed by a footbridge to the rough road on the far side. This leads to Carroglen, and the trackless slopes above are then followed upwards. The going is heavy and rather uninteresting from here to the higher parts of the mountain : the best line is up the Lurg Burn and by the Spur of Creag Mhòr na h-Iolaire and the fence leading up and over the summit plateau.

If it is desired to traverse the mountain to Loch Tay, from Comrie, on returning to Invergeldie the path to the top of Glen Lednock (past Spout Rollo and Bot na h-Acaire) should be taken. This leads high up the hillside, and east of Ruadh Mheall and Point 1557, to the zigzag path down Fin Glen.

Approaching the mountain from Crieff, an easy start is given by the private road to Glen Turret Lodge. This way leads off from the Monzie road ¾ mile after leaving A85 to Comrie. Thereafter, the Turret road rises, steeply in places, to the loch at 1127 ft. and the lodge at its head. From Crieff to here is a little over 6 miles. The loch lies placidly between steep slopes, those of Carn Chois, 2571 ft., on the west being rocky. Beyond the lodge make for the main stream from Lochan Uaine and on the left bank an interrupted track will be found leading over and around the very well-preserved morains which fill the floor of the glen hereabouts. The way becomes wet as Lochan Uaine is approached at 1523 ft., and a route should then be made up the grassy hillside to the west. The slopes on this side are easy and lead without break to the flattish ground leading up to the summit ridge. As a variation on the descent, follow the fence southward to where it slopes off into Glen Lednock and then make a way over peat hags and thick heather to the headwaters of the Allt nan Columan. From here Carn Chois is an easy ascent, or a way can be made much lower down by contouring the slopes a little above Loch Turret and so back to the road south of the loch. The east slopes of Carn Chois, being rocky, should be traversed low down.

From the north and east, Ben Chonzie must be approached by Glen Almond. The road from Newton Bridge in the Sma' Glen follows the north bank of the Almond and is passable for cars for most of its length. The surface improves somewhat after the second gate is passed. A little beyond Auchnafree there is a bridge over the river, leading to Larichfraskhan. From here the best route to the summit is to follow the south

THE CRIANLARICH HILLS FROM BEINN ACHALADAIR.

R. N. Rutherford.

8

STRATHFILLAN, WINTER.

VIEW SOUTH FROM THE CRIANLARICH HILLS.

A. D. S. Macpherson.

bank of the Almond for a further 1¼ miles and mount the corrie between Ben Chonzie and Moine Bheag to the col. Steepish slopes on the right are climbed to the mountain's summit. By continuing along Glen Almond to Dalriech, where the road ends, open slopes lead to the top. This route gives pleasing and expanding views to the north-west. From Amulree (or Kenmore) a lovely route to the north side of Ben Chonzie is by Glen Quaich to Loch Freuchie, then south-west by the track leading up the north side of the wild little Glen Lochan, and over the small col to Glen Almond. This route leads directly to Auchnafree.

Beyond the road end at Dalriech, a track continues west up Glen Almond to Dunan, when it turns more north and leads over the col to Gleann a' Chilleine and Ardtalnaig on Loch Tay. The last part down the glen beyond Tullichglass affords fine views of Ben Lawers rising bluff above the waters of Loch Tay.

The ridge of hills to the north of Glen Almond is of little interest. It is cut into by several deep corries, but the tops above are ill-defined and flat. The highest point, **Creagan na Bheinn,** 2909 ft., lies at the westermost end and is most easily approached from Ardtalnaig by the Glen Almond path up Gleann a' Chilleine. From the top, the Ben Lawers group shows up very well, but Ben Chonzie to the south-east across the Almond appears as a flat-topped mass without character. At the other end of the ridge, and almost separated from the main group by Glen Shervie, **Meall nam Fuaran,** 2631 ft., rises steeply above Glen Lochan and shows fine rocky corries.

The smaller group of tops between Glens Lednock and Almond have more character : the highest summit, Creag Uigeach, 2840 ft. (Creag Uchdag on some maps), is itself a defined peak with rocky outcroppings on all sides, and is readily approached by the path between Ardeonaig and Comrie. This path leads high up on a spur of Creag Uigeach, above the deserted Bot na h-Acaire, and from the highest point the summit of the Creag is gained by a climb of a little over 1200 ft. up roughish slopes of heather and scree. The view back down the Lednock is very pleasing.

PATHS

Comrie and Ardeonaig by Glen Lednock and Fin Glen.—This right-of-way path has been described in the foregoing chapter. It is well worth while leaving the Glen Lednock road, and, by following the gorge path, walk by the Deil's Cauldron. A fine sight this when the Lednock is in flood. The upper part of the road is less interesting, apart from the rushing water-spout at Spout Rollo, and after leaving the ruins of Bot na h-Acaire the path climbs high up the hillside of Creag Uchdag and passes its highest elevation (1930 ft.) about ½ mile short of the watershed (*circa* 1700 ft.). It drops down into Fin Glen in a series of zigzags and commands a magnificent view over Loch Tay to the high peaks of the Lawers group. From Comrie, the distance to Ardeonaig is just over 12 miles.

Newton Bridge to Ardtalnaig by Glen Almond (Right-of-way Path).—From the Sma' Glen a road leads up the north side of the River Almond for nearly 8 miles to Dalriech when it continues as a path, at first well marked, then very faint, to the ruins of a cottage. Here a way is made more north and the course of the Allt a' Chilleine followed down the glen of that name. Beyond Leadour the path improves and leads to Ardtalnaig by the south bank of the stream.

Amulree to Glen Almond.—Follow the road west at the school just south of Amulree Hotel and branch left at the old church on the south side of Loch Freuchie. From here a rough track leads over by Glen Lochan to Auchnafree in Glen Almond. The gradients are easy and the track is a repaying one as it passes under the steep slopes of Meall nam Fuaran on the right and by the little lochans on the left.

Amulree to Kenmore.—From the hotel at Amulree is a choice of routes into Glen Quaich, by roads north and south of the Freuchie. That on the north side of the loch is the more picturesque and continues as a path above the north side of the River Quaich to Garrow. The road on the south side of the river joins it here and the track continues by gentle slopes over the elevated moors to the north-west. Soon after the highest point (*circa* 1650 ft.) a lochan reservoir is passed and the track descends to Kenmore. The last part through trees is charming.

CENTRES

Hotels are available at the following : Amulree, Ardeonaig, Comrie, Crieff and Kenmore.

Youth Hostels at Comrie and Kindrochit (Ardtalnaig).

BIBLIOGRAPHY

" Ben-y-Hone," Note by W. D., *S.M.C.J.*, Vol. 4, p. 179.

" Ben Chonzie," Guide Book Article, *S.M.C.J.*, Vol. 6, p. 244.

" Ben Chonzie on Ski," by J. H. Wigner, *S.M.C.J.*, Vol. 8, p. 133.

" Some Hill Roads in Scotland," by W. A. Smith, *S.M.C.J.*, Vol. 14, p. 95.

*" Some Glenalmond Climbs," by M. B. Nettleton, *S.M C.J.*, Vol. 23, p. 90.

" Easter on Ben Chonzie," by W. M. Deas, *C.C.J.*, Vol. 5, p. 216.

*Chiefly of rock-climbing interest.

XIII

THE DOCHART GROUP

Munro's Tables—Section 3.
Maps : O.S. One-inch Scale Popular Edition, Sheets 62
and 55. O.S. Half-inch Scale, Scotland, Sheet 22.
Bartholomew's Half-inch Scale Revised, Scotland,
Sheet 12. Bartholomew's Half-inch Scale, Great Britain,
Sheet 48.

(1) **Meall Glas,** 3139 ft. (The Grey Between Glens Dochart and
    Mound)   Lochay.

(2) Beinn Cheathaich, 3074 ft. (The $\frac{7}{8}$ mile E.N.E. of (1).
    Hill of Mists'

(3) **Sgiath Chuil,** 3050 ft. approx. $2\frac{1}{2}$ miles N.N.W. from Luib
    (The Back Wing)   Station.

(4) Meall a' Churain, 3007 ft. (The $\frac{1}{2}$ mile north of (3).
    Mound of the Stones)

THIS little frequented and, on the whole uninteresting, range
lies between the valleys of the Dochart and the Lochay. Its
peaks lack character, and are surrounded by so many finer
mountains that it is hardly surprising that the knolly summits
of the group are but little known. From Killin the range
stretches westwards for a distance of 10 miles, and reaches its
highest point in Meall Glas near the western end of Glen
Lochay. Beyond here the furthest headwaters of the River
Lochay, flowing from Loch Chailein, serve to divide the group
from Beinn Chaluim and the other peaks of Mamlorn Forest
to the west and north.

To the east, the final spurs of the range provide a fitting
background to the very lovely lower reaches of the bounding
valleys to north and south, while the most easterly top—
Sron a' Chlachain—broods over the Dochart Falls at the
entrance to Killin. The view to the west from here, beloved
by artists, although not embracing any of the Dochart peaks,
is framed satisfactorily by the slopes of Meall Clachach rising
above the valley.

The hills are typical sheep country with steep slopes of
bent and bracken on the Lochay side. With its knolls and
broken heathery moorland rising from the floor of the Dochart
valley, the group supports a wealth of bird life, and is not
devoid of botanical interest.

Meall Glas, 3139 ft., is locally called Meall Glas Mhòr.
The ascent of this peak is often combined with that of Sgiath
Chùil. If making for Meall Glas, the easiest approach is
from the Lochay side, it being possible to drive a short way
beyond Kenknock. From the road end, a rough track leads
on up the glen to Lubchurran, reached by a footbridge over
the river. The most pleasant approach is now to slant across
the hillside in a south-westerly direction and make for the
north-west ridge of Meall Glas, which is gained high up after
making height in Coire Cheathaich. The ridge is reached near
the 2500-ft. contour and thereafter leads by easy slopes to
the summit, where a good-sized cairn, on a rocky outcrop,
marks the highest point.

Meall Glas may be climbed from Tyndrum or Crianlarich
in conjunction with Beinn Chaluim. From the summit of the
latter peak the descent is made to the, as yet small, River
Lochay by way of the steep east ridge (Stob a' Bhiora). The
river crossed, a stiffish pull up the slopes of Meall Glas takes
one on to the mountain's north-west ridge and so to the
summit.

An easy walk of ¾ mile then takes one round the horseshoe ridge with its slight depressions to the north-east top,
Beinn Cheathaich, 3074 ft., and its small cairn.

From Auchessan in Glen Dochart, the mountain is
approached by the Allt Riobain. Follow the west bank of that
stream to the more level ground above some outcrops of rock,
then make a course north-west over the very hummocky moor.
Two miles of heavy going lead from the Allt Riobain to the
steeper slopes under the summit of Meall Glas.

Sgiath Chùil, 3050 ft.—The height is approximate and
not shown on the Ordnance Survey one-inch map. If coming
at the mountain from Meall Glas, there is a descent from
Beinn Cheathaich of nearly 1100 ft., first of all steep, then on

to peaty ground past a large cairn. From the col (*circa*
1980 ft.) a steep grind south-east, varied by some rocky outcrops, leads to the top of Sgiath Chùil, where there is a small
cairn.

If climbing the mountain by itself, it is most approachable
from the Glen Dochart side, by way of Innishewan Farm.
A footbridge near Luib Station leads over the river to the
farmhouse, from where an old zigzag road leads up through
woods to the open moor. There is then a short spell of heavy
going until the steeper slopes leading up to Sgiath Chùil are
reached. Due north from the summit a rocky ridge leads, in
½ mile of delightful going, to the handsome little peak of
Meall a' Churain, 3007 ft. It has two somewhat rocky and
rounded tops about 100 yards apart, the southern, and
higher, being graced by a small cairn 10 yards west of the
highest top. The other top also has a very small cairn.

The descent can be made with ease to the north, by the
broad ridge running down to the Lochay. The river is
crossed by the footbridge at Lubchurran.

It may be preferred to continue eastwards from Meall
a' Churain, along the ridge of peaks between Glen Dochart
and Glen Lochay, to Beinn Bhreac and Creag Mhòr. The
going is tedious, with many ups and downs. From Creag
Mhòr the best way off is north-east to Corrycharmaig and the
bridge over the Lochay to Duncroisk.

There is a surprising view in every direction from these
modest Dochart hills which just pass the 3000-ft. limit.
Near at hand, on the north, lies Glen Lochay, while to the
south and west lie Glen Dochart and Strath Fillan with their
cottages, river reaches and clumps of pines. Glen Dochart
is dominated by the long, unbroken slopes of Ben More across
the valley. In a sweep to the west are the familiar shapes
around Ben Lui, and, further off, the Cairngorm snows may
be visible.

Parts of the range are suitable for ski running. East of
Sgiath Chùil and Meall a' Churain lies the large Coire Lobhaidh
in which the best ski-ing is obtained. The slopes are comparatively free of stones, and are of the right steepness.

PATHS

There are none over the group. At the Killin end are a number of short tracks through the woods above the Lochay which give pleasant walks but lead nowhere in particular.

CENTRES

Hotels are found at Crianlarich, Killin, Luib and Tyndrum, of which Killin and Luib are the most convenient centres.

Youth Hostels at Crianlarich and Killin.

BIBLIOGRAPHY

" The Glen Dochart Hills," by J. G. Stott, *S.M.C.J.*, Vol. 2, p. 31.
" The Killin Hills," by H. B. Watt, *S.M.C.J.*, Vol. 2, p. 137.
" The Dochart Group," Guide Book Article, *S.M.C.J.*, Vol. 7, p. 28.
" The Highlands in June," by J. G. Stott, *S.M.C.J.*, Vol. 14, p. 259.

XIV

THE FOREST OF MAMLORN GROUP

Munro's Tables—Section 3.
Maps : O.S. One-inch Scale Popular Edition, Sheets 55
and 62. O.S. Half-inch Scale, Scotland, Sheet 22.
Bartholomew's Half-inch Scale Revised, Scotland,
Sheet 12. Bartholomew's Half-inch Scale, Great Britain,
Sheet 48.

(1) **Beinn Heasgarnich,** 3530 ft. 1¾ miles south-east from Loch
    (doubtful)   Lyon.

(2) Stob an Fhir-Bhogha, 3381 ft. ½ mile south from (1).
    (Spur of the Bow-man)

(3) **Creag Mhòr,** 3387 ft. (The Large 2¼ miles south-west from (1).
    Crag)

(4) Stob nan Clach, **3146** ft. (Spur of ⅝ mile south by west from (3).
    the Stones)

(5) **Beinn Chaluim** (N. top), 3354 3¾ miles east-north-east from
    ft. (Malcolm's Mountain)   Tyndrum.

(6) Beinn Chaluim (S. top), 3236 ½ mile south of (5).
    ft.

" MAIM LAERNE is the King's Forest—very riche in deer
lying upon Brae Urchay, Brae Lyon and Brae Lochay, 10 myl
of length." On modern maps " Mamlorn " is restricted to
Brae Lochay alone, and the hills of the group are massed
around the headwaters of the Lochay.

Despite their commanding position in the very heart of the
Southern Highlands these mountains lie in such a tangle of
headwaters that, from a distance, it is difficult to obtain an
adequate view of them. The rugged spurs of Creag Mhòr,
and the huge steep-sided pyramid of Beinn Chaluim stand
guard impressively at the head of upper Glen Lochay. From
this point, however, Beinn Heasgarnich shows no more than
its great uninteresting lower slopes. From the main bridge
over the River Lochay at Killin a good distant view of the

mountain is had, and from there the tremendous bulk becomes apparent. It is from the north that the mountain shows to best advantage, especially when seen from Beinn a' Chreachain north of Loch Lyon. From there the fine north-east corrie of Heasgarnich is visible, with its bold summit rising immediately behind.

Standing so far from the sea, the two larger hills of the group carry great quantities of snow, much of which remains well into the summer. If it were not so inaccessible, Heasgarnich would rival Ben Lawers in popular ski-ing favour. As it is, the mountain is too far from any road end to make it worth while carrying skis to the distant summit.

Also due to their comparative inaccessibility, and to the amount of snow lying upon them, the mountains are noted for the large number of white hares, ptarmigan and snow buntings which make their homes there. The hill fox is also common, though not so easily seen.

The nearest points of approach to the group are Killin, Tyndrum, Crianlarich and Upper Glen Lyon. From Killin it is possible to motor to a point a very little west of Kenknock in Glen Lochay : the road is very narrow, however, and there is a paucity of turning places. In the north, the Glen Lyon road is passable to Invermearan, from which point Beinn Heasgarnich is accessible. This starting point is distant from Creag Mhòr. Beinn Chaluim is more easily approached from the west, from Crianlarich or Tyndrum.

Beinn Heasgarnich, 3530 ft.—The backbone of the mountain consists of a long, and well-defined, rounded ridge, which rises up steeply in an easterly direction from the bealach separating it from Creag Mhòr (Bealach na Baintigh-earna, 2170 ft. approximately), and comes to a subsidiary top of Heasgarnich at 3381 ft. This top, Stob an Fhir-Bhogha, is not marked on the one-inch Ordnance Survey map but appears as the 3300-ft. contour. There is a small cairn. From here, the main ridge becomes confused and, after a very small drop, bends slowly to the north. A gradual rise in a distance of just over $\frac{3}{4}$ mile brings it to the main summit of Beinn Heasgarnich, where there is a 3-ft. cairn a few yards south of the highest point.

H

The main ridge then continues in a north by west direction to the shoulder called Stob Garbh Leachtir, overlooking Loch Lyon. From the main summit, too, a subsidiary ridge runs out in an east and north-easterly direction, and, with the main ridge to the west, encloses the fine northern Coire Heasgarnich.

The slopes are mostly grassy, but on the east side there are signs of glaciation. A number of lochans are found about the 3000-ft. level, of which the one to the south-east of the summit, placed at a height of 3288 ft., is one of the highest in Scotland. It measures about 225 ft. by 125 ft., and is the source of the Allt Tarsuinn, being itself fed by a great patch of snow which is usually so conspicuous in the view from Glen Lochay. The glacier on this side of Beinn Heasgarnich must have been one of the last in the country to disappear.

The easiest way of ascending the mountain is by Kenknock, 7 miles from Bridge of Lochay, by the road through the very lovely narrows of the lower part of the glen. Beyond Kenknock the road becomes very rough, and finally degenerates into a mere track fully 1 mile before reaching Badour. From Killin to this point is 10 miles. The track can be left a little way short of Badour and a way made towards the Allt Bad Odhar, the left bank of the stream being followed to near the 1250-ft. contour. Here, where a tributary from the north-west joins the main stream, is a footbridge which should be crossed. The tributary burn leads straight towards the main ridge of the mountain and easy slopes are climbed to gain the ridge about ¼ mile north of Stob an Fhir-Bhogha. From there to the main summit cairn it is pleasant going along the gently inclined ridge.

The way from Crianlarich is long and tedious, and should not be lightly undertaken, especially in the short days of winter. Cross the River Fillan at Inverhaggernie and go up the burn of that name by the path leading to the west of Lochan Dubh. Beyond this some difficult, heavy country has to be crossed below the slopes of Creag Loisgte, and a way made by the west side of Lochan Chailein. Contour the eastern slopes of Beinn Chaluim as far as the Allt Chaluim, crossing that stream about the 1300-ft. contour. Little is gained by descending towards upper Glen Lochay, rath~: than contouring the hillsides right around, as the way to the valley is wet and laborious. If the Allt Chaluim is crossed near its junction with the Allt Lairig Mhic Bhaidein, the lower slopes of Creag Mhòr are contoured and height is gained around the spur of Sròn nan Eun and so into the valley of the Allt Bad a' Mhaim. The latter stream is joined somewhere near the 1800-ft. contour, and is followed upwards for a little way, when it is crossed, and a direct line made for the summit of Stob an Fhir-Bhogha. From there to the main top of Heasgarnich is ¾ mile of easy ridge.

There are alternative routes from Tyndrum : both again involve considerable walking distances. The first route leaves the main road just to the north of the bridge spanning the River Fillan, 2 miles from Tyndrum. Follow the farm track to Auchtertyre, and, crossing the railway above, take to the left bank of the Allt Gleann a' Chalachain which is then followed nearly to its headwaters. A small tributary stream joins it from the east, the junction being almost 3 miles up the valley from Auchtertyre. The little tributary falls from the low and narrow bealach immediately to the north of Beinn Chaluim and gives a crossing at about 1870 ft. On the other side of the col is the start of the Allt Chaluim which then leads down to where the Crianlarich route, described above, is joined. To this point the route described is much more satisfactory than the Inverhaggernie way by Lochans Dubh and Chailein, and is, in fact, the quickest route from either Tyndrum or Crianlarich to both Creag Mhòr and Beinn Heasgarnich.

The other route from Tyndrum to Beinn Heasgarnich is of an entirely different type. The approach is from the north-west. First, take the main Glen Coe road north to Auch, then use the track up the east side of the Allt Chonoghlais, and over the low pass leading to Loch Lyon. Do not descend to the loch, however, but cross the Allt Tarabhan to Luban. The Abhuinn Ghlas is forded here and a long, rather trying, skirting movement made round the slopes of Meall Tionail and into the Coire Fionn a' Glinne. From here there is a steep grind up to the northern spur of Heasgarnich-Stob Garbh

Leachtir—followed by a pleasant, short, but well-defined ridge to the summit cairn. The walking distance from Auch is certainly not less than 8 miles.

To reach Beinn Heasgarnich from the road in Glen Lyon, it is well to remember the difficulty of crossing the rivers. In times of spate this obstacle may well prove insurmountable for there are no bridges west of Cashlie. At Lubreoch there is a ford of stepping stones which gives a dry crossing when the river is reasonably low. A boat may also be available. At the east end of Loch Lyon there is a ford between Invermearan and the now ruined cottage at Lubheasgarnich : when the river is at all full this ford is impracticable. The road itself is passable for cars to the farthest point, but is very narrow, and has many sharp bends and switchbacks. As the western end of the glen is approached, the surface becomes worse, and the whole way along from Bridge of Balgie it is none too good, although better than the upper parts of Glen Lochay.

If the river is fordable at Invermearan, as it should be after a reasonable spell of dry weather, Beinn Heasgarnich is very approachable from this direction. Follow the spur of Stob Garbh Leachtir which leads straight to the top of the mountain. A knolly part in the ridge is passed about the 2750-ft. contour, and the ridge gives fine views of the great corrie to the north of the mountain.

Alternatively, from the stepping stones at Lubreoch follow the faint track towards the Lairig nan Lunn, about halfway to the old sheep-fank. Break off west and obliquely contour the slopes of Meall a' Chall so as to reach the north-east spur of Heasgarnich. The spur leads by way of some small lochans to the summit.

From the summit of Beinn Heasgarnich the view, naturally, from the mountain's commanding position, is most extensive, sweeping over Atholl, Badenoch and Lochaber. To the south and west it is unique, giving the best point from which to gain an impression of the heights of Creag Mhòr and Beinn Chaluim. The two fine summits are backed by more distant ranges, Ben Lui, Ben More and Stobinian being prominent.

Creag Mhòr, 3387 ft., and Stob nan Clach, 3146 ft.—
Creag Mhòr is a finely shaped mountain which rises up very
steeply for over 1350 ft. from the bealach separating it from
Beinn Heasgarnich. This north-east face is rocky. To Glen
Lyon the mountain throws out a long shoulder culminating
in Meall Tionail (2937 ft.) above the west end of the loch,
while to the upper end of Glen Lochay it presents two very
well-defined ridges. These two ridges, Stob nan Clach and
Sròn nan Eun, form a horseshoe enclosing Coire-Cheathaich,
one of the features of this fine mountain

Like Beinn Heasgarnich, Creag Mhòr is best ascended
from Kenknock, from where, at the road end, a deteriorating
track leads west up the glen as far as Badvaim. From the
west bank of the Allt Bad a' Mhaim, the best route to the top
is by the ridge of Sròn nan Eun, rising straight ahead. A
steep pull of 1500 ft., avoiding a few rocky outcrops, brings
one to the ridge and the top of Sròn nan Eun (2747 ft.). There
is a slight drop before the ascent of Creag Mhòr is completed
by the ridge which bends around the head of Coire-
Cheathaich. A fair-sized cairn marks the top of the flattish,
stony summit, from whence there is a good view, although
this is hardly so fine as that from Beinn Heasgarnich. The
latter mountain turns an uninteresting side in the direction
of Creag Mhòr.

The descent can be varied by the other enclosing arm of
Coire-Cheathaich. Leave the summit in a westerly direction
and after a steepish descent for about 400 yards bear sharply
south to the col beneath Stob nan Clach. This point on the
ridge is not named on the one-inch Ordnance Survey map but
appears as the 3100-ft. contour. There is no cairn, but there
are three distinct tops, the north one being the highest. The
ridge to Glen Lochay is at first gradual over these tops, then
drops steeply for a short distance before fanning out in more
gentle slopes above the valley. It is best to cross the Allt
Cheathaich just below the 1500-ft. contour and traverse the
easy hillside to Badvaim.

The routes from Crianlarich by Inverhaggernie, and
from Tyndrum by Auchtertyre, have been described under
those to Beinn Heasgarnich, in each case to the 1300-ft. level

on the Allt Chaluim between Cam Chreag and Beinn Chaluim. The second route, that by Auchtertyre, is the better. From the Chaluim stream the ascent is usually completed by way of the Stob nan Clach ridge described above.

Creag Mhòr can also be climbed from Auch on the old Glen Coe road, first up Gleann Choillean (the north side of the stream should be taken) to the 1366-ft. watershed just east of Cam Chreag. Skirt the north slopes of that peak and work diagonally up to about the 1750-ft. contour when the Allt Mhic Bhaidein is crossed. Beyond here easy slopes are climbed to Stob nan Clach and the main ridge of Creag Mhòr followed to the summit cairn.

A slightly easier, though longer route from Auch is by Gleann Auch and the path to Glen Lyon (see also under routes to Beinn Heasgarnich). The bridge at Luban and Tomochoarn can be taken and the ascent made south-west by Meall Tionail, 2937 ft., to the summit of Creag Mhòr.

The ascent of Beinn Heasgarnich can be very conveniently combined with that of Creag Mhòr, and it is perhaps preferable, whether from Kenknock or Tyndrum, to take Creag Mhòr first. The steep descent north-east from Creag Mhòr to the bealach between there and Beinn Heasgarnich is unlikely to give trouble unless conditions are very icy. It is well to remember that steep pitches and rocky outcrops occur frequently on this side.

Beinn Chaluim, 3354 ft.—This double-topped peak, from whose springs rise the headwaters of the beautiful Lochay, shows such a modest front where it fans out gently to the much-frequented railways and road in Strath Fillan that, strangely, few realise the bold pyramid formed by its steep and rocky north and east flanks. It is sufficiently isolated also to have had this unique remark made of it : " Beinn Chaluim is a good hill for a rainy day ; standing as it does all by itself, one cannot be expected to tackle any second peak."

The best route to the summit is by Auchtertyre, up the Allt Gleann a' Chlachain to where a stream, descending from the south peak of Beinn Chaluim, enters from the east, about 1¾ miles above the railway. From there to the short western ridge of Chaluim's south top it is a pleasant slope of bent, with, in the winter and spring months, a magnificent view over Strath Fillan to the shining snows of the great Ben Lui corrie opposite. The south top has an unexpected cleft, or fault, whose western edge is a little rocky rampart. A very small cairn on a rock marks the top.

The ridge between the south and main top of Beinn Chaluim gives delightful going, rocky in parts, and is well defined. It stretches for ½ mile due north to the main summit where there is a moderate-sized cairn on the highest point. With such an inner circle of near neighbours as Ben More, Stobinian, Cruach Ardrain, Beinn Laoigh, Beinn Dorain, Creag Mhòr and Beinn Heasgarnich, the sweep of the view from Beinn Chaluim is altogether unexpected in its grandeur. It extends from Ben Nevis to the Lomonds, and from the twin tops of Ben Cruachan to the distant Cairngorms.

From Crianlarich it is really best to make use of the route described above by Auchtertyre, but it is also possible to ascend the peak by way of the path up the Inverhaggernie Burn. Before the Lochan Dubh is reached, bear north and make directly, by stony and rough country, for the south top. It is usual to ascend by one of the routes above described and to descend by the other. If it is desired to descend to Glen Lochay, a way should be made due east from the summit cairn, and the descent made by way of Stob a' Bhiora. The north face of the mountain above the Allt Chaluim is very steep, and rocky in parts, and is best avoided.

PATHS

There are no paths through these hills, although a number skirt the group. Passing reference has been made in the foregoing chapter to the track between Auch and Loch Lyon, as this can be used conveniently as an access route to the northern hills of the group : it is more fully described in the chapter on the Glen Orchy and Inishail hills.

The hill route by the Lairig nan Lunn, immediately to the east of the present area, and between Glens Lochay and Lyon, has already been described under the section on the Killin hills.

CENTRES

There is no near accommodation to the northern hills of the group : the most convenient centres and hotels are at Crianlarich, Killin and Tyndrum.

Youth Hostels at Crianlarich and Killin.

BIBLIOGRAPHY

" The Tyndrum Hills," by J. G. Stott, *S.M.C.J*., Vol. 1, p. 325.

" Beinn Heasgarnich," Guide Book Article, *S.M.C.J.*, Vol. 7, p. 28.

" B. Heasgarnich, Creag Mhòr and B. Chaluim," by F. S. Goggs, *S.M.C.J.*, Vol. 7, p. 366.

" Some Hill Walks from Tyndrum," by J. H. Bell, *S.M.C.J.*, Vol. 9 , p. 1.

" Beinn Heasgarnich and Others," by J. Ritchie, *C.C.J.*, Vol. 4., p. 200.

9

July, 1938.

BEINN DORAIN FROM ABOVE AUCH

E. C. Thomson.

May, 1947.

J. D. B. Wilson.

VIEW FROM THE SUMMIT OF LAWERS.

R. M. Adam

June, 1947.

I D B Wilson

XV

THE KILLIN HILLS

Munro's Tables—Section 3.
Maps : O.S. One-inch Scale Popular Edition, Sheet 55.
O.S. Half-inch Scale, Scotland, Sheet 22. Bartholomew's
Half-inch Scale Revised, Scotland, Sheet 12. Bartholo-
mew's Half-inch Scale, Great Britain, Sheet 48.

(1) **Meall nan Tarmachan,** 3421 ft.   4   miles N.E. of Killin.
     (The Round-topped Hill of
     the Ptarmigan)

(2) Meall Garbh, 3369 ft. (Round-   ½ mile S.W. of (1).
     topped Rough Hill)

(3) Beinn nan Eachan (West top),   1   mile W.S.W. of (1).
     3265 ft. (The Mountain of
     Little Horses)

(4) Beinn nan Eachan (East top),   ¼ mile E. of (3).
     3110 ft.

(5) Creag na Caillich, 2990 ft. (Crag   ¾ mile S.W. of (3).
     of the Old Woman)

(6) **Meall Ghaordie,** 3407 ft. (doubt-   5½ miles N.W. of Killin.
     ful)

(7) Beinn nan Oighreag, 2978 ft.   2   miles N.E. of (6).
     (The Mountain of Cloud-
     berries)

SEPARATED from the Lawers group by the pass of the Lochan
na Lairige, these hills form a fine group running west to the
valley of the Allt Lairig nan Lunn, which then serves to divide
them from the bulk of Beinn Heasgarnich still further to the
west. On the north the area is bounded by Glen Lyon, and
on the south by Loch Tay and Glen Lochay. Two main
masses make up the whole group—the Tarmachans to the
east, and Meall Ghaordie to the west. The deep depression of
the Lairig Breisleich lies between. The character of the
two sections is somewhat dissimilar, the eastern peaks being
by far the more rugged.

The Tarmachan range has long been a favourite amongst hill walkers, as it affords excellent views and some exceedingly pleasant ridge wandering. Furthermore, the hills show an imposing outline to Killin at their feet, and especially so to the traveller as he breasts Glen Ogle and descends on the north side. Meall Ghaordie, however, is not seen at all from Killin and in any case presents its more exciting side to Glen Lyon in the north.

Killin forms the usual centre, although Meall Ghaordie is readily accessible from the north, and the main roads leading over Glen Ogle from the south, and along Loch Tay from the east, give ready access. The road up Glen Lochay is passable for cars a little beyond Kenknock, although the surface is very bad and there is a paucity of turning places.

The Tarmachans, like the Lawers range, are a happy home for alpines and sub-alpines : a variety of saxifrages in particular make these hills of interest to the botanist. The Meall Ghaordie section, on the other hand, is comparatively barren.

Meall nan Tarmachan, 3421 ft., is often approached from the Lochan na Lairige, but is easily climbed direct from Killin by following the Aberfeldy road for fully 1 mile east of Bridge of Lochay and taking to the hillside on the left. A diagonal route is then made across the slopes above a sort of grassy dyke. The track shown on the map is now unobservable, being completely overgrown. When the more level ground is reached beyond the Allt Tir Artair, about the 1250-ft. contour, bear north and make a bee-line for the summit. A lower top, overlooking the small corrie high up on Tarmachan's eastern side, is passed on the way.

From the Lochan na Lairige the best way to the summit is to make height beside the stream descending south of the cliffs below the Lochan an Tairbh-uisge, and, after crossing the floor of the upper corrie, gain the summit from the north. The upper corrie generally holds good snow well into the spring and affords excellent, though short, ski-ing slopes.

From Glen Lyon the approach to the summit is less interesting and considerably longer. It is best accomplished by following the Lochan na Lairige road to a point ¾ mile

short of its highest point and making a way up the dull Coire
Riadhailt by the east bank of the Allt Bail' a' Mhuilinn. The
summit is gained from the north-west.

A good-sized cairn marks the highest point of the grassy
top, and there is a splendid view. Over the trench of the
Lochan na Lairige, the Lawers range stands up well, although
the eastern peaks are hidden, and in the opposite direction
one looks right up the length of Glen Lochy with the bulk
of Beinn Heasgarnich well in evidence. Ben More appears
directly over the shapely summit of Meall Garbh, which itself
is sufficiently lower than Meall nan Tarmachan to afford the
latter peak its true status as the major hill of the range.
Further off on the ridge, Beinn nan Eachan appears as a
rounded hump with the long ridge of Meall Tòn Eich stretching
northwards.

The main ridge leaves the summit of Meall nan Tarmachan
in a southerly direction as a broad, grassy slope. Soon,
however, as the col is approached, the ridge bends south-west
and narrows somewhat, but is still fairly broad. There are a
number of grassy knolls and secondary ridges, and three
small lochans are passed on the way between Tarmachan and
Meall Garbh.

Meall Garbh, 3369 ft.—If approaching from the direction of the col below Meall nan Tarmachan, the ridge to the
highest point of Meall Garbh is pleasantly steep but quite
easy. Just to the east of the summit, an attractive grassy
ridge, pointing directly to the west end of Loch Tay, gives
an excellent approach from Killin, and an easy route of
descent in bad weather provided the start is hit off correctly.
The start lies below the final conical peak of Meall Garbh and
not more than 50 yards from the highest point. From there
steer directly south and, once on the ridge, follow its crest
right down to the more level ground around the 2000-ft.
level, when a way is made south-west round the projecting
spur of Meall Liath.

The summit of Meall Garbh is the most attractive of the
range, being finely pointed and cut off on all sides except to
the west, in which direction a narrow ridge runs out for a
short distance beyond a miniature col. There is no cairn

on the top, but an oblong block of schist marks the highest point. On the north the slopes are at first almost precipitous for a short distance, then steep and very stony into Coire Riadhailt.

The main ridge continues west from Meall Garbh, airy and narrow for perhaps 50 yards, then, turning north-west, broadens and descends steeply to the col below Beinn nan Eachan. This col (Bealach Riadhailt, *circa* 2950 ft.) is a narrow defile between steep, flanking slopes.

Beinn nan Eachan, 3265 ft.—Beyond the Bealach Riadhailt the main ridge is broad, knolly, and a little complicated. The largest knoll forms Beinn nan Eachan's east top (3110 ft.), where there is a small pile of stones. On the west the drop is a good deal deeper than the contours of the Ordnance Survey map would seem to indicate : it is, in fact, nearly 100 ft. of steep descent to the col. If avoiding the east top, contour its slopes on the north-east, passing between smaller knolls, and gain the main ridge beyond, where it becomes more defined and bends to the south-west below the main summit. From here, 350 yards east of the top, a nearly level ridge stretches out northwards for 1 mile to Meall Tòn Eich (2821 ft.) before descending gently to the Lochan na Lairige road at the junction of the Allt Bail' a' Mhuilinn and the Breisleich Burn. This ridge is followed if ascending to Beinn nan Eachan from Glen Lyon, but the route has little interest.

The summit of the hill is grassy, and has a small cairn. Steep, broken cliffs guard the top on the south, while on the north, the hill drops evenly into Fionn Ghleann.

Beyond the cairn the grassy ridge descends gradually, then more steeply, a little north of west to where it bends sharply south-west and continues as a broad highway to the col beneath the last main hill of the range. The total drop from Beinn nan Eachan to the col is around 450 ft.

Creag na Caillich, 2990 ft.—From the col the ridge is again knolly, and ascends to the top in a southerly direction. There are a few stones on the grassy pyramid which forms the highest point of the Creag. From here the view back along the range is very pleasing, and all the tops are visible.

Meall nan Tarmachan appears between the two nearer summits of Meall Garbh and Beinn nan Eachan, while, to the west, the eye is drawn to the upper reaches of Glen Lochay.

There are three distinct little tops on the ridge running south, the summit of Creag na Caillich being the most northerly. The south top, overlooking Killin, has a small, flat pile of stones near the highest point. To the east this ridge is bounded by a series of broken precipices, increasing in height as the ridge runs southward, until, beneath the south top, they reach their maximum height and thereafter swing round the end of the ridge and lose themselves in grass and screes.

If descending from the summit, a steep section at the south end of the ridge is easily avoided by keeping a little to the west. Thereafter a wide shelf of bracken-and-heather-clad moorland is crossed to the steep slopes over Glen Lochay, reached most easily by descending close to the western edge of a small plantation and gaining the road about $\frac{1}{2}$ mile west of Bridge of Lochay. This also forms the best approach if climbing Creag na Caillich from Killin.

West of the Tarmachan range the Killin hills are cut into by the valley of the Allt Dhùin Croisg running up to the watershed at the Lairig Breisleich. The pass is seldom used as a route between Killin and Glen Lyon in spite of the fact that there is very little difference in height or distance between it and the Lochan na Lairige further east. The road in the latter pass, and its more impressive surroundings has made the Lochan na Lairige route the more widely known. The Lairig Breisleich in consequence of its infrequent use has remained practically trackless for most of its length. A faint path runs up the side of the Allt Dhùin Croisg but does not continue to, or over, the Lairig, which is very boggy.

Beinn nan Oighreag, 2978 ft., lies west of the Lairig Breisleich and about $3\frac{1}{2}$ miles north of Duncroisk in Glen Lochay. It is a rather uninteresting and featureless hill and seldom climbed, although the ascent is perfectly simple from either Duncroisk or from Glen Lyon. The latter is the shortest route. As the ascent is made from the Lochan na Lairige road, a good deal of height is gained before starting up the hillside at all. Leave the road near where the Allt

Breisleich joins the Allt Bail' a' Mhuilinn. After crossing the stream, mount the rather boggy stretch of grass and heather to the northerly ridge of the hill, which is then followed to the top by a succession of easy steps.

The summit of the hill is of a hummocky nature and has three distinct tops. On the middle one, which bears the hill's name on the Ordnance Survey map and is the true summit, there is a fairly large cairn. North from here the hill falls gradually to a peaty hollow and then rises slightly to the north top. This is a featureless mound, the highest point of which is about 25 ft. lower than the Ordnance Survey top and nearly 400 yards distant therefrom. There is a small, well-built cairn. South from the Ordnance Survey top, at a distance of about 250 yards, is the south top, which is a smooth knob of rock at practically the same elevation as the Ordnance Survey top. From here south, the hill drops rapidly for about 100 ft. and then runs out south as a broad and nearly level shoulder which can be followed without difficulty to the Allt Dhùin Croisg. The stream leads to Duncroisk in Glen Lochay.

Meall Ghaordie, 3407 ft.—From Glen Lyon the two northerly spurs of this mountain, Creag Laoghain and Creag an Tulabhain, look almost like separate peaks. They enclose Choire Laoghain and are craggy and steep on their north faces. From Stranuich, where the River Lyon can be crossed, the ascent of Meall Ghaordie is best accomplished by Creag Laoghain. A way through the broken rocks is not hard to find by keeping towards the west and, once on the high ground near the 2750-ft. contour, a broad and easy ridge leads southwards to the summit of Ghaordie. There is a smallish cairn on the top. The best feature of the view is the bulk of Beinn Heasgarnich to the west : for the rest, none of the surrounding hills show to any great advantage.

The southern slopes towards Duncroisk in Glen Lochay are boulder-strewn in their upper parts, but are extraordinarily even and regular below the 2500-ft. contour. A descent on this side can be made very quickly into Glen Lochay.

West of Meall Ghaordie lies a tangled mass of flat-topped peaks, extending as far as the Lairig nan Lunn. They are all

easily accessible from the south by open, grassy slopes and
afford fair views of the Dochart hills on the opposite side of
the Lochay, but their summits are ill-defined and give heavy
walking.

PATHS

Glen Lochay to Glen Lyon by the Lairig nan Lunn.—
The path starts ¼ mile north of Kenknock. To reach it,
strike the first burn to the west of the farm and follow it
north until it forks : the beginning of the track will be found
100 yards on, inside the fork.

The pass (1938 ft.) is crossed by its east side on the hillside
above the wet ground of the col. Little height is lost for a
short distance beyond the highest point and then a way is
made down grass slopes to the Allt Lairig nan Lunn which
is crossed. A little over 1 mile further on Lubreoch is reached,
and the River Lyon is forded to gain the valley road on the
north side. In times of spate, the stepping stones at the
ford are likely to be under water. Occasionally a boat is
available, but this cannot be relied upon.

Glen Lochay to Glen Lyon by the Lairig Breisleich.—
The way is trackless and boggy for most of its length. From
Duncroisk (2¾ miles from Bridge of Lochay) a track follows
the Allt Dhùin Croisg for a little way, but from there on the
going is heavy. The bealach itself is open, flat and very wet,
and lies at an altitude of approximately 1870 ft. Descent on
the north is drier and 1½ miles on the east bank of the Allt
Breisleich brings one to the footbridge over the Allt Bail' a'
Mhuilinn, and to the Lochan na Lairige road.

CENTRES

Without transport, Killin is the only convenient centre
having hotel accommodation. For those with some means of
conveyance, Fortingal (Hotel) is a useful base for the northern
approaches.

Youth Hostel at Killin.

BIBLIOGRAPHY

" The Killin Hills," by J. G. Stott, *S.M.C.J.*, Vol. 1, p. 270.

*" Two Climbs on the Tarmachans," by H. Raeburn, *S.M.C.J.*, Vol. 5, p. 70.

" Notes on the Tarmachan Range," by A. W. Russell, *S.M.C.J.*, Vol. 5, p. 88.

*" A Winter Climb on the Tarmachan Cliffs," by W. I. Clark, *S.M.C.J.*, Vol. 5, p. 242.

Guide Book Article, *S.M.C.J.*, Vol. 7, p. 25.

*" Tarmachan and the Creag na Caillich Gully," by A. M. Mackay, *S.M.C.J.*, Vol. 7, p. 61.

" The Heights of Tarmachan," by J. G. Inglis, *S.M.C.J.*, Vol. 7, p. 115.

*" A Climb on the Tarmachans," by J. Macmillan, *S.M.C.J.*, Vol. 7, p. 298.

*" A Winter Climb on Creag na Caillich," by H. Walker, *S.M.C.J.*, Vol. 7, p. 365.

" Beinn nan Oighreag," by J. A. Parker, *S.M.C.J.*, Vol. 19, p. 208.

" Beinn nan Oighreag," by J. G. Inglis, *S.M.C.J.*, Vol. 19, p. 361.

*Chiefly of rock-climbing interest.

XVI

THE LAWERS GROUP

Munro's Tables—Section 3.

Maps : O.S. One-inch Scale Popular Edition, Sheet 55.
O.S. Half-inch Scale, Scotland, Sheets 18, 19, 22 and 23.
The map sheets are ill-divided for this group.
Bartholomew's Half-inch Scale, Scotland, Revised.
Sheet 12. Bartholomew's Half-inch Scale, Great Britain,
Sheet 48.

(1) **Ben Lawers,** 3984 ft. (doubtful)   Loch Tay north side and 2¾
                                          miles N.W. of Lawers Inn.

(2) Creag an Fhithich, 3430 ft.   ½ mile N. of (1).
     (Raven's Crag)

(3) An Stuc, 3643 ft. (The Steep   1 mile N. by E. of (1).
     Rock)

(4) **Meall Garbh,** 3661 ft. (The   1½ miles N.N.E. of (1).
     Rough Hill)

(5) **Meall Greigh,** 3280 ft. (Meall   2¾ miles N.E. by E. of (1).
     Gruaidh—Hill of the Cheek,
     or, possibly, the Herd)

(6) **Beinn Ghlas,** 3657 ft. (The Grey   ⅞ mile S.W. of (1).
     Hill)

(7) **Meall Corranaich,** 3530 ft.   1¼ miles W. of (1).
     (Hill of the Corrie of the
     Brackens)

(8) **Meall a' Choire Leith,** 3033 ft.   2 miles N.W. of (1).
     (Hill of the Grey Corrie)

THIS group of massive, schistose summits lies in the triangle
formed by the River Lyon, Loch Tay, and the road that runs
from one to the other by the Lochan na Lairige. The tops are
somewhat retiring, and it is difficult, from the low ground
about the group, to obtain an adequate impression of the
height of the mountains. From a little way off, and especially
from the tops of the hills south of Loch Tay, the sweeping,
grassy slopes show to better advantage and Ben Lawers—
the monarch of Perthshire—then asserts its true majesty.

From the Ben Chonzie hills is this especially true, and, seen from that angle, the summits around Lawers, as well as exhibiting their whole height, show to shapely advantage.

The group lies close to the centre of Scotland, being nearly equidistant from John o' Groats and the Mull of Galloway, as well as from Mull and the North Sea. In view of their situation, it is not surprising that the hills carry snow well on into the spring and early summer of most years, and this, coupled with the ease of access, the height of the mountains and their open, grassy slopes, has made the area a skier's rendezvous. During spring week-ends there are probably more people in Coire Odhar than in any other corrie of a similar height in the Highlands. The road to the Lochan na Lairige is passable for cars at most times, and there is now an adequate parking place ½ mile short of the south end of the lochan below Sròn Dha Murchdi. From there it is an easy carry to the Scottish Ski Club hut in Coire Odhar, and to the good slopes beyond.

There is probably a good deal of limestone in Ben Lawers, and the mountain is celebrated for its wealth of alpine and sub-alpine plants. A number of rare species have been identified, and the whole range is very repaying to the botanist. A list of the more important species growing is to be found in the Journal of the Cairngorm Club, Vol. 2, p. 125.

The mountains of this group are most usually approached from the Loch Tay side, either from Killin or Lawers, but Fortingal in Glen Lyon is in many ways an excellent base. There are roads on the three sides of the triangular group, and although the one on the west—that by the Lochan na Lairige—is not recommended for large cars, it at least gives easy access into the heart of the hills.

Ben Lawers, 3984 ft., claims sovereignty over all the hills of Perthshire, and, in fact, is exceeded in height by only nine other mountains in the whole of Britain. For all that, it is truly a pedestrian peak for nowhere on it, excepting on a small section to the north-east of the summit, are there any considerable cliffs. Almost everywhere the slopes are open and easy, and for the most part are grass covered. The easiest route to the top is from Lawers, 8 miles from Killin, above the north side of Loch Tay. Leave the road just beyond the school and follow a path on the left bank of the stream. This line is maintained and a way made directly to the east ridge of the mountain. There is no difficulty, and the ridge (reached near the 3000-ft. contour) is then followed to the top. Alternatively, by following the direction of the Lawers Burn, on the left bank of which there is again a path for a little way, one eventually comes in sight of the fine Coire nan Cat. Before reaching the lochan, however, bear left and reach the east ridge of the mountain by climbing the steepish, grassy slopes facing north.

The cairn on the top is much reduced from its one-time magnificence, and is now considerably broken down. There is also a survey pedestal. Originally, the cairn was some 20 ft. high, and the large block of quartzite with which it was crowned was therefore set at an altitude of over 4000 ft. Little of this 1878 cairn remains to-day and a pile of stones some 7 ft. high marks the summit of the mountain.

The view is magnificent, extending from the Cairngorms to the Lothians, and from the Atlantic to the North Sea. Arran and the Paps of Jura appear in the south-west, while, away in the opposite direction, it is possible to discern the blue and distant shape of Ben Wyvis. Nearer at hand, the mountains of Perthshire stand around in splendid confusion, while, seemingly at one's feet, is the dark hollow to the north-east of the summit in which nestle the two small lochans of the Cat corrie.

From Glen Lyon the route to Lawers is longer and more laborious but, nevertheless, very repaying. Leave the road opposite the church 2 miles east of Innerwick and cross the Lyon by the bridge. There is a rough road on the other side which is followed east for a short distance until it crosses the Allt a' Chobhair. Follow the right bank of the stream under Creag Roro for a little over 1 mile, cross the stream issuing from Fin Glen, and ascend the pleasant ridge enclosing that glen on the west. This leads to steeper slopes high up, and the summit of An Stuc is then either crossed or contoured on its west side. The main ridge continues south over the small intervening height of Creag an Fhithich to the summit of Lawers.

From Killin the quickest way follows the Lochan na Lairige road past the Burn of Edramucky, when a disused and faint cart track leads up by the burn and into Coire Odhar. The track continues up the corrie, on the Beinn Ghlas side, and the latter mountain is climbed easily by its stony western slopes. From the summit it is necessary to descend about 400 ft. to the col and continue up the summit ridge of Lawers. Half-an-hour would be average time between the two tops. Below the ridge and near the source of the Allt an Tuim Bhric is an outcrop of rock known as Creag nan Gabhar, while further along the ridge, on the same side, but nearer Ben Lawers, is another small outcrop—Creag Loisgte.

The main ridge can be followed in either direction from the summit of Lawers, and it is very usual to include the highest point in a traverse of a part, or the whole, of the range. Having described the most usual routes to the summit of the parent mountain, it is now proposed to treat the other tops of the ridge as they would be met on a traverse from west to east. It is, of course, unnecessary to traverse the range in a single expedition, as there are easy routes to and from the ridge at many points. The easiest of these will be indicated.

To traverse the whole range involves the crossing of eight tops (six of which are " Munros "), or nine if the subsidiary ridge of Sron Dha Murchdi is included, the aggregate ascent along the ridge from Meall a' Choire Leith to Meall Greigh being nearly 4000 ft. If ascending from Killin, the climb to the first summit is 2600 ft. From Lawers Inn to Meall Greigh involves a climb of nearly the same height, whilst the distance between the end tops, by the ridge, is rather over 9 miles.

Meall a' Choire Leith, 3033 ft. To the north, this hill throws out a long spur to Sròn Eich which then drops steeply to Glen Lyon. On the east of the spur is the little rocky Coire Ban, and the north slopes of Sròn Eich are themselves broken by small outcrops. The hill is accessible from Glen Lyon by crossing the river by the bridge 2 miles east of Innerwick and making use of the rough track towards Gleann Da Eig. Before reaching the Allt Gleann Da Eig, however, bear left up steep slopes and gain the more level ridge of Sròn Eich. This

passes above Coire Ban and leads easily to the summit of
Meall a' Choire Leith. The top is flat, and has a very small
cairn towards the north-west side of the summit plateau.

If approaching from Killin, it is necessary to follow the
Lochan na Lairige road to its highest point, a little way beyond
the lochan, and then, bearing north-east, to cross a small
bealach and contour the head of Gleann Da Eig. The slopes
beyond Coire Gorm lead easily to the summit of the mountain.
This approach is dull, and it is more usual, when coming from
Killin, to gain the main ridge further south, usually by Sròn
Dha Murchdi and Meall Corranaich.

South of Meall a' Choire Leith the main ridge drops to the
col at 2550 ft., with the somewhat rocky Coire Liath on the
east and Coire Gorm on the west. Beyond the bealach the
ridge swings more directly southwards and mounts at first
quickly, then very gradually, to the next summit. **Meall
Corranaich, 3530 ft.**, has a small cairn. This, however, is not
at the highest point, the latter being some 80 yards to the
north-east on almost flat ground. The view into Coire Odhar
is rather attractive. The summit is usually reached direct
from the Lochan na Lairige road, either by Coire Odhar to the
bealach at its head, or over Sròn Dha Murchdi (3040 ft.) $\frac{1}{2}$
mile to the south-west of the main top. The east slopes of this
hill, facing Lochan na Lairige, sometimes give excellent though
comparatively difficult ski-ing. The better-known slopes
around Coire Odhar tend to distract attention from other
excellent ski-ing possibilities elsewhere in the range.

The south-east ridge of Meall Corranaich, leading to the
bealach (*circa* 3050 ft.) below Beinn Ghlas, is steep, and in
places broken, but nowhere difficult, and the line of the ridge
across the col leads quickly to the slopes of Beinn Ghlas on the
opposite side. North of the bealach steep but ski-able slopes
lead to the more level floor of Gleann a' Chobhair, while to the
south are the upper slopes of Coire Odhar. The Scottish Ski
Club hut is situated in the centre of this corrie, less than $\frac{1}{2}$
mile from the bealach.

Beinn Ghlas, *circa* 3740 ft. At this summit, where there
is a small cairn, the main ridge alters direction abruptly from
south-east to north-east before descending to the Ghlas-Lawers

bealach (*circa* 3300 ft.). The slopes of the mountain on the Meall Corranaich side are steepish, and near the top considerably broken by small outcrops of rock, but may be ascended without difficulty almost anywhere. A line of broken and low cliffs runs along under the north side of the ridge, while, in summer, the south-west side is scree-covered. If it is desired to make a descent from Beinn Ghlas, other than by Coire Odhar, there is a good ridge of short grass running south-east towards Loch Tay. This can be followed down quickly to near the 2000-ft. contour, when it is best to bear right and pick up a rough track beyond the stream issuing from Coire a' Chonnaidh, and so to the main road above the loch.

Beyond the summit of Beinn Ghlas, the main ridge continues as a fairly defined edge to the bealach, beyond which the open slopes of Ben Lawers are climbed to the highest summit of the group. Reference to this section has already been made in the normal routes to the summit of Lawers. The main ridge again alters direction at the highest point and as a wide rounded spur descends gradually in a northerly direction, here forming the upper boundary of the deep Coire nan Cat immediately to the east.

Creag an Fhithich, 3430 ft. The Raven's Crag is locally known as Spicean nan Each and rises on the main ridge ½ mile north of the summit of Ben Lawers. On the south side the rise from the col is only 130 ft., the Creag's summit being shown as a small 3400 ft. contour on the one-inch map, but is not named thereon. North of this top the ridge is again fairly gradual to the Bealach Dubh (3042 ft.) beneath An Stuc.

An Stuc, 3643 ft. Like the preceding top, An Stuc, is not named on the one-inch map, nor is its height given—only the 3600 ft. contour. It is without doubt the shapeliest top of the whole range and the only one showing a continuously bold front. Its south-westerly slopes drop precipitously to Lochan nan Cat in a series of broken cliffs and scree gullies, while on other sides the angle below the summit is everywhere steep although not rocky. From the Bealach Dubh a nicely defined ridge leads to the summit. If desired, there is an easy descent to Glen Lyon from this point, following the western retaining spur of Fin Glen. High up, the slopes are steep, and in winter the top of Fin Glen and upper slopes of An Stuc on this side carry a fine steep field of snow. The few outcrops of rock call for care if a glissade is contemplated.

The main ridge now bends to the north-east and descends steeply, by broken slopes, to the An Stuc-Meall Garbh bealach at 3253 ft.

Meall Garbh, 3661 ft. Meall Garbh stands $\frac{5}{8}$ of a mile north-east of An Stuc and is reached from the col between the two mountains by a short and easy climb, the first part by small broken rocks. The summit is well defined and has a small cairn. To the north of the mountain is a corrie, unnamed on the one-inch map. This is Choire Roic, and the bounding ridge to its west gives a very pleasant high level walk to the summit of Meall Garbh from Glen Lyon, starting from Roromore. A way is made up the ridge between Creag Roro and the corrie (Coire Mhaidhein) to the knolly upper portion. A small summit is crossed at 2866 ft. and the gradually rising ridge then leads pleasantly to the summit of Meall Garbh.

If climbing the hill from Coire nan Cat, mount by the steepish spur which ends above the more easterly lochan of the corrie. This is Lochan Uan—an off-shoot of Lochan nan Cat, to which it is joined. A few hundred feet above it on the spur is a fine slabby piece of rock known as Creag a' Bhuic.

Proceeding east from Meall Garbh, the ridge is broad and easy down to the Lairig Innein, 2802 ft. beneath the last peak of the range.

Meall Greigh, 3280 ft. This top is $1\frac{7}{8}$ miles almost due east of Meall Garbh, and from the Lairig Innein it is no more than an easy walk by the broad and rather knolly ridge to the summit. There is a moderate sized cairn at the highest point. Descent is easiest by the south ridge and Lawers Burn. On the way, and above where the ridge eases off into the more level ground above the burn, two outcrops of rock are passed. The more northerly is Sron Mhor.

From the summit it is also possible to descend to Chesthill in Glen Lyon by following the broad north-east spur of the mountain down into Gleann Dà-Ghob.

Paths

There are few in the area. The Lochan na Lairige road from Loch Tay to Glen Lyon is the main walkers' route to the north. An alternative route of descent on the north is to leave the road just short of its highest point and cross the low col into Gleann Da-Eig. The going in places is a little rough, but by following the right-hand bank of the stream a rough track is picked up lower down. This improves as it descends and leads eventually to a bridge over the River Lyon some 2 miles east of Innerwick.

Centres

There are hotels at the following :—Fortingal, Killin and Lawers.

Youth Hostel at Killin.

Bibliography

" Ben Ghlas and Ben Lawers," by J. M. Macharg, *S.M.C.J.*, Vol. 1, p. 158.

" Note on Ben Lawers," by W. Brown, *S.M.C.J.*, Vol. 2, p. 276.

" Ben Lawers," Guide Book Article, *S.M.C.J.*, Vol. 7, p. 23.

" A Tale of Two Days' Tramp," by F. S. Goggs, *S.M.C.J.*, Vol. 9, p. 229.

" The Highlands in June, by J. G. Stott, *S.M.C.J.*, Vol. 14, p. 259.

" Cairn on Ben Lawers," by H. MacRobert, *S.M.C.J.*, Vol. 23, p. 94.

" Note on the Cairn on Ben Lawers," by H. R. J. Conacher, *S.M.C.J.*, Vol. 23, p. 191

" Ben Lawers," W. E. C. Dickson, *C.C.J.*, Vol. 2, p. 192.

*" Snow Climbs in Perthshire," by W. Barclay and E. R. Beard, *C.C.J.*, Vol. 4, p. 177.

*" Ben Lawers," by James McCoss, *C.C.J.*, Vol. 12, p. 264.

*Chiefly of rock-climbing interest.

XVII

GLEN ORCHY AND INISHAIL GROUP

Munro's Tables—Section 3.
Maps : O.S. One-inch Scale Popular Edition, Sheet 55.
O.S. Half-inch Scale, Sheet 22. Bartholomew's Half-
inch Scale, Scotland, Revised, Sheet 11. Bartholomew's
Half-inch Scale, Great Britain, Sheet 48.

(1) **Beinn Dòrain, 3524 ft.** (Peak   2 miles S.E. by E. from Bridge
   of the Otter)   of Orchy.
(2) **Beinn an Dòthaidh, 3283 ft.**   2¼ miles E.N.E. of Bridge of
   (The Mountain of Scorching)   Orchy.
(3) **Beinn   Achaladair,   North**   1¾ miles N.N.E. of (2).
   Top, 3404 ft. (The Mower)
(4) Beinn Achaladair, South Top,   ¾ mile S.S.W. from North Top.
   3288 ft.
(5) **Beinn a' Chreachain, 3540 ft.**   2½ miles N.W. from Inver-
   (Krechan—a drinking shell)   mearan :   head   of   Glen
                                         Lyon.
(6) Meall Buidhe, 3193 ft. (The   1 mile W.S.W. from (5).
   Rounded, Yellow Hill)
(7) Point 3145 ft. -   -   -   -   ½ mile N.N.E. from (5).
(8) Beinn Odhar, 2948 ft. (The   2 miles N. from Tyndrum,
   Dun-coloured Mountain)   L.N.E.R. Station.
(9) Beinn a' Chaisteil, 2897 ft. (The   1½ miles E.N.E. of Auch.
   Peak of the Castle)
(10) Beinn Bhreac-liath, 2633 ft.   1½ miles W.S.W. of Auch.
   (The Grey Speckled Moun-
   tain)
(11) Beinn Udlaidh, 2759 ft. (The   3 miles W.S.W. of Auch.
   Dark or Gloomy Mountain)

THE main tops and finest mountains of this group lie to the
east and north-east of Bridge of Orchy. Here is found a high
range of peaks overlooking Rannoch Muir : a long serpentine
ridge, a lofty bastion, and a fitting western wall to the mountains of Breadalbane in the east. In addition to this fine

range—usually known as the Bridge of Orchy group—are a number of lower summits grouped east and west of the Glencoe road, between Tyndrum and the Orchy

Between Beinn Dòrain and Beinn a' Chreachain the main ridge of summits bends in a general direction from south to east, although in detail the ridge is very much more complicated than would appear with a casual glance at the map. The distance in a direct line between the two end summits is a little over 4¾ miles : to follow the ridge in its entirety, however, involves a walk of over 7 miles between the two highest tops, and an aggregate ascent from the summit of Dorain to the summit of Chreachain of 3000 ft. To this falls to be added the ascent to the first summit, which cannot be less than a further 3000 ft. from whichever point the ascent is made.

The mountains fall steeply towards the west and north, and it is from these angles that the size of the range is most easily appreciated. The views of Achaladair and Dòthaidh from the Glencoe road as it crosses the Black Mount are particularly fine, whilst, viewed from the south, the huge symmetrical cone of Beinn Dòrain is a familiar sight to travellers on the West Highland railway, or to motorists as they cross from Perthshire into Argyll by the new Glencoe road. The great cone reveals its true height as do few of our Scottish mountains. The scar of the railway round its flanks, and the dwarfed viaduct at Auch, serve as a rule by which we can better appreciate the tremendous sweep of grass and scree rising ever more steeply to the craggy summit far above. The highest top of all, Beinn a' Chreachain, is retiring and not seen to advantage from any point accessible to the tourist : to the climber, however, approaching along the main ridge, the mountain gradually reveals its true character, and the view from its summit is the finest of the whole chain.

Available approaches to the main ridge are from the four points of the compass : from the south by Tyndrum and Gleann Auch, from the west by Bridge of Orchy, from the north by Achallader Farm or Crannach, and from the east from the head of Glen Lyon. Of these approaches, that by Glen Lyon is in many ways the most beautiful, but is undoubtedly the least convenient.

Beinn Dòrain (or Doireann ; pronounced Doran), **3524 ft.**
Though not the highest nor the finest mountain in the group,
Beinn Dorain, with its shapely cone and commanding position
apparently athwart the Road to the Isles, is far famed and has
always appealed to the Gaelic imagination.

The simplest approach to the summit is from Bridge of
Orchy, and by the mountain's north ridge. After crossing the
railway, follow the south bank of the Allt Coire an Dothaidh
to where the ground steepens near the 1500-ft. contour, then
bear right up steep slopes well to the south of the precipitous
corrie between Beinn Dòrain and Dòthaidh. The summit
ridge is reached at a height of little less than 3000 ft., and is
followed to the top, where there is a small cairn. A rather
larger cairn is passed on the ridge. This marks the almost
imperceptible north top of Dòrain.

The view is not so fine as that from the other hills of the
group, but includes a pleasing vista over Loch Tulla. Parts of
Loch Awe and Loch Lomond are also visible.

For the descent, a pleasant variation is to follow the north
ridge right down to the col beneath Beinn an Dòthaidh. It is
necessary to bear north-east where the ridge steepens, as the
col is not in direct line. If using this route in mist it is well to
remember the considerable cliffs at the north end of the ridge,
and to make due allowance east in order to strike the col
correctly. From the bealach (2454 ft.) the descent into Coire
an Dothaidh is steep but not difficult : several small cliffs are
encountered lower down, but are easily avoidable. The floor
of the corrie is more level and has a large boulder near its
western edge before the slopes leading to Bridge of Orchy are
reached.

The ascent from Auch is tedious but direct. It gives a fast
route of descent. The belt of rock outcrops met a short
distance below the summit offers no difficulty, and below them
the steep grassy slopes are open and regular right down the
valley. To the south-west some long and surprisingly straight
stream courses give, when packed with snow, very fine
glissading.

Beinn an Dòthaidh (pronounced Doe), **3283 ft.** The
ascent of this mountain is often combined with that of Beinn

Dòrain, as the easiest approach is by the Dòrain-Dòthaidh bealach. This point is reached from Bridge of Orchy by Coire an Dòthaidh, as described above, when it is necessary to turn north up steepish slopes of grass and rocky outcrops. The ground soon becomes more level as the large summit plateau of Dòthaidh is reached. In mist it is often difficult to locate the small summit cairn which lies near the edge of the northern cliffs and is built on a large outcrop of rock. A smaller cairn lies on slightly lower ground to the north-west.

A more repaying route to the summit is by way of Achallader Farm and the left bank of the Allt Coire Achaladair. The railway is crossed by a bridge above the farm and for a short distance beyond a track is followed. The northern corrie of Dòthaidh grows in impressiveness as it is approached. Do not enter the corrie, however, but at a height of about 1500 ft. leave the stream and make for the spur of the mountain enclosing the corrie on the west. This leads up heathery slopes to the higher parts of the mountain when one turns left to the summit. Some fine rock scenery is passed on this route. A descent may be made from the top by going east over a second top and then bearing south-east to the Dòthaidh-Achaladair col (*circa* 2480 ft.). Approaching the col, the route may be confusing as there are three knolls to be crossed with a curious twist in the ridge, south then northeast. The upper part of Coire Achaladair is often wet.

From Beinn Dòthaidh the view is substantially the same as that from Beinn Dòrain except that the prospect to the south is obscured by the bulk of the latter mountain. Stob Ghabhar stands up proudly beyond the wooded shores of Loch Tulla, while an uninterrupted view is obtainable down the length of Glen Orchy.

Beinn Achaladair, 3404 ft., shows a large shield-like front to Rannoch Muir. From Crannach Wood, however, it appears to better advantage, and from that point stands up as a true and shapely peak above the remnants of the ancient Caledonian Forest.

There are two distinct tops, almost 1 mile apart, and joined by a gently curving ridge which is nowhere steep. Along the west slopes below the south top are small rock escarpments and broken ground, while beneath the main summit and facing north-west is a range of broken precipices about 400 ft. high. The corrie to the north-east of the summit is also steep and rocky, being separated from the north-west face of the mountain by a steep rib descending directly below the summit, towards Crannach. On the south-east the mountain is joined to Beinn a' Chùirn and Beinn Mhanach by gentle slopes leading down to the bealach at about 2050 ft. These two hills are easily climbed from this direction and are often taken in conjunction with Achaladair.

From the north, the quickest route to the top is from Achallader Farm at its foot, by the Allt Coire Achaladair and the easy, though steep, western slopes of the mountain to the dip between the north and south tops. Cross the stream a little above the railway and mount the slopes above in a direct line, keeping to the south of the rocky escarpments on the north-west face of the mountain. The sudden view as one breasts the summit ridge is very pleasing, and from the col it is an easy walk to either top. The south top (3288 ft.) is rather featureless, and has a very small cairn. From there to the Achaladair-Dòthaidh col the way is easy by a gently sloping ridge and a steeper descent south-west at its end immediately above the bealach.

As one approaches the main summit from the col between there and the south top, the ridge narrows and drops away very steeply to the north-west. Two small cairns are passed on the gently rising ridge, and the summit is reached at the easterly end. It is marked by a good-sized cairn on the edge of the northerly cliff.

From the top, a good descent is by the steep rib dividing the north and east faces of the mountain. It starts immediately below the cairn and faces north-east, but may be difficult to locate in mist. (Looking down from the top, there are small cliffs to the right and the top of a shallow, slanting gully directly below the summit.) The rib is rocky in the upper part, but as it descends towards Crannach it broadens and becomes less steep.

The descent east from the top is also steep to the Achaladair-Meall Buidhe col (*circa* 2700 ft.), and is enlivened by rock outcrops. In snow conditions it is well to keep a little south of the edge as the top of the corrie—like the summit ridge of the mountain—is often corniced. North from the col a scree-and-grass gully runs down to the Allt na Crannaich, and the valley can be reached easily by this route. Gradual slopes of rough grass lead south from the bealach, and into Gleann Cailliche. This is the best way of reaching Invermearan from Achaladair.

From the col, too, a steep rise of 400 ft. leads to the nearly level ridge of **Meall Buidhe** (3193 ft.). There are considerable cliffs to the north. Once the level part of the ridge is gained, the going is delightful over springy turf by a number of almost imperceptible tops. There are three very small cairns on the ridge before the slight dip under Beinn a' Chreachain's stony flank is reached. From this point an easy scree gully leads down to the beautiful Lochan a' Chreachain, lying beneath the cliffs at a height of 2285 ft.

Beinn a' Chreachain, 3540 ft., is not only the highest, but is also the shapeliest mountain of the group. Rising steeply on all sides except where it is linked towards the south-west with the main ridge, its position jutting out northwards into the Moor of Rannoch makes it one of the finest viewpoints in Scotland.

The structure of the peak is more complicated than appears at first glance. To begin with, the summit lies some 300 yards to the south-east of the main ridge, which at that point forms the top of the cliffs above Coire an Lochain (in the depth of which lies Lochan a' Chreachain). The narrow and graceful ridge to the north, after a slight dip, rises to the 3145 ft. top of Coire Dubh, and then fans out gradually into the moor. It can be very confusing in mist.

Coming by it from Gortan, which lies at a height of nearly 1100 ft., there is a stretch of the Moor, then the gentle slope through the scattered birches of the Bad na Gualainn, until the ridge narrows. At first it runs south-west to the point marked 2914 ft., then swings south after a very small dip. In a short distance it bends further east and rises more steeply to the top of Coire Dubh (3145 ft.). There is a small cairn at this point. From there the ridge runs straight and narrow for

½ a mile beyond the slight dip, when, after a sharp turn to the
south, it merges into the summit mass of Beinn a' Chreachain.
There is a large well-built cairn on the top. In snow conditions
this route is repaying for a descent, particularly the section
from the summit of Chreachain to the 3145-ft. top. The ridge
here is often a narrow edge of snow for quite a distance and
offers delightful walking with the steep drop to Coire an
Lochan on one side, and the little eastern corrie of Beinn a'
Chreachain on the other. This latter (Coire Dubh) has a tiny
lochan at a height of nearly 3000 ft., and in winter its waters
are seldom visible beneath the mantle of snow. From the col
near the 3145-ft. top a good glissade can be had to the slopes
above Lochan a' Chreachain, and from there the descent to
Crannach is easy.

If coming from the opposite direction, along the main
ridge from Meall Buidhe, the slopes of Chreachain are climbed
on stony ground without difficulty to the top. The broad
gully running down from the dip between Meall Buidhe and
Beinn a' Chreachain into Coire an Lochain, is not difficult,
and gives a good glissade in snow conditions.

The view is the finest in the range and embraces a magnificent panorama over Rannoch Muir to the Lochaber peaks
to the north and north-west. The Cairngorms are visible to
the north-east, while to the south the ranges of Breadalbane
are grouped in splendid array. Beinn Heasgarnich in particular shows to advantage.

Beinn Odhar, 2948 ft., and **Beinn a' Chaisteil,** 2897 ft.
These two hills rise to the south of Gleann Auch and are well
seen from the new Glencoe road as it sweeps northwards on
the hillside above Auch. Beinn a' Chaisteil in particular is
imposing from this side, being steep-walled and rocky. The
West Highland railway passes close on the flanks of both
hills, before contouring the slopes of Beinn Dòrain, low down.

Beinn Odhar is most readily accessible from the highest
point on the road and railway between Tyndrum and Auch.
(The railway notice on the summit of the pass gives this
height as 1024.75 ft.!) From there steep slopes of roughish
grass lead to the highest point. A more interesting though
slightly longer ascent is to leave the old road just after where

it bridges the railway south of the watershed, and follow the Crom Allt into Coire Thòin. The ridge bounding the east of this leads by easy slopes to the summit. Lower down the ridge, and in the corrie, it is often possible to get good ski-ing. North of the summit, a fairly wide band of broken rock stretches across the face, and below are steep grassy slopes to Auch.

Beinn a' Chaisteil presents its defences to the front and it is best, unless a deliberate rock-scrambling route is required, to walk up Gleann Auch, by the path on the south bank of the Allt Chonoghlais, until it is possible to strike up the hillside to the south, through rock outcrops. A wide, open ridge then leads to the small cairn at the 2897-ft. point. The true summit is cairnless, and lies 100 yards to the south-east. The view has little to commend it apart from the long sweep of Beinn Dòrain, which certainly is revealed in all its height.

Beinn Bhreac-liath, 2633 ft., and **Beinn Udlaidh,** 2759 ft., are the highest points in the small group of hills lying in the triangle between Glen Orchy, Glen Lochy and the Glencoe road between Tyndrum and Bridge of Orchy.

The ascent of Beinn Bhreac-liath has little of interest apart from the rather fine water-eroded grass ridges in Coire Chailein above the Glencoe road, from where the hill is most easily climbed. On the west, the hill is connected to Beinn Udlaidh by a col at a little over 1900 ft., from which point the latter hill rises in rough grass and rock outcrops to its main top near the east end of a broad summit ridge running a little south of west. The broad ridge running north from the top, and into Glen Orchy, offers an easy route of descent.

PATHS

Auch to Invermearan (Glen Lyon head). A right-of-way path runs up the south bank of the Allt Chonoghlais, passing the site of Auch Chapel and burial ground, after crossing the stream to its north bank. Beyond the ruin of Ais an t-Sithein the track is faint but follows the course of the Allt a' Chuirn to the low bealach beyond (*circa* 1200 ft.). Crossing this it descends low down on the side of Beinn Mhanach to the west end of Loch Lyon. The north shore of Loch Lyon is then followed to Invermearan and the Glen Lyon road.

Bridge of Orchy to Bridge of Gaur (Loch Rannoch). This is part of the very old drove road between Loch Rannoch and Dalmally. From the Glencoe road at the east end of Loch Tulla, a farm track (passable for cars) leads to Achallader farm, beyond which the way continues as a progressively less defined path. At Barravurich, Tulla Water is crossed by a bridge and the path follows the north bank of the river past Crannach Wood. Beyond the lonely cottage at Gortan, the way is rough and heavy, and in wet weather, especially, it may be preferable to follow the railway after crossing the stream. A little way beyond Madagan Moineach, a route is found by boggy and rough ground to the Duibhe Bheag stream where it bends sharply to the north-east. Contour the slopes of Meall Leachdann nan Each and drop into Gleann Chomraidh. A good track is found at Grunnd nan Darachan which then leads to the main road and Bridge of Gaur. The distance from Achallader farm to Bridge of Gaur is more than 16 miles, of which fully a third is virtually trackless and gives very heavy walking.

CENTRES

There are hotels at the following :—Bridge of Orchy, Inveroran and Tyndrum.

The train can sometimes be stopped at Gortan Siding.

Nearest Youth Hostels are at Crianlarich and Dalmally.

BIBLIOGRAPHY

*" Beinn an Dothaidh and Beinn Doireann," by Gilbert Thomson, *S.M.C.J.*, Vol. 3, p. 76.

" A Long Day in the Hills in March," *S.M.C.J.*, Vol. 3, p. 127.

" The Corries around Achalladair," by H. C. Boyd, *S.M.C.J.*, Vol. 4, p. 92.

*" Notes on Beinn a' Chaisteil," by E. M. Corner, *S.M.C.J.*, Vol. 5, p. 315.

Guide Book Article, *S.M.C.J.*, Vol. 7, p. 29.

" Some Hill Walks from Tyndrum," by J. H. Bell, *S.M.C.J.*, Vol. 9, p. 91.

" The Achallader Accident," by George Sang, *S.M.C.J.*, Vol. 17, p. 179.

*Chiefly of rock-climbing interest.

K

XVIII

THE LOCH LYON HILLS

Munro's Tables—Section 3.
Maps : O.S. One-inch Scale Popular Edition, Sheet 55.
O.S. Half-inch Scale, Scotland, Sheet 22. Bartholomew's
Half-inch Scale Revised, Scotland, Sheet 11. Bartholo-
mew's Half-inch Scale, Great Britain, Sheet 48.

(1) **Beinn Mhanach,** 3125 ft. (The   Head of Glen Lyon.
Monk's Hill)

(2) Beinn a' Chùirn, 3020 ft. (The   ¾ mile west by south from (1).
Hill of the Rocky Heap)

AFTER stretching west for over 25 miles from Fortingal, the
Glen Lyon road comes to its furthermost point at Invermearan,
close to the eastern end of the Loch from which the Lyon
issues. It is a lonely spot, for the last miles of the road are
very bad and hardly encourage the motorist. Besides, there
is no through road, and anyone wishing to proceed west must
perforce use their legs. Beyond the road end at Invermearan
a good track continues by the north shore of Loch Lyon, and
leads, by way of the bealach south of Beinn a' Chùirn, and the
Allt Chonoghlais, to Auch. As one looks up Auch Gleann
from the new Glencoe road one sees two rounded grassy
summits right at the head of the glen, and framed between the
steep slopes of Beinn Dòrain on one side and Beinn a'
Chaisteil on the other. The left-hand summit is Beinn a'
Chùirn, and the right-hand one the higher Beinn Mhanach.
The latter hill rises directly from the north shore of Loch
Lyon and the Allt Tarabhan in long grass slopes and is well
seen, blocking the head of Glen Lyon, when one is approaching
Invermearan from the east.

The two hills form an inner-guard to the high range of
mountains stretching in a great semi-circle from Beinn
Dòrain to Beinn a' Chreachain, and are connected to the
centre of this semi-circle by a pass along which runs the county

134

march between Perthshire and Argyll. Beinn Mhanach lies wholly in Perthshire ; the county march crosses the summit of Beinn a' Chuirn and continues a short distance east to the col below Beinn Mhanach before descending to the low bealach between Loch Lyon and Auch Gleann.

The two hills are most frequently climbed in connection with one or two others of the greater Bridge of Orchy mountains, but they may be approached easily from either Auch to the south-west, or from Invermearan in the east.

Beinn a' Chùirn, 3020 ft., is not now classed as a separate summit in the Munro list. It is most readily reached from Auch by the path by the Allt Chonoghlais. Leave the path where it bends eastwards by the Allt a' Chùirn, and mount the easy grass-and-scree slopes of the south-west side of Beinn a' Chùirn. Less than 1 hour after leaving the path, the mountain's flat top should be to hand. There is no cairn, only a few stones at the highest point. From here easy open slopes lead down, a little north of east, to the col separating Beinn a' Chùirn from its higher neighbour.

Beinn Mhanach, 3125 ft. A rounded ridge runs up to the summit of this hill from the col, and the cairn should be reached easily within 20 minutes of leaving Beinn a' Chuirn. The small cairn is quartz-topped.

Descent can be made either to the west end of Loch Lyon and by the rough track along its northern shore, or directly east down the knolly ridge, to Invermearan. There is a small footbridge over the Allt Meran.

If descending from Beinn Mhanach, and returning to Auch, it is best to return a little way towards Beinn a' Chùirn and descend grassy slopes to the headwaters of the Allt a' Chùirn where the track will be regained.

From the summits there is a most comprehensive and charming view of Loch Lyon and the smooth-contoured upper reaches of the glen, with, across the loch, the great bulk of Beinn Heasgarnich rearing upwards. To the south-west, where the Allt a' Chuirn, flowing from the low 1200-ft. watershed, joins the Allt Chonoghlais, Gleann Auch is hemmed in by the steep slopes of Beinn Dòrain on the north-west, and those of Beinn nam Fuaran and Beinn a' Chaisteil on the south-east.   The contrast between this, and the view down Glen Lyon is very pleasing.

PATHS

The only one is that from Auch to Invermearan, Glen Lyon.   This has been described under the Glen Orchy and Inishail Group. (q.v.).

CENTRES

Hotels are somewhat distant, the nearest being at Bridge of Orchy.   Other centres with hotels near enough for those with transport are Crianlarich, Inveroran and Tyndrum.

Youth Hostel at Crianlarich.

BIBLIOGRAPHY

Guide Book Article, *S.M.C.J.*, Vol. 7, p. 32.

XIX

THE UPPER GLEN LYON AND WEST RANNOCH GROUP

Munro's Tables—Section **3**

Maps : O.S. One-inch Scale Popular Edition, Sheet 55. O.S. Half-inch Scale, Scotland, Sheets 22 and 18. Bartholomew's Half-inch Scale Revised, Scotland, Sheet **12**. Bartholomew's Half-inch Scale, Great Britain, Sheet 48.

(1) **Stuchd an Lochain, 3144** ft. (The Peak of the Little Loch) Between Glen Lyon and Loch Giorra.

(2) Sron Chona Choirein, **3031** ft. (doubtful) ¾ mile E. by S. of (1).

(3) **Meall Buidhe** (Garbh Mheall), 3054 ft. (Yellow Rounded Hill) Between Lochs Rannoch and Giorra.

(4) Meall Buidhe, S.E. top, 3004 ft. ¾ mile S. by E. of (3).

THERE are no more lonely or secluded hills in Perthshire than those forming the lofty plateaux to north and south of Lochs Daimh and Giorra. Here, if anywhere, Stevenson's

" Essential silence
Cheers and blesses, and forever in the hill recesses
Her more lovely music broods and dies."

So quiet and retiring are they, that, when first the Guide Book was issued through the S.M.C. Journal, they escaped being recorded at all. The two plateaux, and the associated high ground to the west, form the catchment area feeding Lochs Daimh and Giorra, which in turn drain into the Allt Conait flowing to join the River Lyon some miles west of Bridge of Balgie. The magnificent beech and lime avenues alongside Meggernie Castle, near where the Conait joins the Lyon, form a fitting and glorious approach to the higher reaches of the glen.

Stuchd an Lochain, 3144 ft., forms the ridge between
Glen Lyon and Gleann Daimh. The main backbone of the
mountain runs roughly east and west, but throws off spurs to
north and south. The two overlooking Cashlie in Glen Lyon
drop steeply to the valley and enclose between them the little
corrie down which falls the Allt Cashlie. On the opposite side
of the hill, facing Glen Daimh, the north ridge of the hill,
and an eastern spur, Creag an Fheadain, hem in the steep-
sided Coire nan Cat with its lochan at over 2300 ft.

Around Cashlie are the now faint remains of the ancient
" Forts " of Glen Lyon: massive towers probably built by
the early Celtic Feinne tribe to protect themselves and their
cattle in troubled times. The theory that the Forts were
originally built as watchtowers seems hardly tenable as the
positions are unfavourable. All that remains today is, here
and there up the glen, rough circles of overgrown stones, a
poor reminder of the magnificence of the original Forts,
which, from the size of the remains, must have had walls not
less than 7½ ft. thick.

Many centuries after the building of the Forts (around
1590 in fact) Mad Colin Campbell of Glen Lyon—he who
built Meggernie—made the ascent of Stuchd an Lochain with
his man, for his own dark purposes. " On the brow of the hill,
Stuic-an-Lochain—a huge rock beetling over a deep circular
mountain tarn—they encountered a flock of goats." It is one
of the earliest records of an ascent of a Scottish mountain, and
an accurate description of the north-eastern face of the hill
with its steep, broken rock terraces plunging down some 800 ft.
around the dark Lochan nan Cat.

The ascent may be made equally easily from Lochs Farm
on the north, or from Cashlie on the south. Lochs Farm is
about 1350 ft. up, and Cashlie about 1000 ft. The motorist
can take his choice. Coming up Glen Lyon, the road for Lochs
breaks off to the right, a little over 1 mile west of Meggernie
Castle, and leads up the lovely little glen of the Allt Conait.
The surface is very bad, and the road narrow, but it is not
much worse in this respect than the main Glen Lyon road.
There is a footbridge across the Allt Conait, about ½ mile
below Loch Giorra, which takes one on to the Coire Ban ridge,

if it is not intended to go right to Lochs and make the ascent from there. Above Lochs there is a bridge across the Daimh water, which leads on to the Creag an Fheadain ridge. On the top of the Creag (2909 ft.) is a small cairn from which one looks right over Lochan nan Cat to the main summit, nearly 1 mile away. A broken-down fence can now be followed along the ridge. First a march cairn is passed, and after bending more to the west the ridge is followed to the summit of Sron Chona Choirein (3031 ft.). This top is unnamed on the O.S. one-inch map, appearing thereon as a fairly large 3000-ft. contour. The ridge from here is almost due west, and leads, after a very small descent, to the next top at 3005 ft. The latter is shown as Point 2971 ft. on Bartholomews' half-inch map. Thereafter the ridge again descends almost imperceptibly, and bends to the north-west before ascending steeply to the main summit of Stuchd an Lochain. A small, roughly-built cairn marks the highest point.

From Cashlie in Glen Lyon, the ascent is easy past the bold peak of An Grianan. A path from the sheep fank above the lodge leads up the east side of the Allt Cashlie for about 1000 ft. into the corrie, and from its end a north-north-west course is taken over simple ground to the foot of the main top, up which it is a very easy scramble.

If one has come over the Lairig nan Lunn from Kenknock in Glen Lochay, and crossed the River Lyon at Lubreoch by boat, an easy route lies up the Allt Camaslaidh. If the weather has been wet, the Meall nan Odhar ridge to the north gives easier going than the corrie. From the top of Meall nan Odhar (2668 ft.) a ¾-mile walk along the broad ridge leads to the summit of Stuchd an Lochain.

There is a very striking view from the summit. Glen Lyon shows its depth and narrowness between Ben Lawers and Carn Mairg, away towards Chesthill. An unusual view is also obtained of the bold eastern flank of the great Bridge of Orchy range.

Meall Buidhe (Garbh Mheall), 3054 ft. The local name for the main top is Garbh Mheall, but on the O.S. one-inch map this name is applied to the northern summit of the mountain. Bartholomew's half-inch map gives the local nomenclature to the highest top, and the name Meall Bhuidhe does not appear.   The mountain stands 4½ miles south of Bridge of Gaur at the west end of Loch Rannoch, and is conspicuous from that point.   Seen from the north, the name Garbh Mheall (rough hill) is certainly appropriate, but to the south the mountain merges into the pastoral type.   Its summit ridge consists of a wide backbone of hill from Garbh Mheall, 2991 ft., to the main top, ½ mile south by west. From there the almost level turf of the high ridge stretches in crescent form to the south-east peak, 3004 ft., which appears as a small 3000-ft. contour on the O.S. map and is unnamed. After a slight drop the ridge continues almost due east to Meall a' Phuill, 2882 ft., the last of the tops on the 1½-mile-long horseshoe.

A number of excellent paths lead up the valleys from Bridge of Gaur and Camghouran on Loch Rannoch's south side.   These very greatly facilitate the ascent of the Meall Buidhe range from this direction.   Probably the easiest approach of all is from Bridge of Gaur by a path which starts at a height of under 700 ft. and leads by the little Allt an Fheadain, and its longer tributary the Allt a' Mheanbh-chruidh, to the slopes of Meall Caol, near the headwaters of the tributary stream.   A short distance along the hillside, above the low watershed, brings the path to the left bank of the Allt Sloc na Creadha and a bothy by a footbridge over the stream.   From this point one can either attack Garbh Mheall direct to the stony top, or continue up the path to its conclusion, cross the burn, and descend straight to the main Meall Buidhe summit, where there is a large cairn.   Beyond the main summit the scimitar ridge gives easy and nearly level going to the south-east top at 3004 ft.   A small cairn is passed on the way.

The descent to Lochs Farm is best accomplished from this point, by the broad and easy shoulder descending straight to the west end of Loch Giorra ;   the same route gives a useful way of ascent if coming at the mountain from Glen Lyon direction.   Alternatively, if descending from Meall Buidhe to Glen Lyon, it is possible to continue east along the main ridge, and over Meall a' Phuill, when a gradual descent round

April, 1924　　SCHICHALLION AND LOCH RANNOCH.　　*Hugh Gardner.*

10

June, 1925.

C. E. Andreae.

SPEARHEAD ARÊTE, NARNAIN.

Angus Smith.

BEN IME FROM BEN NARNAIN.

W. Holmes.

THE BRACK, NORTH FACE.

the outjutting shoulder of Creagan nan Gobhar leads to the road a little over 2 miles west of Bridge of Balgie.

If an alternative descent to the north is required, there is a path by the Allt Easan Stalcair in the valley, just to the east of Garbh Mheall. The slopes of the hill on this side are fairly steep, and small outcrops of rock occur towards the north end. The path in the valley joins with the well-marked path by the Luban Feith a' Mhadaidh, and leads to Camghouran.

One further route to the summit of Meall Buidhe remains to be mentioned. It is from Gortan siding on the West Highland railway, and is long and rough. Cross the footbridge over the Allt Learg Mheuran and make due east for the northern slopes of Creag Riabhach and Meall Cruinn, gaining height round the latter and crossing Coire Dubh at its upper limit. The little col beyond is crossed and Coire Gorm entered on the other side. Meall Buidhe is ahead, and easily climbed by its south-west shoulder. The distance from Gortan siding is nearly 8 miles, and it seems more, for much of the way is rough and heavy.

To the west of Loch Daimh is a group of hills rising nowhere to the 3000-ft. level. The highest, Meall Buidhe, 2976 ft., is unnamed on the half-inch map, this name being given thereon to the 2813-ft. peak ½ mile to the east. West of here is the long, steep-sided ridge of Meall Daill, 2858 ft., at the extreme end of Glen Lyon and bounded on its west side by Gleann Meran. These hills are best ascended from the upper reaches of Glen Lyon by the Eas Eoghannan, or from Gortan siding to the north-west of the group.

Paths

Glen Lyon to Loch Rannoch, by the Lairig Meachdainn. Follow the road to Lochs Farm from Glen Lyon for about 1 mile from the branch in the valley and take to the trackless hillside on the north. A stream can be followed almost due north to the bealach (*circa* 2320 ft.) east of Meall a' Phuill—the Lairig Meachdainn. After crossing the open col it is necessary to steer north-west, and, obliquely descending the shoulder of Meall a' Phuill known as Carn nam Fiadh, to drop into the valley of the Allt Easan Stalcair. A path is found close to the stream and on its right bank, and this leads to the Luban Feith a' Mhadaidh where there is a choice of routes. The way to the right leads to Camghouran and the road on the south side of Loch Rannoch : that to the left leads to Bridge of Gaur. Distance from Bridge of Balgie in Glen Lyon to Bridge of Gaur is 12 miles, of which over 3 miles are trackless over the highest part of the route.

The fine shooting paths leading into the hills from Bridge of Gaur and Camghouran are dead-ends, but may be linked up to give splendid walks amongst the lower hills south of Loch Rannoch.

CENTRES

Hotel accommodation is far distant from the area. Fortingal and Kinloch Rannoch have the nearest hotels and transport is necessary to reach the group from either place. It is sometimes possible to get a bed at Bridge of Gaur.

BIBLIOGRAPHY

" Stuchd an Lochain and the Upper Part of Glen Lyon," by F. S. Goggs, *S.M.C.J.*, Vol. 8, p. 235.

" Mheall Garbh, Glen Lyon," by E. M. Corner, *S.M.C.J.*, Vol. 11, p. 120.

XX

THE CARN MAIRG RANGE

Munro's Tables—Section 3.
Maps : O.S. One-inch Scale Popular Edition, Sheet 55.
O.S. Half-inch Scale, Scotland, Sheets 18 and 19.
Bartholomew's Half-inch Scale Revised, Scotland,
Sheet 12. Bartholomew's Half-inch Scale, Great Britain,
Sheet 48.

(1) **Càrn Mairg,** 3419 ft. (meirg— rusty ; The Rust-coloured Cairn) — 4 miles north-west by west from Fortingall.

(2) Meall Liath, 3261 ft. (The Grey Lump) — ½ mile east by south from (1).

(3) Meall a' Bharr, 3315 ft. approx. (doubtful) — ¾ mile west-north-west from (1).

(4) **Creag Mhòr,** 3200 ft. approx. (Large Crag) — 3¼ miles west-north-west from Fortingal.

(5) **Meall Garbh,** 3200 ft. approx. (The Rough Hump) — 2¼ miles west from (1).

(6) Meall Luaidhe, 3035 ft. approx. (The Round Hill of Lead) — ¾ mile south-east by east from (5).

(7) An Sgòr, 3002 ft. (The Rocky Peak) — ⅝ mile south-west from (5).

(8) **Càrn Gorm,** 3370 ft. (The Blue Heap) — 4½ miles north-west by west from Invervar, Glen Lyon,

NEAR its foot, Glen Lyon is enclosed by two great ranges, the peaks of the Lawers group to the south, and the mass of Càrn Mairg and its satellites to the north. The slopes of both ranges descending into Glen Lyon are steep, and in places thrust their grassy buttresses right to the river's banks. The narrowest section of the glen is, however, not really between the two mountain groups, but a little to the east of them, right at the mouth of the glen. The formation is most attractive, and at the pass of Lyon the river is hemmed in between rocky walls, the rushing waters, overhung by ancient and noble trees, making a picture of great beauty.

As one approaches Glen Lyon along the road from Fortingal, it seems hardly possible that the crooked narrow entrance,
between high hills, could be the mouth of Scotland's longest
glen. Beyond the narrows, the glen opens out, however, and
assumes a more normal character, with a nearly flat bed
along which the river pursues its more leisured course.

Càrn Mairg, then, encloses the mouth of the glen to the
north, the most easterly spurs of the group reaching out
above the narrows and fanning out in easy slopes north of
Fortingal. Westwards, the range extends to the Lairig
Chalbhath, a pass of 1600 ft., through which runs the " Kirk
road " from Innerwick, in Glen Lyon, to Dall on Loch Rannochside. To the north, Càrn Mairg is separated from
Schichallion by the wastes of Gleann Mòr and the headwaters
of the Allt Mòr.

Approach to the range is from Glen Lyon, reached from
Loch Tay by Fearnan, or from the east by way of Fortingal.
The latter village, a model of its kind, is without doubt the
most convenient base from which to explore the group.

The range occupies a large area over 2500 ft. and the
flattish summits are in some ways reminiscent of the Cairngorms : Càrn Mairg, however, has none of the magnificent
mural cliffs so common in the great granite mountains of the
east. Due to the unimposing shape of the summits, the group
is infrequently visited, although the traverse of the whole
range gives a hill-walking expedition of considerable interest
and length. Parts of the range are ideal for ski-ing.

In the following description of the mountains of the range,
it is proposed to treat the group as though it were being
traversed. Access to the hills is most easy from the two ends
of the range, which lies in the form of a great crescent. To
reach the summits in the centre of the chain, separately from
the others, involves tedious and long walks up the southern
corries. The east end of the range is the preferable start.

Creag Mhòr, 3200 ft., approx. The one-inch O.S. map
applies the name to a smaller rocky summit to the east of the
main top, and on the ridge descending to Beinn Dearg, north
of Fortingal. The name, however, refers equally to the higher
mountain rising directly above Chesthill in Glen Lyon. It is

possible to climb directly from Woodend, or Chesthill, to the summit by way of a curving ridge above the steep slopes of Creag Dhearg. The going is laborious for nearly 2000 ft. above the glen, and the more simple, though longer, approach is by making use of the excellent path leading across the hillside from Balintyre. This path rounds the western shoulder of Creag Mhòr, and enters Coir' Chearcaill. It leads to a bothy in that corrie, at a little over 1750 ft. From Invervar Lodge another zigzag path mounts the hillside to join the one from Balintyre, at the 1250-ft. contour. Another convenient approach is from below the ruins of Carn Ban castle by the right bank of the stream descending past a round clump of trees some little way up the hillside. Whichever way the path is gained, follow it just into Coir' Chearcaill and take to the west ridge of Creag Mhòr. This broad ridge curves gradually to the south-east and leads without intervening tops to the west summit of Creag Mhòr where there is a flattish cairn. The O.S. one-inch map shows the top of the mountain as a large 3100-ft. contour. In actual fact there are two summits, separated about ⅓ of a mile. Both are over 3200 ft. and the dip between is certainly over 50 ft. A near approximation of the heights of the two tops is—east top, 3240 ft.; west top 3230 ft. A gradual descent from the west top to the flattish col, and a subsequent rise, takes one to the higher top which is rocky and has a cairn on its highest point.

From here, to continue the traverse of the range towards Càrn Mairg, it is necessary to return most of the way towards the east top when the spur leading due north is followed to the col. The going is gradual and easy, almost to the col which is very wet and peat-haggy at the bealach. There is a stone-man immediately to the north of the col. The ridge beyond leads up by easy slopes, and quartzite boulders, to the ridge connecting Càrn Mairg with its easterly outlier, Meall Liath, the junction being close to the latter hill.

Meall Liath, 3261 ft., is an uninteresting rounded summit, from which one has a fine outlook over Gleann Mòr to the south side of Schichallion. There is a fair-sized cairn on the flattish, stony top. **Càrn Mairg,** 3419 ft., lies due west of Meall Liath, and is connected by a broad ridge and a col at *circa* 3100 ft. Following this ridge from Meall Liath, and on the Càrn Mairg side of the col, one picks up a very faint track which leads up beside screes and through a broken wall. The ridge near the top is covered with quartzite boulders, and leads directly to the large summit cairn. South of here the slopes drop steeply into Coir' Chearcaill and are precipitous in places near the top.

From the highest summit of the range, a short descent on large scree, in a north-westerly direction, leads to an attractive, nearly level ridge running out to the most easterly and highest top of **Meall a' Bhàrr, 3315** ft. approx. A broken-down deer fence runs along the crest nearly to the end, which is rocky and has a small inconspicuous cairn just to the north of the highest point. The ridge is almost level and the top is hardly distinguishable when approaching from Càrn Mairg.

From the end of the rocky part, a course is taken due west, and a slight descent made beside the deer fence to a col. This is not so deep as the O.S. map would indicate.

The ridge of Meall a' Bhàrr (O.S. map shows the name ½ mile to the south of the ridge) is a gently undulating hog's-back stretching west and north west from its highest point. Towards its western end, the ridge curves gradually more and more to the north, until just before it descends to the next col it is facing only a few degrees west of north. The deer fence runs the length of the ridge over a number of tops barely distinguishable from the cols. On a high point at the west end of the ridge, there is a small cairn and a little wooden hut a short way down the slopes to the south. There is also a well-built, 3-ft. cairn on the east side of the col immediately below this point. If it is not desired to continue on to the next summit of the range, an easy descent from the hog's-back ridge of Meall a' Bhàrr may be made into Coir' Chearcaill. Make for the path in the corrie—the bothy cannot be seen from the ridge above.

The main ridge now bends west again and descends to the col below Meall Garbh. There is a 4-ft. cairn at the corner of the deer fence, where it bends sharply west to the descent, and a further square cairn about 100 ft. lower down. The descent is easy to the broad and bouldery col (*circa* 2880 ft.). From this point Glen Sassunn shows its great expanse of heathery wastes to monotonous effect : a descent, and even more, an ascent, on this side of the range is to be avoided.

Meall Garbh, 3200 ft. approx. The main ridge bends gradually to the south-west, and, from the col, Meall Garbh is reached by the broad shoulder, liberally sprinkled with quartzite boulders. The deer fence, followed from Meall a' Bhàrr, continues over the summit now being approached. A considerable area on Meall Garbh is enclosed by the 3000-ft. contour and there are four distinct tops. The highest (the first one reached when approaching from the east) has a moderate-sized, well built, cairn about 70 yards south of the deer fence. On the ridge, beside the fence, is another flat and stony top, almost equal in height to the highest point. There is no cairn on this second top.

South from the main summits a broad and dirty ridge leads out to a further top some 30 ft. lower in altitude than the main top. There are two small cairns on the ridge. Beyond the higher of these cairns, the ridge continues in a southerly direction by a gradual and boggy downward slope to a wide col below **Meall Luaidhe,** 3035 ft. approx. This top is unnamed on the O.S. map and is indicated as a shoulder by the projecting 3000-ft. contour south-east of Meall Garbh. Bartholomew's half-inch map names the peak and gives its altitude as 3035 ft., although the probability is that the true height is slightly in excess of this figure. It is boggy on the col between Meall Garbh and Meall Luaidhe, and the ascent to the latter summit is very slight, probably just over 50 ft. There is a small cairn on the summit.

By contouring south-east from here, a way can be made directly into the Invervar corrie but the way is heathery, high up, and gives pretty heavy going. An ascent by this route is not recommended.

If it is intended to continue along the main ridge, it is now necessary to retrace one's steps to the summit of Meall Garbh and to follow the deer fence once more as it descends the hill in a westerly direction. 200 ft. down the fence turns sharply to the north-west. One leaves it at that point and continues down the grassy hillside for a short way further, before bearing south to the col below the next little peak of the ridge. A 5-ft. stone-man is encountered near the col on the north side ; the col itself is narrow and wet.

An Sgòr, 3002 ft., is unnamed on the O.S. one-inch map and indicated by a very small 3000-ft. contour. Bartholomew gives the name and height. The little summit is the most shapely of the range, and rises steeply on all sides. A sharp pull of 250 ft. on grass leads from the col to the rounded top. There is a small flat pile of stones on the highest point with steep slopes a few yards to the east. Descent to the next col is again just over 250 ft. and the depression is reached by steepish slopes, at first due west, then south-west to the bealach.

Càrn Gorm, 3370 ft. This is the last summit of the main ridge. It is reached without difficulty from the col below the Sgòr by the north ridge, well defined in its lower reaches, but broadening out higher up. There is a large cairn on the summit, from which point all the tops on the main ridge are visible.

To the west-north-west of the cairn is a long, flat ridge with a shoulder of just over 3000 ft. It is hardly a top as the rise from the muddy col connecting it with Càrn Gorm is not quite 50 ft.

The easiest descent from Càrn Gorm is by the spur, south-east of the summit. Steepish slopes are descended from the cairn for nearly 700 ft., when a peaty section is encountered. The headwaters of two small streams almost unite here and the descent can be continued by either of the burns. The easier way is by the ridge enclosing the east-flowing stream. This route takes one to Invervar and to the starting point of the traverse of the range. The other descent, by the south-. flowing burn, is by steepish grassy slopes and brings one to the road in Glen Lyon, just west of Slatich farm.

To traverse the whole of the Càrn Mairg range, making deviations where necessary to include those tops not on the main ridge, involves a walking distance of over 14 miles and an aggregate ascent of fully 5250 ft. For those with a car the expedition can be made most conveniently by starting the climb from Invervar and finishing at the same point. The views from the ridge are somewhat marred by the dreary wastes immediately to the north. Schichallion, however, is well seen from tops east of Meall Garbh, while the Lawers group across Glen Lyon provides a fine and ever-changing picture in the south.

PATHS

Innerwick to Dall by the Lairig Chalbhath. This is a right-of-way, and locally known as the Kirk Road. On the opposite side of the road from the little chapel at Innerwick, about 1 mile east of Bridge of Balgie, a path runs north, up the valley of the Allt a' Mhuic. Beyond the trees it zigzags and climbs diagonally above the Allt Chalbhath right up to the pass (*circa* 1600 ft.).

Easy slopes, and a good track, now lead down on the north for 2 miles, when the way forks. The left fork makes through scattered trees to Dall and Loch Rannochside in a further 1¾ miles : the right fork goes to Carie by way of the Allt na Bogair. If making for Kinloch Rannoch, this latter is the preferable route. Much of the Black Wood of Rannoch has been cut. From Glen Lyon to Dall by the right-of-way, is just less than 7 miles.

CENTRES

The most convenient is Fortingal, where there is an hotel. Other hotels at places not too distant for those with transport are found at Aberfeldy, Coshieville (1½ miles east of Fortingal at junction of main road), Fearnan (Loch Tayside), Kenmore and Kinloch Rannoch.

BIBLIOGRAPHY

" The Glen Lyon Hills," by J. G. Stott, *S.M.C.J.*, Vol. 1, p. 131.

" Deep Glen Lyon," by J. G. Stott, *S.M.C.J.*, Vol. 2, p. 113.

" Càrn Mairg," Guide Book Article, *S.M.C.J.*, Vol. 6, p. 247.

" A Tale of Two Days' Tramp," by F. S. Goggs, *S.M.C.J.*, Vol. 9, p. 229.

" The Carn Mairg Range," by J. Gall Inglis, *S.M.C.J.*, Vol. 16, p. 161.

XXI

SCHICHALLION

Munro's Tables—Section 3.
Maps : O.S. One-inch Scale Popular Edition, Sheets 55 and 56. O.S. Half-inch Scale, Scotland, Sheet 22. Bartholomew's Half-inch Scale Revised, Scotland, Sheet 12. Bartholomew's Half-inch Scale, Great Britain, Sheet 48.

Schichallion, 3547 ft. (or Schie-   4 miles south-east by east of
hallion)   Kinloch Rannoch.

SITUATED almost centrally in the country, and isolated on all sides by deep valleys, the graceful cone of this mountain is one of Scotland's most familiar hill-shapes. It appears in the distant view from many mountains, and is easily recognisable from most directions. Seen from Rannoch Muir, or the mountains of Glencoe, the peak is not so regular in outline as from other quarters, and from there its upper slopes lie back on one side, near the top, giving the mountain an unusual truncated appearance. From Loch Tummelside, too, some of the symmetry of shape is lost : the perfect cone is revealed when one looks south-east from Loch Rannoch. This viewpoint is one of the most favourable for a number of reasons, and the silver birches by the road on the north side serve as a perfect foil for the waters of the loch and the towering cone of the mountain behind.

The evenly weathered quartzite of which Schichallion is composed has given rise to the mountain's regularity of contour : a regularity which encouraged Maskeleyne, then Astronomer-Royal, to carry out his pendulum experiment in the determination of the earth's mass. Bare quartzite crops out along the summit ridge, and the upper slopes of the mountain are strewn with screes from this rock, which, in certain lights, give the peak a beautiful rosy tint.

Access is easy from north or east. The road from Aberfeldy cuts north through the hills by Strath Appin, reaching the River Tummel some 3 miles west of the Loch. The road thereafter continues to Kinloch Rannoch. From near the highest point on the road from Strath Appin to Tummel a secondary road branches to the west, and, crossing the lower slopes of Schichallion, approaches Kinloch Rannoch from the south side of the Tummel.

This secondary road gives the quickest route to the summit for those with a car. Leave the road near where it crosses the Allt Strath Fionan, and mount the slopes above by the line of a remarkably straight wall descending the hillside. The ascent is easy all the way to the ridge which is struck about ½ mile east of the summit. The ridge is a little tiresome in places, on account of large boulders, but it is nowhere difficult, and leads direct to the small summit cairn.

This route, although the quickest, is certainly not the best for getting maximum enjoyment from the mountain. Probably the most repaying approach is by the east ridge from the Aberfeldy-Tummel road. A little over 2 miles north of Coshieville Inn (at the junction of the road to Fortingal) and just south of Glengoulandie Farm, a good path breaks off to the west, and, following the slopes above the north bank of the Allt Mor, leads on to the east ridge of Schichallion. When the ridge is reached, it is worth while to keep on the south side until the upper slopes are gained. In this way the magnificent prospect over Rannoch is revealed suddenly, and with effect. The east ridge may also be reached by a path crossing the northern slopes of Dun Coillich. The main road is left just north of White Bridge, and the path then followed almost due west to the Aonach Ban ridge of Schichallion.

From Kinloch Rannoch the ascent is usually made direct, by the rather broader west ridge of the mountain. Follow the secondary road, across the Tummel, for about 2 miles to Tempar farm. The burn of that name is now followed, there being a path for part of the way on its left bank. Beyond the headwaters, the ridge of the mountain narrows and steepens, and leads directly to the summit cairn.

All the above routes are equally suitable for descents. The

direct approach to the mountain from the south is more suitable for descent than ascent, and the following description is therefore given when descending from the summit and making towards Fortingal. The southern slopes of the mountain are fairly steep and very much scree-covered, in their upper reaches. Lower down, and in Gleann Mor, there is thick heather. Make for Glenmore Bothy, south-east of the junction of the Allt Mor and the Allt Creag a' Mhadaidh. There is a path here, which followed, leads over the bealach between Meall nan Eun and Meall Gruamach, and into Gleann Muilinn. Thereafter, descent is by the beautifully wooded glen of the Allt Odhar to a point in the valley near Fortingal.

The view from the summit of Schichallion is most extensive, but possibly a little marred by the uninteresting bulk of the Càrn Mairg range, close to the south. Beyond that range, Ben Lawers stands up well, and the view to the west is delightful. At one's feet, to the north, is a wealth of loch scenery and deep wooded valleys, all in rich contrast to the barren wastes immediately to the south.

Paths

Kinloch-Rannoch to Fortingal by Gleann Mor.—A good third of the way is trackless. Follow the road from Kinloch Rannoch over the Tummel, as far as Tempar, then branch up the left bank of Tempar Burn. Cross the bealach (*circa* 1930 ft.) west of Schichallion and descend the narrow and wet valley north of Creag an Earra. Cross the Allt Mor and make for the bothy on the slopes above the stream's south bank. Here there is a path leading over the ridge above, and into Gleann Muilinn, and a way is then made to Fortingal by the Allt Odhar.

Tummel Bridge to Fortingal by the hills. Follow the main Aberfeldy road east, then south, to Daloist, when a track leads up the hill on the right. This takes one above the Allt Kynachan to the road leading round the slopes of Schichallion to Kinloch Rannoch. Follow this road west for a little over 1 mile, then mount the slopes of Tigh an 't-socaith to the south. Cross the headwaters of the Kynachan and continue to the east ridge of Schichallion, crossing it as high up as inclination dictates. The south slopes leading into Glen Mor are steep. Once in the glen, one may follow the Allt Mor by its left bank, and by a path lower down, so reaching the main road some 2 miles north of Coshieville. Alternatively, one may continue more directly to Fortingal over the next ridge by the path from Glenmore Bothy described above.

CENTRES

Hotels are found at Coshieville, Fortingal and Kinloch Rannoch.

Nearest Youth Hostel is at Strathtummel (Allean House, 1½ miles east from east end of Loch Tummel).

BIBLIOGRAPHY

" Schichallion," Guide Book Article, *S.M.C.J.*, Vol. 6, p. 245.
" From Ballinluig to Lawers over Schichallion," by W. Garden
 S.M.C.J., Vol. 7, p. 15.

APPENDIX I

Rock-climbs in the Arrochar Group

The lower slopes of all the hills, with the exception of Ben Ime, are covered with Forestry Committee plantations. There have already been several disastrous fires and climbers are requested to keep to the recommended routes and to take every possible precaution against fire.

The climbs are on The Brack, The Cobbler, Narnain, Creag Tarsuinn, A'Crois and Ben Ime. On The Brack the cliffs face north, on all the other peaks the cliffs face east and hence are free of snow at a much earlier date than the Glen Coe peaks. In each case the climbs are described from left to right, looking towards the cliffs.

THE BRACK

The north face of The Brack forms one of the most impressive rock masses in the Arrochar district. At its western end, the face takes one unbroken sweep to the boulder-strewn corrie, but towards the east it is bisected by a diagonal rake, into two distinct tiers of rock, the lower one being more broken up by caves, fissures and vegetation.

Further to the east the crags bend round to form the north-east face which is divided by two wide grassy gullies, and presents a less coherent grouping of rock features. In the upper and lower corries, there is also a great profusion of massive boulders which cannot be equalled for size anywhere else in the district.

Split Pinnacle.—A conspicuous wedge of rock on the skyline of the high pass east of the summit.

Edge Route (50 ft., M.).—A steep climb up eastern edge of pinnacle. Good holds.

Gimcrack, (50 ft., M.).—The crack which completely severs the pinnacle.

Bobcrack, (50 ft., D.).—A crack on a small rock face to north of pinnacle and at same level (cairn). First pitch 20 ft. chimney climbed either on outside or as through route.

Second pitch, a 30-ft. crack

North of this and at same level. Four distinct rock steps bounding a short gully with a pinnacle on its left side.

Four Step Ridge (150 ft. (cairn).—Pitch I. (45 ft.). Either of twin chimneys. One on left deep-cut and permitting several variations. Right hand chimney is shallower. There are three pitches and the third is very difficult.

Inglis Clark Arete (300-400 ft., M. and artificial (cairn).— The " knife edge " arete of an early Journal account. It lies on the angle of the crag between north-east and north faces, and on the lower tier of crag. The line of climb follows the crest of the left wall of a well marked gully, and is marked by a conspicuous pointed pinnacle on corrie floor.

May Route (350 ft., D.).—Upper tier from the rake. Steep vegetation, cracks and slabs.

Now comes a stretch of crag, high and very steep, with one well-defined groove (unclimbed) running up centre to ledge known as Gallery. Before attempting groove, climbers might well take preliminary survey from Gallery where it will be seen that most of face is badly inclined, water worn and not too sound in upper part.

Elephant Gully (300-350 ft.,D. in summer conditions).—This deep rift in the western end of the north face is in three distinct sections, each marked by a cave-like recess. All the climbing is in the gully bed or on right wall.

Whilst this gully is no more than *difficult* in summer, in proper snow and ice conditions it might well be a formidable climb.

THE COBBLER

To avoid confusion the numbering in the original Cobbler Guide has been retained. 4A indicates an entirely new route, not mentioned in that guide, while 5a indicates a variation of an existing route.

SOUTH PEAK

1. *South-east Arete* (300 ft., M.).—The original route by the skyline. There are two variations to the first ledge pitch—by a chimney a little higher to the left, or by a direct climb on an edge to the right. Above this there are numerous variations, generally easy to the left, more difficult to the right.

2. *Jughandle* (350 ft., V.D.).—Starts in a shallow gully 60 ft. to right of col (cairn) and consists of a series of upward and traverse movements keeping to right of skyline whole way to the summit.

3. *Grassy Traverse.*—The first climb made on the north face. Starts about centre of face (cairn) where a ledge leads up to the left to a steep grassy slope and traverse over steep and treacherous grassy and mossy ledges to join Route 1 (should be avoided).

4A. *North Wall Groove* (S.).—First two pitches as for 4, then one continues upward instead of traversing—7 pitches.

4. *North Wall Traverse* (300 ft., severe and exposed.).—The first pitch is as for 3. From the apex of the steep grassy slope a shallow groove leads upwards for 70 feet till it merges with overhanging rocks above (crux) then a difficult traverse movement to a large block (only belay for remainder of climb). Now four pitches by turfy ledges and slabs to join route 5 below the nose—dry weather essential.

5. *Nimlin's Direct Route* (250 ft., V.D. to S.).—This fine climb follows the angle between north and north-west faces (which shows up so well in photograph). 1st Pitch—Smooth face with small holds leading up and slightly left to finish at small stance and flake belay. Route now follows a series of walls and grass ledges, until buttress narrows to a steep nose. Finish on top of semi-detached block, known as " Jock."

5a. *Slack's variation* (280 ft., V.D. to S.).—Starts on low rock rib at right hand side of north wall near prominent chimney—three pitches, of which the second is very severe, to reach end of first ledge on ordinary direct

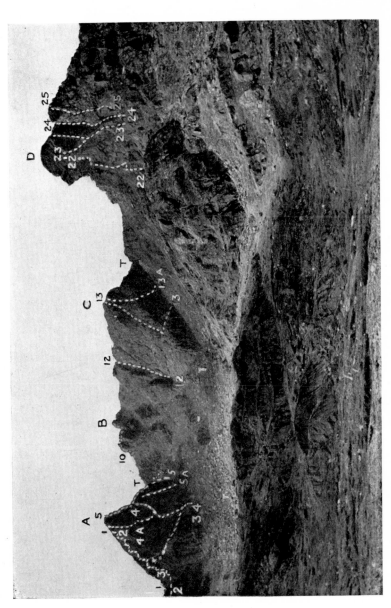

March, 1931

THE COBBLER FROM THE UPPER CORRIE.

B. H. Humble

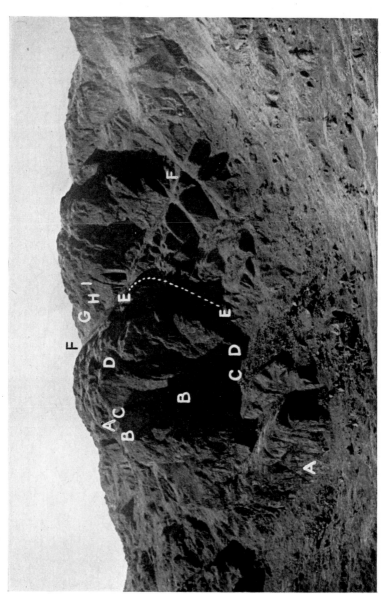

Douglas Scott.

CREAG TARSUINN.

A. Buttress various routes   B. Slab and Groove   C. M°Lay's Gully   D. M°Lcore's Chimney   E. Currier Gully   F.

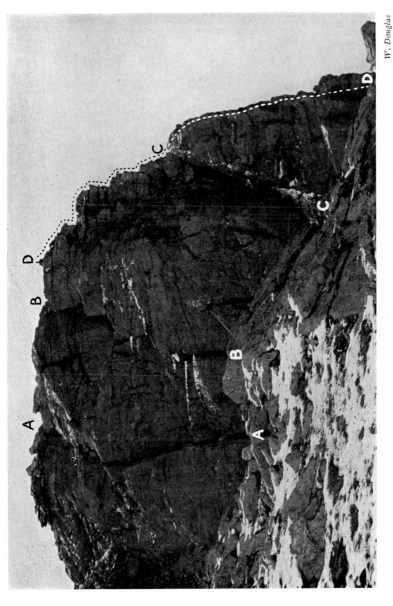

BEN NARNAIN: SUMMIT CLIFFS.

W. Douglas

South
Buttress.

Crois
Gully.

Centre
Buttress.

Pinnacle
Gully.
Pinnacle
Buttress.

R. H. Humble

April 1947

route. This can be joined, or another and harder route taken to the left.

6. *Sloping Ledge* (D.).—From the col follow a narrow but well-marked ledge to the left. At further end climb direct upwards to upper ledge of original route. From here, either join original route, continue direct by 12-ft. wall to summit, or move round sloping ledge to the ledge to the left, to join finish of Route 5.

7. *Original route* (M.).—The usual route when traversing the peak by obvious ledge to right of col (not seen in photo.).

8. *North-west crack* (60 ft., S.).—Starts at end of ledge of 7. One pitch usually repulsively wet.

9. *Ardgartan Wall* (200 ft., V.D. to S.).—The climb is on the south face overlooking Ardgartan policies. It is somewhat artificial as escapes are possible to the right at every pitch.

CENTRE PEAK

10. *The Arête* (D.).—Continues the classic route on the traverse of the peaks, first by a 50-ft. crack, then an easy traverse, then a long sloping slab with good holds to the east window of summit rock. In icy conditions there are easy variations to the right at both pitches.

11. *McGregor's Ledge* (D.).—Short and strenuous from west to east window, and involving a muscle-up on to mantelshelf which leads to sill of east window.

CENTRE PEAK BUTTRESS

12. *Centre Gully*.—The steep narrow gully almost in centre of the mountain gives a nice little climb under snow, and there may be a cornice at exit.

13. *Cave Route* (D.).—Starting from a large patch of grass about a third of the way up the face, a well-marked shallow gully runs up to summit (photo). Easy to cave about 100 ft. up; climb to narrow ledge on right wall, or make exposed traverse right round corner. This leads to smaller upper cave, then to continuation of main gully.

13A. *Chimney Route* (200 ft., V.D.).—Starts about 80 ft. down from col on right-hand side of buttress (cairn). Six pitches with a V.D. right-angled chimney midway.

NORTH PEAK

14A. 100-ft. *Wall* (S.).—The left-hand wall of route 14—very steep and very fine holds.

14. 100-ft. *Chimney* (V.D.).—The first obvious chimney to the left of this peak. Good sound rock. Climb to ledge below huge overhang, then an exposed traverse left on sloping holds and indifferent grips.

15. *Cat Crawl* (120 ft., Severe and exposed).—Starts 3 ft. to right of 14. An awkward stomach traverse, a few feet above start, is technically difficult.

16. *Right-angled Gully* (D.).—The best-known climb on this peak. The holds on first pitch now much worn. First two pitches up bed of gully, then traverse right and scale a 10-ft. wall.

17. *Direct finish* (S.).—This is the continuation of the gully from top of second pitch of 16.

18. *Right-angled Groove* (120 ft., very severe and exposed).—Starts lower and to right of 16 and finishes on outer rim of broad ledge of ordinary right-angled gully route. The holds are small and sloping and the whole route very exposed. Can only be done as a single pitch, balance climbing throughout.

19. *Ramshead Ridge* (120 ft., D.).—This is the short ridge between right-angled gully and ramshead gully. The crest can be reached from the right side. Fine well-cut holds—finish on terrace below 18.

20. *Ramshead Wall* (80 ft., V.D.).—This route lies on wall at top of Ramshead Gully and gives a fine face climb on reliable quartz holds. Forms a good finish to the Recess Route or McLay's Crack.

21. *Ramshead Gully* (200 ft., severe and exposed).—This gully splits the mountain from top to bottom. The gully is climbed at an easy angle for 80 ft. to deep-cut chimney on right. Then 1st pitch (60 ft.)—climbed completely inside chimney on excellent holds. Very exposed and sensational exit left to steep upper gully. 2nd pitch (15 ft.)—Climb gully on bad holds to smooth pitch smothered in vegetation and debris. 3rd pitch—Huge boulder choked-rubble.

22. *Recess Route* (300 ft., V.D., S. pitch 6.).—The finest climb, not only on the Cobbler, but in the whole Arrochar district. Starts at lowest point of rock between Ramshead Gully and Great Gully—8 pitches.

1st Pitch (50 ft.)—A slabby wall is climbed to left on balance holds to grassy ledges.

The hardest pitch is No. 6.—that above the halfway terrace, where it starts at right end. From end step into a corner with a crack in it. The crack is holdless, but can be climbed by jamming the right arm in it and using sketchy holds on left wall, but very exposed, and very small holds. (To escape from this pitch without climbing down, one can traverse left, along " Half-way Terrace," to reach Ramshead Gully). Two cave pitches above this which can be avoided by traversing right, along ledge to final pitch and McLay's Crack Route, while they can also be used as a finish to that route.

23. *McLay's Crack* (200 ft., D.).—Starts about 20 ft. lower and to left of Great Gully. A smooth wall in a corner is ascended into a turfy chimney, often very slimy. After 60 ft., chimney branches and left branch is followed.

24. *Great Gully* (E. to M.).—Often very slimy and not recommended in summer.

In hard snow it gives an interesting climb, when the two usually easy pitches will be difficult.

25. *North Rib* (200 ft., V.D.).—Starts 20 ft. to right of Great Gully and goes up rib crowning north wall of gully.

About 200 yards west of 25, a line of crags rises from a field of huge boulders. There are possible short routes here, and the area is best reached by continuing up the burn from the Narnain Stone in the direction of Ben Ime, then striking uphill to the left.

BEN NARNAIN

Although Ben Narnain is a particularly rocky mountain with extensive outcrops from the 2000 ft. level to the stony summit plateau, the actual rock-climbing is confined to an outcrop only 200-300 ft. below its summit. This outcrop, the

Spearhead Ridge, is a level-topped wedge of rock which abuts from the summit plateau on to the upper slopes of the south-east ridge.

The whole ridge is no more than 150 ft. long and averages 100 ft. in height. The rock falls steeply to north and south of the ridge and its nose is formed by two abrupt steps, the lower, steeper one forming the Spearhead. Routes are well shown in photo between pages 156-157.

Restricted Crack (60 ft., M.).—Starts about 6 yards up scree slope from Jamblock and follows a pronounced fault.

Engine-room Crack (70-80 ft., D. and Strenuous).—This subterranean route is entered more easily from north side of ridge, but a restricted entry may be found on south face. Strenuous back and knee climbing in almost total darkness.

Jamblock Chimney—(85 ft., D. and strenuous if exit made by manhole).—A deeply cut chimney which demonstrates a variety of technical moves. From the upper cave there is an interesting exit by a manhole in the roof. Stoutish climbers are advised to make their exit by the more open routes to south and north.

Spearhead Chimney (40 ft., D.).—A fold on south face some yards west of Arete. Climbed on right wall on small holds. Finishes on top of Spearhead.

The Spearhead Arête (150 ft. of actual ascent, D. to V.D. according to variation chosen)—A classic route by any of its variations.

Secondary Spearhead.—A smaller replica of the Spearhead as viewed from the south-east Ridge. Actually the butt end of a small outcrop.

N.E. Corner (40 ft., D.).—A steep little climb by a corner and crack.

S.E. Corner (30 ft., D.).—Direct climb on south side keeping near corner of crag.

CREAG TARSUINN

A considerable buttress of rock at the south end of Creag Tarsuinn, which encloses the head of Coire Sugach. The buttress is partly detached from main crag by an easy scree-filled gully on the south side and a steep gully (McLay's) to the north. The face of the buttress has a southern aspect.

Original Buttress Route (400 ft., D.).—Starts at lower corner of upper rock tier and bears left over heather ledges and short rock faces to edge overlooking gully to south. Upper part tends back right to " Pulpit " and finishes up " Knife Edge."

Direct Buttress Route (400 ft., D. to V.D. according to variations taken).—Starts at same point as No. 1 and goes directly up series of faces and heather patches. Steep nose 300 ft. up is most difficult section. May be avoided by chimney on right. Finish by " Pulpit " and " Knife Edge." Several variations possible. Holds small but well defined.

Garrick's Route (100 ft., D.).—Goes up centre of lower rock tier from rock platform and finishes on terrace between upper and lower tiers.

(Note : There are several other variations up to V.D.)

Slab and Groove (130 ft., V.D.).—The angle between rock wall and great slab on north side of " Knife Edge." Start in lower part of McLay's Gully by a slab traverse into groove. Steep upper part provided with splendid belay on large flake at foot of rock wall. Finishes at top of " Knife Edge."

McLay's Gully (200 ft. 100 ft. of rock climbing V.D.).— A dangerous gully filled with loose debris. Climbing confined to two steep waterslides 60 ft. and 40 ft.

McLaren's Chimney (V.D. to S., 7 pitches).—This chimney is the most obvious feature of the crags to right of Buttress, huge chokestone half way up—route in gully bed and left wall.

Curving Gully.—Starts to right of McLaren's Chimney. Lower pitches turned on right wall.

The cliffs are now divided by a rake, running downwards from south to north. It is easy in summer, but in snow it gives awkward traverse movements over iced slabs.

1st gully on south end of rake. M. 60 ft. Steep grass.

2nd Gully. 80 ft. M. with several loose sections—rather dangerous.

Face route. 120 ft. S. in boots.

A long traverse on very small holds finishes to left of unclimbed gully.

Now come the four unclimbed gullies more in the nature of grooves, all very steep with possibilities of face routes between them.

A'CROIS

These cliffs are well shown in the photograph opposite page 157.

Easy Gully.—Small pitch in lower section easily avoided on right.

South Buttress (400 ft.).—Easy angles except at northern end overlooking gully, where climbs of more difficult quality are possible.

Crois Gully (300 ft., D.).—Varies with snow conditions. Fine well marked gully with sometimes 2 short ice-pitches.

Central Buttress (350 ft. Up to D.).—Depending on variation.

Pinnacle Gully (250 ft. Up to D.).—Varies with conditions. 1st pitch climbed on left or by a through chimney. Upper parts may present short ice-pitches.

Pinnacle from Gully (100 ft., D.).—Only recorded route to top of pinnacle. Steep and vegetatious with awkward steep section near top.

North Gully.—Wide gully which sometimes gives good step—cutting on upper part. Cornices easily avoided.

BEN IME

The climbing on Ben Ime is confined to the north-eastern face, the wide northern gully and the upper rocks of the short, steep ridge at the angle between the two faces.

NORTH-EASTERN FACE

Easy Gully.—A short easy gully which leads up to a wide, fan-shaped scoop from which a variety of exits may be taken. In winter this initial gully may show an ice-pitch and an extensive but easy cornice may form on the rim of fanshaped scoop.

Fan Gully Buttress.—This is the highest single crag on Ben Ime. The edge overlooking easy gully can be followed, and there are many variations. The only real climb done so far is—

Ben's Fault (400 ft., D.).—Starts by shallow gully to the right, but may possibly be climbed by a more direct gully with a rock pitch near its top. This approach has not been tried. 100 ft. up a series of short and, in come cases, deep-cut chimneys lead directly to flat top of crag.

Fan Gully (Ice pitch 15-20 ft., V.D.).—Final gully and approach slopes 300 ft. In summer, gully is uninteresting and barred by one unpleasant slimy wall which forms ice pitch. In winter it gives a very good climb if approach slopes have well frozen snow. At narrow section the rock wall forms an ice pitch with a cave below it. Upper gully is easier.

Fan Gully Chimney (50 ft., D. in summer to S. in winter).—It is an alternative to ice pitch, and it may be found by traversing right, up to steep chimney from point 20 ft. below ice pitch.

By following the right branch of the burn from the sheep-fold, one reaches north face of Ben Ime, where there are several gullies, one of which has been climbed.

APPENDIX 2

KILPATRICKS AND CAMPSIES

Kilpatricks (Auchineden Hill, The Whangie).—On the
west slope of the hill's northernly spur is a remarkable formation, consisting of a narrow wall of rock, fully 100 yards long,
split off from the main mass of the hill. The fissure between the
rock wall and the hill is narrow in places and has an average
depth of fully 30 ft. Two gaps divide the wall into three
portions. Of these the southern and middle portions present
no difficulty, and may be traversed in either direction.

The northern portion (The Pinnacle) is harder, and is
gained from the north by a number of alternative routes.
Once on the ridge, the edge seems very narrow and precarious
to the small grassy top, and the rock is unreliable. Following
the ridge beyond the top, one comes to a vertical drop at the
south end. This can be ascended or descended with the
assistance of a rope and gives a hard climb of 35 ft.

Campsies.—The bulk of the climbing is to be found
amongst the rocks facing Blanefield on the hillside between
Dumgoyne and the Ballagan Burn. On most of the routes the
rock is untrustworthy, and everywhere has to be treated with
the greatest respect. A good deal of turf and other vegetation
grows on the cliff : this adds to the interest but not to the
security.

(1) *The Long Gully* (450 ft., M.).—This is the first
prominent gully, south of Dumgoyne, in the cliffs of Slackdhu.
The worst bits are avoidable and the gully gives an interesting
scramble. It is inclined to wetness and is very loose in places.

(2) *Coffin Gully Buttress* (250 ft., V.D.).—In the centre of
the Slack Dhu face is a deep, black cleft known as Coffin
Gully : the buttress to the left (north) of this is the climb. The

route is well scratched and is probably the best in the Campsies.
Most of the way the rock is as good as anywhere in these hills,
the last pitch being the most doubtful. The start is indeterminate, but, higher up, the way becomes more defined. Above
a short scrambling section about 70 ft. up, the second pitch is
reached. This is started on the right and a traverse made to the
left across a split rock in the face. The pitch is short. A little
higher and to the left is a shallow chimney which is climbed—
largely on vegetation—to another scrambling section on very
loose rock. This ends at a good ledge which, if followed to the
right, leads to the crest of the buttress. The final pitch is
difficult and exposed, being climbed on doubtful rock up the
crest. An alternative is to follow the ledge to the left for a few
yards, when an easy way upwards will be found among little
pinnacles and the top gained by a short scramble.

(3) *Jenny's Lum Arête* (40 ft., S.).—This lies immediately
to the right of the " Lum," a peculiar little crack down which
pours a small burn from the plateau. It is situated high up on
the hillside a short way to the north of Blanefield, and is
approached from there by way of the burn descending from
the direction of the " Lum." When approaching from below,
the Arete is the near edge of the precipitous rock to the left
of the crack. The climb is very strenuous and best tackled
with a rope from above. There is also an easy little chimney to
the left of the rock by which the Arete may be gained.

On the Jenny's Lum rock itself and among the rocks to
its right, are numerous short climbs of varying difficulty.
About 50 yards to the right is (4) *The Pinnacle*, a 40-ft.
basalt pillar, which offers access to its upper parts by moderate
chimneys on either side. The best climb, however, is the
Pinnacle Arete (60 ft., A.S.), which follows the nose of the
pinnacle to its small summit. The most difficult part is low
down. From the top of the pinnacle, a long step is made
across space to the cliff beyond and the climb finishes by easy
ledges.

Further right is another pinnacle known as Jacob's
Ladder, which provides a strenuous but short climb.

(5) The prominent large gully above Blanefield is bounded
on the left by a moderate ridge, which may be completed by

M

climbing up a gully to the left (*The Staircase*). This terminates just below the top of the cliffs, and the finish is exposed. If a way is made up the large main gully, a rather unsatisfactory climb (100-*ft. pitch*) is found starting on the left wall. A traverse right after a few feet leads to a long rock slide which is climbed to the top without much difficulty.

(6) *The Black Craig* is the steep face to the right of the gully above Blanefield. It has been climbed on more than one occasion by the series of nearly vertical scoops and faces between narrow ledges. The rock is very bad and the climbing thoroughly dangerous.

Elsewhere in the Campsies there are a number of short climbs. In the middle of the south face of Crichton's Cairn, near Campsie Glen, is a line of cliffs about 150 yards long. The cliffs are crossed by two ledges, of which the upper is easy. In the lowest section of cliff is a small pinnacle behind which is the Moabite Chimney (30 ft., V.D.). The cliffs above can be climbed in a nearly straight line, starting at the foot of the chimney, and crossing the two ledges.

Above Ballikinrain and a little east of Earl's Seat, there is a short cliff of columnar basalt on which are one or two climbs on sound rock. In the two corries further east—the Corrie of Balglass, and the one from which issue the headwaters of the Balglass Burn—are some fine cliffs. In the Corrie of Balglass is a gigantic slab set at a high angle. This has been climbed with a rope from above.

OCHILS GROUP

ROCK-CLIMBING on the Ochils is confined to small areas. The rock is almost universally unsound, being for the most part composed of volcanic breccias or " pudding stone." The cliffs on Dumyat are the most extensive, although a high line of crag appears on Craig Leith, above Alva. The rocks on that hill offer little encouragement, and, although it has been attempted more than once, the gully in the centre of the cliff does not appear to be possible. On Dumyat, the bulk of the climbing is to be found on the sides of the open gully (The Great Glen), separating the main summit from the western top. From the road, the crags above Blairlogie appear to be climbable but closer inspection proves the opposite.

The Great Glen should be gained from the old road running east from Blairlogie through trees, and a little up the hillside. About 400 ft. up, near where the gully begins to narrow, a small buttress will be noticed. This gives a climb of about 50 ft. on friable rock, with the main difficulty near the top.

The cliffs to the east of the Great Glen are the highest, on them being found the finest climbing. Many of the routes are short and difficult and care should be taken with the rock, for although some of the climbs are reasonably sound, others are quite the reverse. In the face on the east of the Great Glen, and fairly high up, will be seen two prominent gullies. The right-hand, narrow one, is Raeburn's Gully, and the wider left-hand has been named the Cirque Gully. The latter contains no climbing, but is bounded on the north side, at the neck, by the wall of Raeburn's Pinnacle.

Raeburn's Gully (120 ft., V.D.).—Rock fairly sound at difficulties. A short pitch above the initial looseness leads to a platform of wedged blocks. The next part is climbed in the chimney, which is complicated by briars and a good pitch over a projecting piece of rock then leads to a stance below where the gully widens near the top. The best finish leads to the left, by way of an upward sloping ledge. The position is exposed and the holds small and shelving. After rounding the corner at the far end the difficulties cease. The direct ascent of the gully top, by way of a conspicuous rock flake, and, above, a short section of slightly overhanging rotten rock, is only accomplished with the help of a pull from above. It is also possible to step right from the top of the flake and climb a steep wall of grass and rock to easier ground.

Raeburn's Pinnacle is about 60 ft. high and lies immediately to the left of Cirque gully. A severe route has been made directly up the long side, but only with a rope from above. The rock is very rotten. To the left of the face route is a little chimney whose top is split by a jammed rock : the way to the right of this is easy, that to the left severe. From a grass ledge above, and to the right, a short climb leads under a slight overhang to a narrow cleft and the Pinnacle's summit. The top of the Pinnacle is, however, most easily reached by way of a short secure chimney in the wall of Cirque gully.

Further up the Great Glen on the same side will be found two further climbs. The first of these is the *Fork-Chimney* (45 ft., S.), which is easily recognised. The main difficulty is concentrated at the fork and the left-hand branch is taken. The rock is unsound. Higher up again is the *Knife Chimney* (20ft., V.D.), which is short but strenuous.

To the right of Raeburn's Gully and some distance below, is a steepish, oblique gully, overhung on the left by a rounded boss of rock. This gully narrows a little way up and gives a severe pitch of about 30 ft. The difficulty is to gain the bulge of rock to the left by a bad step across, followed by an awkward pull up the face. Above this the grass slope is climbed to the upper part of the gully which is crossed to a grass ledge on the right. This leads up to the *Hornbeam Gully* (100 ft., V.D.), which is formed by a steep cliff on the left and a very steep, smooth slab to the right. The gully is named from the large tree in its lower part. The start is on the right wall slab, but higher up one is forced more into the corner among the branches of the tree. The last section of the climb lies up the corner above a platform formed by the roots of a second tree.

The cliffs on the west side of the Great Glen offer little that is possible, the rocks of the upper terrace being vertical for most of the way. Above the level of Raeburn's Gully there is a boss of rock which gives a scramble of about 120 ft. This is not difficult. By following the terrace to the south, and round the corner of the hill in a westerly direction, an impressive crack will be found. This is the *Black Crack* (60 ft., D.), which is climbed by wedging tactics. The rock is none too sound but there is a good belay at the top, from whence the second may be protected.

High up on the hillside to the east of the Great Glen, the rocks are disappointingly loose and few routes are possible. Some distance across the terrace there are a number of pinnacles, one of which gives its name to the *Lizard Chimney* (35 ft., V.D.), lying between the pinnacle and the main cliff face. The chimney is climbed on sound rock, the main difficulty being at the top.

Further east again the rock becomes increasingly bad and offers no possibilities. The largest face (Mushroom Wall) contains a number of revolting upper chimneys, all of which overhang.

Near the corner, overlooking Menstrie, the rocks are lower and two climbs have been effected. Great care is needed as the rock is most unreliable. The first of these climbs is by a 40-ft. rib of reddish conglomerate with a very difficult pull out at the top. The second follows the straight and very difficult crack near the extreme eastern edge of the cliff. The exit is again the most difficult part.

A short distance below the summit of Dumyat, on the south-west side, is a steep little cliff of reasonably sound rock. This gives at least five short climbs of about 30 ft. and a difficult girdle traverse.

In the wide gully well to the west of the summit and running down to the reservoir, off the Sheriffmuir road, is a further small cliff, along the top of which runs a fence. There is a steep slab near the centre of this, which gives three routes of 35 ft. The girdle traverse of the cliff is also possible although one section near the middle is very hard. The rock is sound.

Apart from Raeburn's Gully and Pinnacle, most of the Dumyat routes were first climbed by J. H. B. Bell.

THE LOMONDS

THE rock is mainly dolerite, very rotten in parts, and still decaying. In places it supports a vigorous growth of vegetation which has to be treated with extreme care. Outcrops of white sandstone occur in minor degree : this, too, is very friable but cleaner than the dolerite. Apart from the climbs on Craigengaw all the routes are short.

The climbing is divided into three groups :—

    (a) CRAIGENGAW CLIMBS.

    (b) BISHOP HILL CLIMBS near MIDDLE SUMMIT.

    (c) OUTLYING ODDMENTS.

(a) *Craigengaw Climbs.*—The main mass of dolerite on the West Lomond consists of the cliff of Craigengaw, which lies north-east of the summit, and beneath the rim of the plateau. A wide gully (the Great Gully) runs up to the plateau and divides the cliff into two, the portion to the east being considerably lower than the main cliff on the west. On the east cliff is a small pinnacle which has been climbed, and higher up the Great Gully are two short wide chimneys on the left. Both have been climbed, the deeper cut one (Professor's Chimney, 30ft., S.) yielding a difficult exit on the west wall.

The north and east faces of the cliff, west of the Great Gully meet along a nearly vertical rock edge, conspicuous as a sort of double edge enclosing a right-angled groove. This is known as the Split Nose. To the left, on the east face of the cliff, are a number of routes. The easiest is the *Moonshine Gully* (125 ft., D.). The way lies up the fairly conspicuous narrow gully, a little to the right of a prominent block of rock high up—the Anvil—and the most difficult section is at the top. A 15-ft. chimney halfway up is also sporting.

The Anvil, from the Great Gully, gives a severe climb of 50 ft. The initial pitch is awkward and starts at the foot of the cliff, directly below the Anvil's top. Higher up, a difficult pull is necessary to gain the ledge running round the outside of the Anvil's base, and the climb is completed by traversing this exposed and sloping ledge and reaching the top from the south east side.

The Split Nose (130 ft., V.S.)—The route gives the most difficult and longest climb on the Lomonds. Belays are very few and, in places, the vegetation is particularly troublesome : crampons have been recommended for dealing with parts of the climb. The start is at the lowest point of rock, right beneath the " Nose." There are two alternative 25-ft. cracks, both difficult, leading to the indefinite ledge beneath the Split Nose. The easterly crack is the easier. The Split Nose, 60 ft., very exposed and difficult, comes next. The lower part is vegetatious and requires extreme care : higher up the rock is cleaner but offers few holds. The top 15 ft. are by a narrower chimney which is almost overhung, and the exit is by a sensational movement outwards, and across the eastern wall. This leads to the Copestone of the Split Nose, which is then left by a delicate traverse to the rather grassy rocks on the west of the nose. The crest of the ridge is regained 16 ft. higher, on the unmistakable Nettleshelf, beyond which the top of the climb is reached by some cracked slabs leading back across the ridge and upwards. The finish, on the large sloping Outlook Slab, commands a wide view, and forms a fitting end to a very difficult climb.

The Lateral Split Nose route starting from the chimney, half-way up the Moonshine gully, gives 30 ft. of very difficult climbing to the Copestone of the Split Nose. From there the direct route is followed as above. This route in its entirety is severe.

(b) *The Bishop Climbs* are situated on a dolerite cliff, just north of the middle summit. The cliff is rather inconspicuous from below, as it lies in a concave part of the edge of the plateau, and just below the rim. The main feature is a weird pinnacle known as Carlin Maggie, whose top appears most insecure and which has so far not been reached. The long side of the pinnacle is very steep but the neck at the back can be reached by a difficult crack on fairly sound rock. Opposite the pinnacle is the Pinnacle Ridge (30 ft., V.D.), which gives a sound climb with an exposed finish.

The climbs on the main mass of rock are a series of chimneys, the best one of which lies some way east of Carlin Maggie. It gives a pleasant climb of 30 ft. on fairly trustworthy rock.

(c) *Outlying Oddments.*—Some way beneath the western summit of the Bishop is a small dolerite face yielding one or two possible routes.

South-east of the West Lomond summit a rounded grassy ridge runs down to an outcrop of rock giving 40 ft. of scrambling in two sections.

In the narrows of Glenvale a terraced cliff of white sandstone occurs on the east side. The rock is none too good but there are easy ways between the terraces. In the centre is John Knox's Pulpit, from whence a good 15-ft. pitch on the left leads to the amphitheatre above. A very hard pitch leads from this point straight to the top of the cliff, and there is an easy way at the south end.

The Maiden's Bower lies on the north slopes of the West Lomond at about 800 ft. The Bower is a circular cave with floor at ground level. On the other side of the rock is the Bannetstane, a mushroom-shaped block connected below by a narrow stalk. The top is gained from the side next the main rock by a stride and a good pull over. On the east side, above the Bower, are one or two entertaining traverses and a circular rock window. The steep arete on the north-west of the base of the Bannetstane also gives a short climb.

High up on the north-east slope between the Maiden's Bower and Craigengaw is the *Corboff Pinnacle*. It is a double pinnacle which affords a good climb from the valley side (35 ft., V.D.). The start is by a narrow crack leading up and through to the upper side of the gap between the pinnacles. This point is again on ground level. From here, the gap between the pinnacles is climbed to the lesser top, and the other summit reached by an airy step from one top to the other. There is an easier way off.

MINOR ROCK CLIMBS ON THE FIFE COAST AND MAY ISLAND

ABOUT ¾ mile along the path running east from St. Andrews, above the bay, one reaches a peculiar thin tower of sandstone—the *Maiden Rock*. It rises from sloping grass, and the shore, and is about 25 ft. high at the " land " end and nearly double that at the other, due to the slope of the ground at its base. Seen end on, it has the appearance of a true pinnacle with steep sides, but its nearly level summit ridge extends for about 25 ft., and is very narrow. There are 13 distinct routes to the top on sound rock, the well worn one in the middle of the east face being the easiest. If care is taken to keep at mid-height, there is also a difficult girdle traverse right round the rock (75 ft.). The hardest portion is the crossing of the narrow " land " face. The *Sea Ridge* (45 ft., D.) is the most pleasant route to the top, which can then be traversed, and a descent made by the *Land Ridge* (25 ft., D.). An east to west traverse would be best accomplished by climbing the *Sea Chimney* (45 ft. A.S.), which lies in the angle to the east of the Sea Ridge. The chimney is very short and shallow, and it is most easily climbed by the rocks immediately to the left. The summit ridge is then traversed nearly to the " land " end, and a descent made by the *Right Cave* route (28 ft., V.D.). This route is severe in descent and starts down a recess just short of the Land Ridge. The step to the cave, a shallow depression in the west face, about mid-height, is the most difficult move. The *Left Cave* route on the other side of the depression is easier (30 ft., D.). Between the Cave and Land Ridge is the nearly vertical *Budget Wall* (25 ft., S.), giving a strenuous climb if care is taken not to go right or left of the most direct line. The other routes are gymnastic problems.

The *Rock and Spindle*, situated ½ mile further from St. Andrews than the Maiden Rock, gives one route to the top. It is easy to within 12 ft. of the summit, when a very disagreeable traverse is made right, and then upwards. The rock is most unsound and marks one of the vent " pipes " of a volcanic age.

The Buddo Rock is again composed of sandstone. It lies near Buddo Ness about 3½ miles south-east of St. Andrews, and is reached from the coast road via a farm track and two fields, or by the coast itself. There are several obvious routes to the top, which is grassy and flat. The rock is split and one can walk through from one side to the other. The most entertaining route—The *Arch Traverse* (40 ft., S.)—starts from near the rock arch at the south-east side and goes right, up greasy sandstone, to the top. The main difficulty is half-way up.

The *May Island* is the largest island in the Forth, and is reached most easily by fishing boat from Anstruther. The rock is excellent and clean on much of the cliff, the best climbing being centred around Pilgrim's Haven, at the south-west corner of the island. Here the walls are very steep and give a number of short, good climbs of between 15 ft. and 50 ft. The main feature of the cove is a large pinnacle rising sheer out of the sea. It is close on 80 ft. high and vertical on three sides, the only way to its top being by the sea-facing ridge. It is usually necessary to swim to the start of the climb, but once there, the route to the gap between the tops is not

BIBLIOGRAPHY

" The Maiden Rock," by H. Raeburn, *S.M.C.J.*, Vol. 7, p. 48.
" The Isle of May and the Bass Rock," by W. Ross McLean, *S.M.C.J.*, Vol. 20, p. 167.
" The Isle of May," by H. W. Turnbull, *S.M.C.J.*, Vol. 21, p. 53.

particularly difficult. There are two tops, the landward being the easier, and is climbed by a steep slab from the gap. The other top is very small and may be climbed from the gap by the edge of a flake of rock, or by the steep ridge facing out to sea. The outlook from the top is sensational.

COWAL AND ARDGOIL

Beinn Mhòr Group (Loch Eck).—Climbing is confined to the Coire an t-Sith sides of Beinn Mhor and Clach Bheinn. On the former there is a good deal of indiscriminate scrambling and bouldering, but nothing definite. The rock is wet and vegetatious. Clach Bheinn has a number of pinnacles which afford short problems, and lie on the north slopes at about the 1400-ft. contour. The most easterly (known locally as the *Kneeling Bishop*) is about 100 ft. high on the long side. The west ridge gives a good climb to a grassy ledge, which is then followed, right, to the east side of the pinnacle and the top gained. The deep crack on the south side would yield a difficult climb. A quarter of a mile west of this pinnacle are two others at a slightly lower level. The south face of the more definite of these gives several good short scrambles. (A. Arthur: R. Anderson.)

Beinn an Lochain.—A few hundred feet below the summit of the mountain, the north-east ridge forms the upper and east wall of a fair sized corrie, the south side of which consists of an extensive, steep, rock face sloping up from west to east. It is considerably broken up by grass ledges. Rather more than half-way down towards the middle of the face is a remarkable, unstable, pinnacle which may be gained easily from its neck. This point can be reached by an ill-defined climb, starting a good way to the west of, and 300 ft. below, the pinnacle. From the pinnacle neck, the climb may be continued diagonally upwards to the east, by the line of least resistance. (1st ascent: H. Raeburn.)

BEN LOMOND DISTRICT

APART from minor problems, the climbing on Ben Lomond is confined to the rocks of the northern corrie, which is reached most easily by the scree slope a little way east of the summit.

The rock is far from ideal and the corrie is better adapted to winter climbing, when some of the gullies give good sport under snow conditions. In the winter also, the narrow gullies on the north slopes of the summit bastion can give nice snow climbing. In summer the rocks are intermingled with a good deal of grass, and much of the cliff is indefinite.

The corrie is bounded by the main summit on the west and three minor tops stretching eastwards. The first of these subsidiary tops east of the summit is the culminating point of a broken and easy cliff. East of this is a scree slope followed by the second section of cliff, which is considerably steeper and more extensive than the first. The east edge is bounded by an easy gully, and the line of cliffs bends sharply eastwards. The third section of cliff is again higher and steeper, and about twice as long as the other two sections combined. Towards the north-east, it tapers off in height and finally merges into the eastern bounding ridge of the corrie.

The western half of the second section is broken up and offers little difficulty. Further east are two ribs beyond a shallow gully which give defined climbs (MacLay and Naismith) of moderate standard.

The third section is crossed diagonally by an easy ledge, from the foot of which the Pinnacle route (Inglis Clark and Shannon) leads almost straight to the top of the cliff. This route is difficult, but offers easy escapes. Between this route and the gully crossing the diagonal ledge is a prominent chimney, which gives a " steep vegetable, rather interesting and difficult climb" (Newbigging), starting from near the foot of the ledge.

The prominent gully in the centre of the cliff is climbable to near the top, where it is blocked by a projecting capstone. A way can be made out to the right from a little lower down, and the cliff top reached without difficulty by the shallow gully on the right (Naismith and Maclay).

On the east shore of Loch Lomond the Cailness burn offers a fair amount of scrambling of the wetter variety.

The lower hills to the west of Loch Lomond are mostly smooth and without rock, but here and there will be found occasional outcrops which may give a scramble to the diligent searcher. Further north, the " Ardlui Boulder," situated close to the road, and about 1 mile south of Ardlui, gives some short problems.

The steep crack in the left-hand side of the Pulpit Rock (facing from the road) has been climbed ; the easiest route to the top, however, is by the slab on the opposite side of the rock.

BEINN BHUIDHE, LORNE AND KNAPDALE

Beinn Bhuidhe.—The rock of which the mountain is composed is a gritty schist, and it is unfortunate that it only crops out in limited quantities. There are no recorded routes, but a certain amount of scrambling can be had on the south slopes.

Lorne.—All the rock on the coast is conglomerate, and sound routes are few. The small cliffs at Ganavan, north of Oban, yield one or two short climbs, but for the most part the rock is untrustworthy. The Dog Stone, situated just off the Ganavan road and close to Dunollie Castle, has been climbed, but cannot be recommended. The overhanging lower section is turned by a recessed chimney near the south-east corner, facing the woods, and the wall above then followed upwards on loose vegetatious rock (45 ft., S.). Descent is best accomplished on a doubled rope (G. A. Collie). The overhang around the base was reputedly caused by Fingal's dog, Bran, when that celebrated animal was chained to the rocky monolith.

The line of cliffs above the shore road south of Oban are most uncompromising and the rock is particularly unsound. There are a number of hidden routes on the cliff, where it curves round to the little bay at Gallanach. These go up deep clefts in the rock, and are almost hidden in the undergrowth. As the floors of the clefts generally slope at only a moderate angle, there is no inherent difficulty, other than that of wedging the human frame into the narrow cracks.

As one approaches the village of Easdale, the cliffs above hold out promise of climbing, but here again the rock is bad. The only recorded climb (150 ft., D.) starts a few yards right of the lowest point of the rocks, up an earthy gully between a somewhat diamond-shaped buttress and the main cliff. This leads in 25 ft. to the crest of the buttress at a little col, and the

crest is then followed more or less direct to a ledge above (40 ft.).
Traverse ledge for 15 ft. round a corner and ascend upper wall
by short, rather difficult chimney in face (15 ft.).   Some
scrambling follows (G. A. Collie).

Knapdale.—In North Knapdale the roughly parallel
ridges are often rocky along their sides, and on them a good
deal of scrambling is to be found. The west face of Cruach
Lusach is mostly rock, and a section 300 ft. below the summit
has three steep cracks separated by rocky ribs, which provide
climbing of almost any standard required. Further west is
Creag nan Iallaig, a steep stretch of good rock. Scrambling
can be discovered on Cruach nan Chilean, on An Stuchd, and
on a 610-ft. top above Loch na Bric. Best of all is Creag nam
Fitheach, 1 mile up the Lussa. On its 100-ft. high, almost
vertical face, are some very steep and difficult cracks, a most
exposed arete and an easier slab and crack climb (A. C. D.
Small).

TROSSACHS GROUP

THE rock of the group is for the most part mica schist, which
in Ben Ledi and Ben A'n shows a fine crystalline appearance.
These Ben Ledi grits are clean and firm, and afford small but
good holds. On many of the hills are rocky outcrops which
give short and difficult problems. Ben A'n alone gives more
or less continuous climbs.

Ben Venue.—The side facing Loch Katrine is steep, and
in places rocky, but the schist is vegetatious and more than
occasionally loose.   Numerous   short   problems   abound,
especially west of the usual route to the top from Achray. On
the slopes beneath the higher summit, starting about 400 ft.
above the loch, is a prominent gully. This was first climbed in
winter by A. W. Russell. At this season it gives a fairly easy
climb on snow. In summer the upper part of the gully has a
number of short rock pitches, rather loose, but not difficult.
This part is narrow and quite steep : lower down, the angle
eases. Classification M.

Ben A'n.—The south face has enough bare rock to draw
the cragsman's eye, particularly at the top, where there is a
bare scarp with tempting rifts. The rock is sound and although

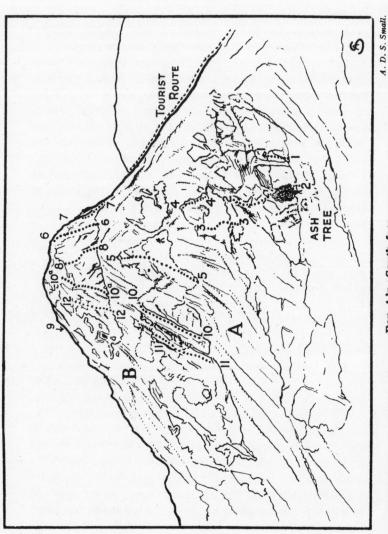

Ben A'n. South face.

A. D. S. Small.

the climbs are all short there are enough recorded routes to give a full day's climbing of a fairly high standard. Lying to the sun, the face dries quickly after rain.

The rocks group themselves into three tiers, broken by cracks and shallow gullies, and separated by sloping terraces of heather. They have an upward tilt from west to east and extend the whole width of the southern slopes. Ranging from 30 to 80 ft. in height, the rocks support a vigorous growth of stunted trees, creepers and brambles.

The lowest tier of rock lies low down and rather towards the east side of the face. An ash tree grows against the cliff and forms a useful landmark. In the following description the order of climbs is arranged roughly ascending the hill and moving westward, more or less, as one might encounter them.

(1) *The First Thirty* (30 ft., D.).—A few yards right of the ash tree there is a shallow gully bounded by a rocky bluff. The face of this gives a straightforward climb on sound rock.

(2) *The Ash Wall* (50 ft., S.A.).—Behind the tree is a narrow flake which may be climbed direct or reached by a traverse from its right end. From top of flake a steep wall leads to a shallow depression. Thereafter the route goes up a steep wall on small holds to a good ledge. This is the crux of the climb. It may be avoided by an alternative line of ascent beginning right, from the shallow depression, but the alternative is vegetatious. From the ledge above the wall, another 20 ft. of climbing on polished slabs leads to the foot of Route 4. To reach Route 3, a slight deviation is made to the left.

(3) *The Birch Wall* (40 ft., S.).—The first section is on very thin holds to a shallow angle, with no resting place. A delicate move is now necessary to cross to the left of the angle, where larger holds lead up to a sturdy rowan. This tree gives both a belay and a name to Route 4.

(4) *The Rowan Rib* (35 ft., D.).—This is a bluff of rock with a steep, almost overhung, base but the holds are mainly large.

The heather slopes above this route mark the top of the first rock tier. From here a leftward slant leads up to a small hawthorn at the foot of the next rock tier.

(5) *The Hawthorn Rib* (130 ft., D.).—The route is rather indefinite until it narrows and steepens between two light-coloured slabs. It has many ledges and large holds, and may be extended to 130 ft. of climbing. The slabs also have well-marked routes across them.

The second heather terrace is now reached and a rightward slant will lead to the final rock tier. Here the crag bends from south to east and at its corner is a rock face bounded by two shallow gullies.

(6) *The Last Eighty* (80 ft., S.A.).—The climb goes straight up this face. The first few feet are overhung and strenuous and the whole climb has a fine exposure. The last section, a little hanging rib to the right of a shallow groove, is most exhilarating on small but well-cut holds.

A variation to the lower section starts a few feet up the right-hand gully. This is a horizontal traverse, starting from a small holly to a point about half-way up the " Eighty." From the top of the " Eighty " a minute's walk takes one to the summit of Ben A'n.

(7) *The Rent* (30 ft., S.).—This route is just beyond the right-hand gully. It consists of a strenuous groove which gives a hard, straight climb with few positive holds, and little freedom of movement. Jamming tactics are employed above the first few feet, which overhang slightly. Higher up the holds improve to a grassy recess at the top. Beyond this there is a further 20 ft. groove pitch to easy ground.

(8) *The Oblique Crack* (70 ft., V.D.).—This climb lies to the left of the " Eighty " and goes up to some jammed stones with a shallow cave above. An awkward slab is tackled on the left, and finally a vegetable section finishing in a steep 20-ft. wall.

(9) *The Record Slab* (20 ft., M.).—It consists of an easily inclined slab running up the south side of the summit rocks.

The twin gullies cleaving the middle of the second tier of rocks were the first climbs to be explored. They are easily reached from below the foot of the rocks, or by descending from the upper to the lower heather terrace and traversing westwards.

(10) *The Right-hand Gully* (100 ft., S.A.).—For 50 ft. the gully consists of fairly easy rock and a thick growth of briars and brambles. Above this it steepens abruptly into a chimney which is climbed on good rock to an overhang. A tricky move is made right on small holds and then directly upwards. The top of the wall is complicated by vegetation. Beyond this the gully rises at an easy angle to the upper terrace.

(10a) Across the terrace the gully continues. At 30 ft. an overhang is passed on the right. Then follows a 40-ft. stretch of steep heather, topped by a vegetable pitch of 15 ft. which is dangerous rather than difficult. Above is a short heather stretch and a little chimney.

(11) *The Left-hand Gully* (100 ft., V.D.).—This is a pleasant climb. The first pitch, 15 ft., is vegetatious and inclined to dampness. The next section is a 15-ft. chimney on the right which finishes on a short arete. A variation is to pass the chimney and climb the steep wall, on good holds, again to the arete. A thicket of holly has to be passed to reach a short, strenuous chimney which leads to the final pitch. This consists of a fine 25-ft. chimney which is ascended by back and knee. Above the exit the gully becomes ill-defined.

(12) *McLay's Chimney* (100 ft., V.D.).—The climb is easily identified from the upper terrace, by a great jammed rock forming an arch in the chimney about half-way up. The route gives fine back-and-knee climbing.

First recorded ascents are as follows :—No. 2, W. White, 1930 ; Nos. 3, 6, 7, J. B. Nimlin, 1937, 1930, 1934 ; No. 8, H. Raeburn, 1898 ; No. 10, W. W. Naismith, 1898 ; No. 11, Gilbert Thomson, 1896 ; Nos. 4, 5 and 7 were climbed prior to 1933.

Ben Ledi.—Apart from scrambling high up on the side above Coireachrombie, rock climbing on the Ben is confined to the south side of the Stank Glen. Immediately west of the stream descending from the small upper corrie below the summit, is a tangled mass of boulders and tiny cliffs. Higher up is a line of pinnacles which, seen from beneath near the Stank burn, assume bizarre shapes, and are seen against the skyline in a serrated outline. Higher again, on the north side of the spur enclosing the upper corrie, are low cliffs of crumbling schist, intersected by short, but steep, scree gullies.

Directly below the summit, the slopes of the upper corrie give a good glissade of about 400 ft. in winter.

Boulders.—These are situated at the foot of the slopes to the west of the stream above mentioned and may be reached in ¾ hour from Stank by the path up the glen and a short climb over thick grass. They are just to the south of a deer fence and are four in number, with some smaller blocks lower down, nearer the burn.

No. 1, *"The Cottage,"* is the largest boulder, and is split into three unequal pieces, the centre piece being the highest (25 ft.). This, itself, is split at right angles near the west side and the resulting crack gives a nice climb in the boulder's bosom. The best climb, however, is a traverse of the three pieces of boulder, in as direct a line as possible, from north to south. A steep face (15 ft.) is climbed on good holds direct to the highest point, and a descent made for a short distance on the other side to a heather ledge. This point may also be reached from the north by a short, strenuous crack. From here it is necessary to bridge the gap to the centre piece of boulder : a knob of rock in the heather helps the step off, and a hold for the left hand on the far side affords some traction. Once over, an easy climb of 20 ft., up slabs, leads to the highest point, which is crossed and a descent made on the south to the ground level. The southern piece of boulder is in the form of a thick flake with a very sharp summit ridge. The top is reached by an easy shelf on the north, and the descent to the ground on the south side made in a nearly direct line on small, but sufficient holds. The route by the west end of the boulder is easier. The east face of the centre piece of boulder has also been climbed.

No. 2 *Boulder* (15 ft.) is climbed most easily on its east side by a traverse on sloping holds. The south side gives a severe climb on tiny holds.

No. 3 *Boulder* (15 ft.) is vertical on three sides and over-hangs on the south. The only route to the top, at the east corner of the south side, on good holds, is very strenuous, and should be done quickly or not at all. A purist descent is harder than the ascent.

No. 4 Boulder (12 ft.) is a little way west and easier than the preceding.   When ascending the hillside above the boulders, make for a conspicuous slab of rock some distance below the pinnacles.   This gives a moderate scramble by a crack and ridge beyond.

Pinnacles.—The lowest of the pinnacles is now ahead, its top a little lower than the main line of rock on the skyline. When approaching from below, a straight, narrow crack will be noticed at the foot of the pinnacle in an angle of rock. This forms the start of the *Crack and Ribs* (70 ft., S.).   The initial crack is very strenuous, without positive holds, and leads in 15 ft. to a slanting groove, at the foot of which is a resting place.   The groove (20 ft.) is vegetatious in its upper part and debouches on a grassy ledge which is then followed a few feet left to a point almost beneath the pinnacle top. Here are found two parallel grooves, separated by a holdless rib, and 20 ft. up, these lead to the pinnacle neck.   This section is vegetatious and exposed.   From the neck the pinnacle is gained easily in 12 ft., by the west side (W. E. Christie).

The main line of pinnacles lies ahead.   The sides next the mountain are very short, but on the other the rock extends to 50 ft.   At the base of the twisted pinnacle on the left is a cavern which can be entered at ground level.   The exit from here upwards is damp and difficult, and lands one below the short side next the mountain.   The pinnacle's summit, which is very small, can only be gained with the aid of a lasso, although a route on the outside edge has been made from below to within 15 ft. of the top.   From the twisted pinnacle the crest of rock can be traversed west without difficulty, the steep drop at the far end being descended rather on the south side.

The cliff on the north of the spur above the pinnacle is loose and, apart from the scree gullies, offers little hope of any climbing.

Ardnandave Hill holds promise of rock climbing, but the face above Loch Lubnaig is indefinite and vegetatious.   It can be climbed without difficulty by the diagonal terraces running up from north to south, and the low cliffs separating the terraces are climbable at a number of points.

The north face below the summit has three small corries, all more or less boulder strewn. In addition, the centre corrie has a small jutting-out pinnacle, not unlike the Cioch in Skye, which is accessible from its neck.

Beinn an t-Sithein shows a rocky scarp below the top and facing Strathyre, which can be climbed with difficulty near the centre on friable rock and vegetation. It is not recommended.

The other hills of the group have nothing to offer the rock climber apart from **Stob a' Choin,** which gives some short scrambles on the side facing the Lochlarig valley. The rock in places is loose and supports much moss.

THE TYNDRUM GROUP

THE rock of the district is mainly schist, vegetatious and, in places, very loose. Intrusive dykes of basalt and dolerite have given rise to the gullies, which are often scree-filled and in common with the rock are loose.

Beinn Laoigh.

(1) The *south-east ridge* gives an easy scramble of about 300 ft. and leads to the main summit. It is the true bounding ridge of the corrie.

(2) *South Gully.*—In spring this is a wide ribbon of snow lying between the south-east ridge and south rib. Higher up it steepens and divides, the top being enclosed by low cliffs. The left branch leads out on to the south-east ridge by way of shelves and easy rocks to the left. Straight ahead the branch finishes in a narrow gully which steepens abruptly before emerging on the south-east ridge. The right branch leads more directly to the summit of the mountain and from it a way can be made on to the south rib above all difficulty.

(3) *The South Rib* is the scimitar-shaped buttress descending almost directly below the summit of Lui. In summer the route starts at the lowest point of the rocks and follows the ridge crest as closely as possible. The difficulties are concentrated in the first 200 ft., at the top of which is a difficult

step round a corner. The rocks of this section are steep, beyond which the ridge degenerates and yields little more than scrambling to the top.

In winter the lower section may be impossible, in which case it is possible to strike the ridge crest, above the difficulties, from the south gully.

(4) *South-central Gully* is a little hard to locate. With good snow it gives a fine climb to the left of the rocky masses separating it from the Central Gully. The middle section is steep and leads to the slopes beneath the final cornice close to the direct line of the Central Gully.

(5) *The Central Gully* is one of the classic snow-climbs of the Highlands. Its difficulty, of course, varies with the state of the snow. One time it may be nothing more than a laboriously steep snow-plod to the summit ; on another it may yield a hard struggle all the way up to a formidable cornice through which it may then be necessary to tunnel. It is usually possible to find a route to the summit ridge by going right or left at the top without having to resort to tunnelling. The route is generally obvious as an unbroken ribbon of snow descending nearly straight from between the two tops of Lui to the floor of the corrie 1000 ft. below. The average angle increases as one ascends, but apart from the section immediately beneath the cornice the steepest bit is usually about 300 ft. below the top. In summer, the gully is mostly scree and steep grass.

(6) Some distance above the corrie floor and below where the Central Gully becomes more confined, and steepens, it is possible to bear right and make towards the north top of Lui by way of the *Upper Snowfield*. It is usual to strike the bounding ridge of the corrie some distance below the north top.

(7) Some distance to the right of the foot of the Central Gully is a rounded indefinite rib running up to the northern bounding ridge of the corrie. This is the *North Rib*, which gives 300 ft. of moderate scrambling in summer.

(8) Nearer Stob Garbh, and north-east of the North Rib, is an open gully which gives a short, easy snow climb to the ridge of Stob Garbh, which can then be followed to the north

summit of Lui. Stob Garbh itself appears to give no climbing of a sufficiently defined character.

Beinn Dubhchraig.—The best climbing is to be had on the crags at the head of the corrie between Dubhchraig and Oss. The rocks are very broken and loose, but some short, defined routes are possible towards the east.

Beinn a' Chleibh has a steep face above the Eas Daimh, opposite Beinn Laoigh. The rocks are intersected by numerous long gullies which give fair snow climbs in winter and a certain amount of scrambling in summer. The rock is very loose.

Beinn Chuirn, 2878 ft., is easily approached from Coninish. In its eastern face is a small corrie at the head of which is a line of cliffs upwards of 150 ft. high. The cliffs are flanked by gullies at either end, and yield two climbs, both vegetable and rather unsatisfactory. The first lies up the crags near the left-hand gully and the second follows a V-shaped gully in the centre of the face. This gully disappears in the cliff half-way up after which a steep face has to be negotiated on loose, earthy ledges and much vegetation.

LEAD MINES ABOVE TYNDRUM

For an " off-day " from Tyndrum the mines on the hillside above the Oban railway are well worth a visit. There are several workings and the shafts leading into the hillside should be treated with care. A long rope and suitable form of illumination are necessary. Much water finds its way into the workings, and the walls are very slimy.

On the left bank of the stream which runs past the mines there is a steep cliff about 70 ft. high. This would give a variety of routes of varying degrees of difficulty. The easiest-looking route has been classed as difficult (Macdonald), but identification is not easy. The rock is largely sound and gives small, though plentiful, holds.

CRIANLARICH GROUP

MUCH indiscriminate scrambling is possible in these hills, but there is no possibility of defined rock-climbs, and the area is better suited to winter ascents. The hills usually carry a good deal of snow until the spring and parts of the range give excellent winter-climbing practice.

Beinn Chabhair possesses sizable outcrops of rock, mostly to the south-east of the peak but these are easily avoided and at the best give only scrambling.

On the south-east slope of **Beinn a' Chroin** are some scattered boulders which give good short scrambles. Higher up the hillside is a fine 40-ft. chimney, climbable direct on sound rock.

Cruach Ardrain has a great buttress on the south-west, lying between Coire Earb and Ishay Glen. This is Stob Glas, and is the rockiest face of the whole group. From time to time some scrambling has been done on it, but the climbing is not of a sufficiently definite nature for recognised routes to have become established. The north face of Cruach Ardrain is scarred by the " Y Gully." This gives a favourite snow-climb from Crianlarich. The angle is not excessive and the eastern branch, leading straight up to the slight niche on the skyline, immediately west of the summit, is the one usually taken. The rocks to the right of the branch are loose and turfy, and should be avoided.

Ben More has some loose and unsatisfactory cliffs on the east side of the north-east ridge running down towards the ruins of Rob Roy's house. The cliffs are situated at a height of between 2500 and 3000 ft. Below them, on the same side of the ridge, and within the tree limit, is Rob Roy's Cave.

The east side of Stobinian, and the corrie between it and Stob Coire an Lochain afford opportunities of good snow-climbing. The face is not, however, divided into gullies or ridges and may be attacked at almost any point. The cornice on the ridge above is likely to be the greatest difficulty of the ascent.

At the head of the Kirkton Glen above Lochan an Eireann-aich is a steep buttress—the Leum an Eireannaich—but it affords no possible route. Near the lochan is a huge boulder, vertical on two sides. The easiest route to the top lies on the south-east.

LOCH EARN GROUP

THE possibilities of this group have not been fully explored. While it is true that no rock-climbs of any great length are to be had, there is a great deal of clean, bare schist to be found on the hills of the Forest of Glenartney, and south of Loch Earn, opposite St. Fillans. The lovely Strath a' Ghlinne, running north-west from Glenartney Lodge, is rocky in its farthest reaches and has a very steep buttress south of Coire na Cloiche.

Ben Vorlich offers only bouldering. The steep south face has some broken rocks but little of interest, and the cragsman's eye will be drawn away to the cliffs of Stùc a' Chroin on the opposite side of the Gleann an Dubh Choirein.

Stùc a' Chroin.—Some summer climbs can be had on the north-east spur, but on the whole it is disappointing, and offers easy going near the crest. Further south, the rock is very turfy and wet, and is better adapted to winter ascents, at which season several good climbs can be got on the face.

By contouring south-west from the foot of the north-east spur, by way of some huge boulders, one reaches a terrace running along the east face of Stùc a' Chroin below the upper cliff, and above a broken rock face below. Almost below the summit are two conspicuous gullies which unite at the foot of the cliff. The most southerly is easy and gives a quick route to the top : the other offers a pleasant and not difficult snow-climb (Thomson and Naismith). The rocks to the left of this gully also have been climbed, from a point half-way up, nearly to the top. North of the gully is a broken face of rock, bounded on the right by the Northern Gully. On the face between is a prominent rock rib giving a good climb of some 250 ft. in all. The foot of the rib is reached from the Northern Gully, a little above its base, by way of steep slopes of grass and broken rock, and the rib itself is climbed from its foot, a little left of the base, directly to the top. Steep slopes lead from there to the summit ridge on the mountain (W. Garden). The Northern Gully gives a direct and easy route from the terrace to the summit ridge (Naismith).

side of the mountain, to the right of the
s a broken rocky face above Choire Fhuadar-
plit by a wide gully running up directly to
summit ridge, and giving an easy snow-climb.

Ben...ach's east side is steep and rocky, but there
appears to be no defined route. There are numerous outcrops
on the ridge leading to Stùc a' Chroin and some very good
scrambling, particularly a little north of the Bealach nan
Cabar. On the west side of the hill above Glen Ample, a
little buttress of shattered rock gives an entertaining climb
of 50 ft.

BEN CHONZIE AND GLEN ALMOND GROUP

The hills are smooth-contoured and show little bare rock
apart from one or two isolated outcrops. Ben Chonzie itself
has a line of low cliff on the slopes above Lochan Uaine at
the head of Glen Turret, and some irregular outcrops a little
further north, but there is no satisfactory climbing to be had
on the schist of which they are composed.

Carn Chois rises steeply above Loch Turret. The broken
rocks of this face are very grassy, but afford some pleasant
scrambles, especially towards the north. The large, indefinite,
face overlooking the north end of the loch can be climbed
almost anywhere by a series of ledges and short scrambles.
Further south and high up on the hillside is a small defined
buttress of clean and rough schist. This has given a rather
difficult but incomplete climb for half its height.

On the east side of Loch Turret and above the Barvick
corrie, screes give way to small outcrops and low cliffs. There
is nothing of a defined nature. The same can be said of the
hills at the head of Glen Lednock, although the ascent of
Creag Uigeach can be enlivened by some " bouldering."

Two corries on the south side of Glen Almond are more or
less rocky : the finest is the north-facing one on Meall Dubh.
To reach it, follow the Glen Almond road for about 1½ miles
to the second gate (parking place), and cross the river near a
small island a little further on. Here and there is a path up
the hillside leading to the hanging corrie above. West of the
path are some entertaining boulders. The corrie is entered

beside the stream, and has a rocky face of schist on its west side. To the north, this face is bounded by reddish scree : lower down an overgrown talus slope leads to marshy ground at the foot of the corrie. The buttress above is somewhat diamond shaped, and on its south side has an indeterminate gully winding up the face. Its true boundary on the south is a straight-cut gully leading to the top of the cliff. A path runs round the extreme base of the rocks and terminates at the foot of the south bounding gully.

Pinnacle Gully (200 ft., M.).—In summer this south bounding gully is a wettish scramble, with, near the top, a small cave pitch and an alternative through route on the left. In winter the gully gives a nice climb.

The Pinnacle (35 ft.,V.D.).—On the left of the South Gully, at, and a little above, the small cave pitch is a detached flake of rock. Its top is reached from the gully below the cave by a pull up the slightly overhanging wall on to a narrow ledge, which is then followed to the left. The ledge may also be gained by a delicate traverse from above the cave pitch in the gully. From the top of the pinnacle it is neces- sary to lean across the small gap and climb the steep arete on good holds to a stance some 10 ft. higher. Scrambling follows to the top of the broken buttress above (Nettleton and Marquand).

Central Gully (300 ft., D.).—In summer, this indeterminate gully, lying to the right of South Gully, is unsatisfactory and the top pitch, which is steep and slippery, apparently has not been climbed. It is much more enjoyable to climb the top half of the cliff by a subsidiary branch to the south. This provides three good pitches of the chimney variety. In winter the main line of the gully has been followed and provides a fine route (Nettleton, Poore and Spence).

North Buttress (350 ft., D.).—This is the main mass of rocks, north of which is the bounding scree. The buttress is diamond shaped and in summer gives a number of scrambling routes on the face. It is best attacked from the lowest point (where there are two defined ridges) ; the upper part admits con- siderable variation and is crossed by numerous non-continuous ledges (Nettleton and others).

The Sma' Glen itself is steep sided. About 1 mile south of Newton Bridge on the other side of the Almond, and quite low down on the hillside, is a considerable rock face. This gives an excellent ridge climb of over 200 ft. on sound rock (Cram). The small cliffs on the west side of the Sma' Glen, above the road, are cut obliquely by a shallow gully which offers an easy snow-climb in winter, while the bounding ridge on its right provides some scrambling.

DOCHART GROUP

THERE is no record of any rock-climbing in the group, and, although there are small cliffs in part of the range, especially around Sgiath Chuil, it is unlikely that these would yield anything worth while. The rock is vegetatious schist.

FOREST OF MAMLORN GROUP

THERE is little encouragement for the rock-climber in these hills. The approaches are long and tedious, and what rock there is, is scattered and unsatisfactory. It is not surprising, therefore, that there is no record of any climbs having been made in, for example, Coire Heasgarnich where, for most people, it is sufficient accomplishment to reach the summit and return to the base which may be a good many miles away.

Coire Heasgarnich would give some good sport in snow conditions, including some fairly broad and easy gullies high up, and just to the east of the summit. The best approach is from Glen Lyon at Invermearan.

A considerable amount of rock crops out on Creag Mhòr, but scrambles have to be sought and are nowhere extensive. In Coire-Cheathaich, almost directly below the summit, is a gully which gives a short scramble (J. H. Bell), and to the left of this is a mass of steeper rock. There is no record of any climbing. Some scrambling can be had on the enclosing spurs of Coire-Cheathaich, notably on Sròn nan Eun.

The north side of Beinn Chaluim is mostly grass and steep screes, with small cliffs here and there. One or two gullies might give fair winter ascents.

THE KILLIN HILLS

THE rock is schist.   On the Tarmachans especially it outcrops in considerable areas, but the cliffs are very vegetatious,
and when wet the climbs are only doubtfully safe.   In common
with most of the hills in the Southern Highlands, the group
affords the best climbing during the winter and early spring,
when a number of the routes gives excellent sport.

Meall nan Tarmachan,—Above the south end of Lochan
na Lairige is a bold mass of rock about 400 ft. at its highest.
It faces south-east and lies to the south of the stream draining
the small lochan (Lochan an Tairbh-uisge) on the north-east
spur of Meall nan Tarmachan.   The cliffs are best adapted for
winter climbs, as the gullies are very grassy in summer and
what clean rock there is, is separated by numerous vegetatious
ledges.   The height of the cliff increases from right to left
when viewing from a little south of the Lochan na Lairige.
Near the right-hand end, where the cliffs are lowest, they are
cut obliquely by a deep gully closed at the top by an overhang.   This gully does not appear to have been climbed,
but would yield to an attack from the left at the start, and a
right-hand turning movement round the overhanging finish.
It is about 150 ft. high.   Left of this a wide, indefinite gully
goes up the centre of the face and fans out near the top.
This gives a moderate climb of 300 ft.

Arrow Chimney (350 ft., D.).—In summer it is difficult to
locate this straight cut, very shallow chimney which lies still
further to the left and a little up the hillside from the highest
section of cliff.   In winter it gives a hard snow-climb, starting
by difficult ledges some distance out on the left wall and
entering the chimney above a chockstone.   After a further
steep pitch, the gully widens a little, and the angle eases to
where the walls again come together.   It is here bounded by a
straight right-hand wall and yields several short pitches to
the top (H. Raeburn).   In summer the gully is barely distinguishable in the face as a narrow band of grassy pitches.
At that time of the year it is unpleasantly loose and unsatisfactory.

Below the summit of Tarmachan, on the east, are some small cliffs which give hardly more than scrambling on loose rock. The central gully yields an easy snow-climb and finishes on the summit ridge and close to the top of the mountain.

Meall Garbh (Cam Chreag).—All along the south-east side of the ridge from Tarmachan col to Meall Garbh is a line of broken and grassy crags. A wide, twisting gully cuts the cliffs towards the east. On the left wall of this, high up, are some very steep, narrow chimneys all grass filled, which give fine winter ascents. They are very short. Two gullies run up to near the summit of Meall Garbh. The left-hand one has three short rock pitches in summer and a snow slope of no great angle in winter (A. M. Mackay).

Beinn nan Eachan.—The south face is rocky, but the only defined route would be the shallow gully crossing it diagonally from east to west and finishing to the left of the summit. There is no record of an ascent.

Creag na Caillich.—The best rocks on the range are found at the south-east end of this ridge, the cliffs there being more or less continuous on the south-east, east and north-east sides. On the north-east side, where the height of the cliff diminishes, a wide gully gives an easy climb to the summit ridge. On the left of this, and more on the east face, is a revolting mass of dark, wet schist, crossed by non-continuous ledges. Left again, the cliff lies back at a rather more accommodating angle and is considerably broken up by grassy ledges. The buttress is climbable towards its south side by a series of shallow gullies, low down, followed by indefinite face climbs linked by ledges. The exposure is considerable and the rock loose (400 ft. D. by the easiest of a number of alternative routes).

South of the buttress is a gully—*the Great Gully* (400 ft., V.D.)—which narrows at about a third of its height and is overhung by a great slab of schist on its right. Above the narrow rocky section, the gully is crossed by a ledge which runs almost continuously across the greater part of the face, and above this again the gully fans out into very steep grass and outcropping schist. The start is low down, with 130 ft. of steep grass and wet, slabby schist, avoidable by a traverse to the left. Then comes the narrow, rocky section, about 70 ft. in all, and in three portions. Two short, strenuous chimneys lead to an awkward finish above the wet and slippery left-hand wall. A further pitch of 20 ft. leads out above the ledge crossing the face, and an escape may be made to the left. The gully continues in a straight line, but is very disagreeable on steep grass. There are five nominal pitches, but no real resting places. (Lower half of gully climbed by H. Raeburn ; whole climb, A. M. Mackay.)

Well to the left of the Great Gully is an unattractive face of slabby schist and very steep grass which continues to the south side of the hill before losing height. Low down in the corrie below the cliffs is a semicircle of clean, sound schist, some of it ice worn. There are numerous short problems upwards of 50 ft. and some fine slabs towards the south end of the semicircle.

Meall Ghaordie.—On the two spurs overlooking Glen Lyon there is a fair bit of broken rock and, on Creag an Tulabhain, a gully which gives an easy snow-climb. The rocks on Creag Laoghain are too much broken up to afford more than scrambling.

THE LAWERS GROUP

OUTSIDE of the cirque above Lochan nan Cat there are no rocks of any worthwhile size on these hills, although the north slopes of An Stuc give some easy snow-climbing. The rocks of An Stuc facing south-east are the most extensive in the area, but are not adapted to good summer climbs as they are very much broken up and lie at an easy general angle. In winter, however, the cliffs provide a number of pleasant snow gullies of which the best is probably *The Cat Gully* (500 ft.). It starts some 800 ft. above the lochan, branching left from the main gully running up to the An Stuc-Meall Garbh col, and finishes at the summit of An Stuc.

On Creag an Fhithich the *Ravens Gully* (400 ft.) starts in the high corrie below Bealach Dubh and runs up the north side of the Creag. There is a steep pitch of 20 ft. about half-way up (J. McCoss).

GLEN ORCHY AND INISHAIL GROUP

In spite of the fact that many of the hills are steep-sided, there is surprisingly little bare rock in the group. Beinn an Dòthaidh is the most notable exception, but even there the northern cliffs have weathered sufficiently to leave only a relatively small series of cliffs. The rock varies from a shale to a hard mica-schist and is nowhere ideal from a rock-climbing point of view. On Achaladair there is a considerable area of garnetiferous schist, the surface of which seems rough and trustworthy. The crystalline structure is, however, unsound.

Beinn Dòrain.—On the east side, overlooking the Allt Chonoghlais, are some low cliffs of sound rock. No defined routes are possible, but a good deal of scrambling can be had. The corrie above Bridge of Orchy is steep-sided, and, from the road, appears to offer fair scope. Closer inspection shows otherwise for the higher parts of cliff are overhung in many places and the easier spots offer little more than scrambling. The only defined climb is on the Dòrain side of the corrie, high up, where there is a conspicuous sloping crack At the top of this a difficult exit must be made to the left, on to a ledge, and thereafter a steep chimney has to be climbed to the easy slopes leading on to the north ridge of the mountain.

Beinn an Dòthaidh.—Quite the finest feature of the mountain is the north-easterly corrie, and in winter conditions there are a number of excellent climbs in the gullies of this face. There are three main gullies, that furthest west bifurcating at about a third of its height. The right-hand branch slopes to the west and continues uninterruptedly to the summit plateau above a steep rock face. The left-hand branch is lost amongst broken rock immediately below the summit of Dòthaidh. The two gullies further east are more conspicuous and broader. Neither of them is as steep as the west gully, and both lead easily to the summit plateau. In winter the main difficulty of the gully climbs is likely to be the summit cornice, which, at times, is considerable. (First ascents seem to have been made as follows : the right-hand branch of the West Gully—W. Ramsay and party ; Central Gully—Naismith and Douglas; ill-defined buttress between Central and East Gullies by a zigzag route and shallow gully—Boyd, Ramsay and Thomson; East Gully—unknown. All these routes are easy.)

Beneath the right-hand branch of the West Gully is a considerable mass of steepish schist about 200 ft. high and lying near the head of the upper corrie enclosed by the north spur of the mountain. It is split into three portions, of which the middle one is the largest, by two steep and very shallow gullies. These do not appear to have been climbed but should yield under suitable snow conditions. The buttresses are crossed by ledges, but there has been no recorded ascent.

Ghyll Buttress (270 ft., V.D.).—Towards the north end of the cliffs is a buttress separated by a deep chimney from a series of slabs running up to a broken face and three arrow-shaped rocks discernable from the Glencoe road. The start is on a large boulder leaning against the buttress, and is marked by a cairn. Two short pitches on the crest lead to the crux. From a ledge one climbs over a short overhang and up 10 ft. of vertical rock. A steep face is then to be climbed on small holds to the mossy ledge at the top of the pitch which is fully 65 ft. From here it is necessary to move to the right and up by a shallow gully to a pitch of loose, mossy boulders. Above this is another slight overhang, avoided on the left, followed by a traverse right, over slabs, and round a corner to a broad ledge. A 25-ft. chimney with good holds brings one to a large belay on a grass ledge from whence it is possible to walk up an easy rock and grass gully, and thence by scrambling to the summit (R. E. Peel).

Beinn Achaladair.—The north-west face of the mountain below the summit ridge is a disagreeable place of loose rock and very steep scree, and is best avoided. To the north-east of the summit, however, and between there and Meall Buidhe is a fine corrie with steep cliffs rent in many places by straight-cut gullies. The rock is loose and has yielded no satisfactory routes in summer: in winter a number of the gullies give good snow ascents. Directly below the summit on this north-east side is a steep but shallow gully, sloping up roughly parallel to the north rib of the mountain. About 250 ft. below the top it crosses a band of cliff and narrows to a groove in the schist. It is the hardest part of an ascent which is nowhere very difficult and one which leads directly to the summit. The gullies further east are all straight-forward, and none of them offers difficulties in excess of steep snow slopes. The one leading to the Meall Buidhe-Achaladair col is the broadest and most gently inclined and gives the easiest route from the floor of the corrie to the upper reaches of the mountain. On the extreme left of the ½-mile line of cliff, a steep and narrow snow gully gives about the most defined climb from the corrie (Brown and Boyd).

Beinn a' Chreachain.—Rocks line Coire an Lochain for about ½ a mile. Meall Buidhe encloses the corrie in the west, but the greater mass of rock is on Chreachain itself. There are three main masses divided by two broad gullies, both easy—the one from the Chreachain-Meall Buidhe col gives a good glissade—and the masses themselves are much broken up by grassy ledges. The largest face, that immediately below the summit ridge of Chreachain, may be climbed almost anywhere in summer.

Rocks in the small eastern corrie are negligible.

Beinn Odhar and Beinn a' Chaisteil.—Small cliffs outcrop on the north slopes of Beinn Odhar and yield some scrambling. The mural sides of Beinn a' Chaisteil seem to hold hope of some climbing, but are hardly attractive. On the Gleann Choillean face are several gullies separated by broken rock. At the angle between Glens Choillean and Auch is a large pyramidal tower between two sloping gullies. The tower itself is mostly steep grass, but on its left side steep rocks drop into the bounding gully. The latter gives a climb on rather unsound rock. It is entered by a trap chimney about 30 ft. high, this being followed by 60 ft. of trap rock with small holds. It is now necessary to break out to the ridge on the right by a vegetatious wall. Thereafter the ridge is followed for about 100 ft., when it is possible to traverse back into the now easy gully and follow it to the top.

o

Beinn Udlaidh.—East and west of the main top are some pleasing schistose cliffs, to the east in Coire Ghamhnain, and to the west circling Coire Daimh. The latter corrie faces a little west of north and is ringed by broken cliffs. Low down and near the centre is a very steep cliff of quartzite, nearly 100 ft. high, and split by two prominent chimneys. The right-hand one—*West Chimney*—is moderately difficult and can be followed by steep grass to the higher parts of the mountain. The other, 100-*ft. Chimney*, appears as a formidable, and none too secure, rift, but is easier than it looks and the rock is reasonably good (100 ft., V.D.).

A few feet to the west of the 100-ft. chimney is the start of the *Central Gully* (170 ft., D.). Two easy introductory pitches of 30 ft. each lead to a steep slab which forms the crux of the climb and is surmounted by a delicate route near the centre. The slab is about 30 ft. high. Above this a grassy slope leads upwards to the top. *Ramshead Gully* (300 ft., D.) is in the upper cliff, and starts above, and a little to the east of, the 100-ft. chimney. It provides a very good scramble on good schist, with one or two short pitches and a large, overhanging rock at the top which gives the gully its name.

Well to the east of the Ramshead Gully, and immediately under the summit of Beinn Udlaidh, is a steep wall of rock bounded on either side by shallow gullies. This cliff gives a good climb slanting up to the right, and is known as the *Black Wall* (250 ft., V.D.). There are some surprisingly commodious ledges of clean rock and fine exposures. The most difficult pitch is near the top.

The bounding gullies have not been followed in a direct line, that on the right (*South Gully of Black Wall*, 200 ft., V.D.) being climbed on its left side for about 60 ft. of difficult rock, then by a zigzag route on easier rocks to the summit. The left bounding gully (*Quartzvein Scoop*, 170 ft., D.) is climbed on the rocks to its left. Near the top it is possible to traverse right and finish the climb on excellent rock for the last few feet.

In the rocks just to the north are two deep fissures, roughly parallel, and partially filled in with stones. They are connected by a third fissure near their midpoints.   To the north of this again is a 60-ft. slab, *Fissure Slab* (60 ft. D.) which gives a pleasant climb on good rock.

On the other side of the hill, on the west side of Coire Ghamhnain is a prominent ridge of rock.   This is known as the Coolin Ridge and gives excellent scrambles up to 80 ft. in height.   Near its top is the *Fold Buttress* (90 ft., V.D.), so called on account of the very noticeable bending in the schist of which it is composed.   A strenuous chimney leads steeply from the foot of the buttress and its roof is turned on the left.   Thereafter a short traverse to the right enables one to attack the top pitch.

(First ascents Beinn Udlaidh climbs—Nimlin, Slack and Hutchison.)

THE LOCH LYON HILLS

THE hills are mostly smooth-contoured, with grass and scree slopes.   On the north side of Beinn Mhanach, facing Gleann Cailliche, there is a line of broken cliff.   The rocks are intersected by several gullies, the best of which lie towards the east end of the rocky mass.   There is no record of any climbs and it is unlikely that anything more than steep scrambling could be found.

UPPER GLEN LYON AND WEST RANNOCH GROUP

THERE is no record of any climbs in the area, and it is unlikely that anything satisfactory will be discovered.   The slopes around Lochan nan Cat on Stuchd an Lochain are precipitous, but offer no chance of defined routes, while on the northern part of the group there are some crags with gullies on the north-east side of Garbh Mheall. On the east side of the summit ridge of Meall Bhuidhe there are steep rocks but of no great extent.

THE CÀRN MAIRG RANGE

THE quartzite of which this range is composed has weathered evenly, giving slopes devoid of cliffs. The steepest face is directly below the summit of Càrn Mairg itself, but this offers no climbing and is disagreeable on account of large boulders, precariously perched.

Low down the hillsides above the road in Glen Lyon there are some small outcrops of rock on Creag Mhòr at the east end of the range and on Càrn Gorm at the west These small cliffs present clean rock and some short scrambles.

SCHICHALLION

A LITTLE scrambling may be had by diligent searchers on the south side of the summit ridge, but none of the climbs could exceed 30 ft. The quartzite is surprisingly pleasant to climb. Elsewhere on the mountain there is nothing for the rock-climber.

INDEX

Note :—Refs. in italics denote illustrations.
Refs. beyond page 153 denote rock-climbs.

A' Chrois, 37, 162, *157*
An Caisteil, 77
An Sgor, 148
An Stuc, 122, 194
An Stuchd (Knapdale), 177
Andrew Gannel Hill, 12
Ardgartan, 26, 29
Ardgoil, 26, 29, 174
Ardnandave Hill, 63, 183
Argyll's Bowling Green, 26
Argyll National Forest Park, 25, 29, 36
Auch, 127, 132, 134-136
Auchineden Hill, 7

Backhill, 12, 14
Bannetstane, 17
Benarty, 18
Bentie Knowe, 13
Bishop's Hill, 16, 17, 18, 171
Blairdenon Hill, 13
Brack, The, 26, 27, 154, *141*
Brackland (Bracklinn) Falls, 88
Burn of Sorrow, 14
Beinn, Ben
  A'n, 60, 177, *178*
  Achaladair, 128, 196, *93*
  Arthur (Cobbler), 32
  Bheag, Cowal, 21, 23
  Bheula, 22, 24
  Bhreac, Cowal, 21
  Bhreac, L. Lomond, 49
  Bhreac, Trossachs, 60
  Bhreac-liath, 132
  Bhuidhe, 52, 176, *52*
  Buck, 11, 14
  Chabhair, 74-76, 187
  Chaluim, 106, 191
  a' Chaisteil, 131, 197
  Cheathaich, 97
  Chonzie, 90, 91, 189
  a' Chreachain, 130, 197
  a' Chroin, 77, 187
  Chuirn, Tyndrum, 186

a' Chuirn, 135
a' Chleibh, 69, 70, 186
Cleuch, 11, 14
Dhubh, 39
Donich, 26, 27
Dorain, 127, 195, *108*
an Dothaidh, 127, 195-196
Dubhain, 22, 25
Dubhchraig, 66, 186
Each, 87, 189
nan Eachan, 112, 193
Eich, Loch Lomond, 49
Ever, 11
Ghlas, 121
Heasgarnich, 101
Ime, 38, 162, *140-141*
Laoigh (Lui), 68, 184, (*Frontispiece*), *60, 61, 68*
Lawers, 118, 194, *109*
Ledi, 61, 181
Lochain, Cowal, 22, 25
an Lochain, 26, 28, 174, *28*
Lomond, 43, 174, *44*
Mhanach, 135, 199
Mhor, Cowal, 21, 23, 174
More, Crianlarich, 79, 187, *76, 77*
Narnain, 35, 159, *140-141*, *156-157*
Odhar, 131, 197
nan Oighreag, 113
Oss, 68
Reithe, 26
Reoch, 49, *44-45*
Ruadh, Cowal, 21, 23
Shee, 12, 14
an t-Seilich, 26, 28
an t-Sithein, 63, 184
Tharsuinn, Cowal, 22, 25
Tulaichean, 78, *77*
Udlaidh, 132, 198-9
Vane, Loch Sloy, 39
Vane, Trossachs, 63
Venue, 59, 177, *60-61*
Vorlich, Loch Earn, 84, 188, *85*
Vorlich, Loch Sloy, 39

Campsie Fells, *4*, 8, 164
Carn Chois, 189
Carnach Mor, 22, 25
Carn Gorm, 148, 200
Carn Mairg, 145, 200
Cashlie, 138
Castle Campbell, 12
Cauldron Linn, 19
Clach Bheinn, Cowal, 21, 23, *20*
Cleish Hills, 18
Cnoc Coinnich, 26, 27
Cnoc Reamhar, 57
Cobbler, The, 32-35, 155-159, *28, 29, 156*

Coire, Corrie
Cheathaich, 97, 105, 191
na Cloiche, 188
Ealt, 24, 29
Fhuadaraich, 189
Ghamhnain, 199
Heasgarnich, 191
Lobhaidh, 98
Odhar, 118, 120
Sugach, 36, 160

Colsnaur Hill, 13
Coninish Glen, 67, 70
Covenanters Glen, 17
Cowal, 20, 29, 174
Craigentaggert Hill, 12
Creachan Mor, 21, 24
Craigengaw, 16, 169

Creag, Creagan,
na Bheinn, 93
na Caillich, 112, 193
an Fhithich, 122, 194
nam Fhitheach (Knapdale), 177
nan Iallaig, 177
Macranaich, 82
Mhor, Glen Lyon, 144, 200
Mhor, Glen Lochy, 105, 191
Tharsuinn (Cowal), 21, 24
Tarsuinn (Arrochar), 37, 160, *156-157*
Uigeach, 93

Cruach Ardrain, 78, 187, *76-77*
Cruach a' Bhuic, 21
Cruach nan Capull, 21, 22
Cruach a' Chaise, 21, 24
Cruach nan Chilean, 177
Cruach Eighrach, 21
Cruach Lusach, 57, 177
Cruach nam Mult, 22
Cruach Tairbeirt, 49
Cults Hill, 19

Deil's Cauldron, Glen Lednock, 91, 94
Dog Stone, 176
Doune Hill, Loch Lomond, 49
Dubh Eas, 41, 53, 71
Dumglow, 18
Dumgoyne, 9, *4*
Dumyat, 13, 14, 166
Duncolm, 8

Earl's Seat, 8
Easdale, 176, *53*
Eas Daimh, 69, 70, 71
Eas Morag, 69
East Lomond, 16, 17

Fife Coast, 172
Fin Glen, Campsies, 8
Fin Glen, Loch Tay, 94
Frandy Reservoir, 12
Fynloch Hill, 8

Gallanach, 176
Ganavan, 176
Gannel Burn, 12, 14
Garbh Meall, Meall Buidhe, 199
Geology, 1

Glen
Almond, 90, 91, 94, 189
Ample, 86, 88
Artney, 84, 85, 87
Bee, 12, 14
Croe, 34
Devon, 12, 14
Dubh, 82
Douglas, 49, 50
Falloch, 41, 71
Finglas, 65
Fruin, 49, 50
Fyne, 41, 53
Keltie, 87
Kin, 29
Kinglas (Ardgoil), 26
Lednock, 90, 92, 94
Lochay, 115
Loin, 37
Luss, 49, 50
Lyon, 115, 138, 141
Mor, 152
Nant, 55, 56
Quaich, 90, 93, 94
Quey, 12, 13, 14
Sherup, 12

Shira, 53
Turret, 90
Tye, 13, 14

Glenquey Reservoir, 12
Glentye Hill, 13
Glenwhinnel, 11

Hell's Glen, 20
Highland Boundary Fault, 1
Holy Loch, 21

Innerdownie, 12, 13
Inveruglas, 34, 36, 40, 41
Isle of May, 172

Kelty Water, 85, 86
Kilpatrick Hills, 7, 164
Kilsyth Hills, 8
King's Seat, Ochils, 12
Kirkton Glen, 81
Knapdale, 56, 177
Knox's Pulpit, John, 17
Knock Hill, 19

Lairig Breislich, 115
Lairig Chalbhath, 149
Lairig nan Lunn, 115
Lairig Meachdainn, 141
Law, The, 11
Leum an Eireannaich, 187
Little Bin, 8
Lomond Hills, Fife, 16, 169
Lorne, 55, 176

Loch, Lochan
    Avich, 55, 56
    Awe, 55
    a' Chaisteil, 76
    Eck, 21, 29
    Freuchie, 90, 93
    Fyne, 20
    Goil, 20
    Humphrey, 8
    Katrine, 64
    na Lairige, 120, 121, 124
    Leven, 8, 16
    Lomond, 37
    Long, 20
    Lubnaig, 88, 60
    Rannoch, 133, 141, 140
    Restil, 28
    Sloy, 39, 40, 41
    Turret, 92
    Voil, 85

Maddy Moss, 12
Maiden's Bower, 5, 17
May Island, 172
Meikle Bin, 8
Mickle Corum, 13
Mill Glen, 12, 14
Mines, Tyndrum, 186

Meall
    a' Bharr, 146
    Buidhe, Achaladair, 130
    Buidhe, Garbh Mheall, 139
    a' Choire Leith, 120
    Corranaich, 121
    na Dige, 80
    Dubh, Glen Almond, 189-190
    nam Fuaran, 93
    Garbh, Carn Mairg, 147
    Garbh, Lawers, 123
    Garbh, Tarmachans, 111, 193
    Ghaordie, 114, 194
    Glas, 97
    Greigh (Gruaidh), 123
    Luaidhe, 147
    Liath, 145
    nan Tarmachan, 110, 192

Mullach Coire a Chuir, 22, 25

Navity Hill, 18
Nebit, The, 11

Ochil Hills, 10, 166

Puck's Glen, 25, 21
Pulpit Rock, 176

Rest-and-Be-Thankful, 28
Rumbling Bridge, 19

Saline Hills, 18, 19
Scad Hill, 12, 13, 14
Schichallion, 150, 200, 140
Sgiath Chuil, 97, 191
Sgurr a Choinnich, Cowal, 21
Silver Glen, 11
Skythorn Hill, 12, 14
Sliabh Goil, Knapdale, 57
Sma' Glen, 90
Spout Rollo, 92, 94
Sron nan Eun, 191
Sron Gharbh, 77
Sron Dha Murchdi, 121
Stank Glen, 181, 183

Stob
  Breac, 64
  a' Choin, 64, 184, *77*
  nan Clach, 105
  Coire an Lochain, 80, 81
  Creagach, 80
  an Eas, 26, 28
  an Fhir Bhoga, 101, 103
  Garbh, 78
  Glas, 77, 187
  Invercarnaig, 80

Stobinian, 80, *66-67*
Strath a' Ghlinne, 188
Stuc a' Chroin, 86, 188, *84*
Stuc Odhar, 62
Stuchd an Lochain, 138, 199,

Tarmachan Range, 110, 192,
  108-109
Tarmangie Hill, 12, 13
Tyndrum Lead Mines, 186

Uamh Bheag, 87
Uamh Mhor, 87

West Lomond, 16, 17
Wether Hill, 18
Whangie, The, 7
Whitecraigs, 16
Whitewisp Hill, 12, 13